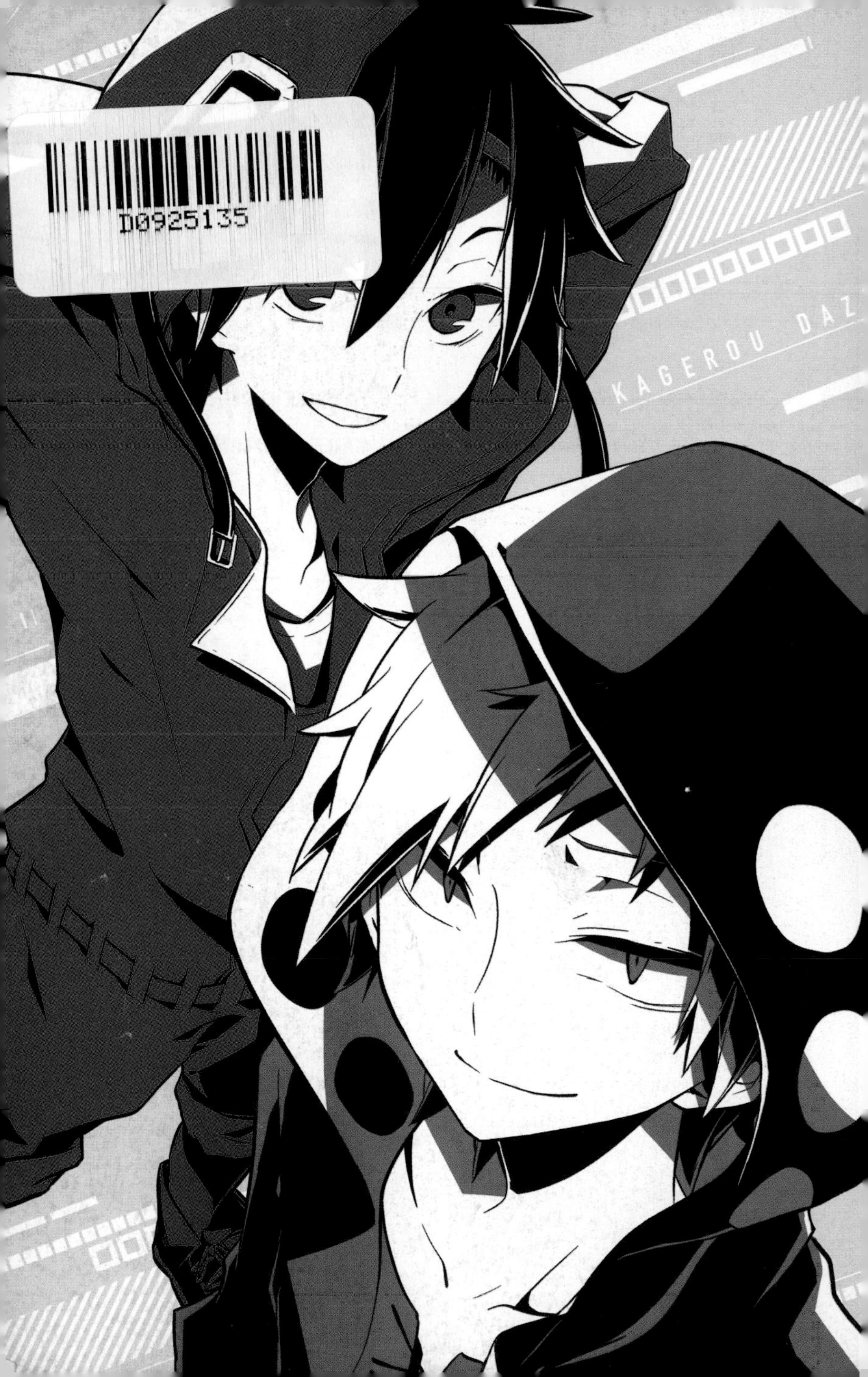
KAGEROU DAZ

KAGEROU DAZE 6
C O N T E N T S

25 SHOUNEN BRAVE II ····· 003

26 SHOUNEN BRAVE III ····· 019

27 FANTASY FOREST I ······· 045

28 FANTASY FOREST II ······ 079

29 FANTASY FOREST III ····· 105

30 KAIEN PANZERMAST I ···· 133

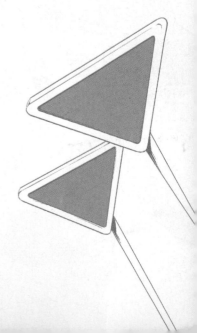

25 >> SHOUNEN BRAVE II

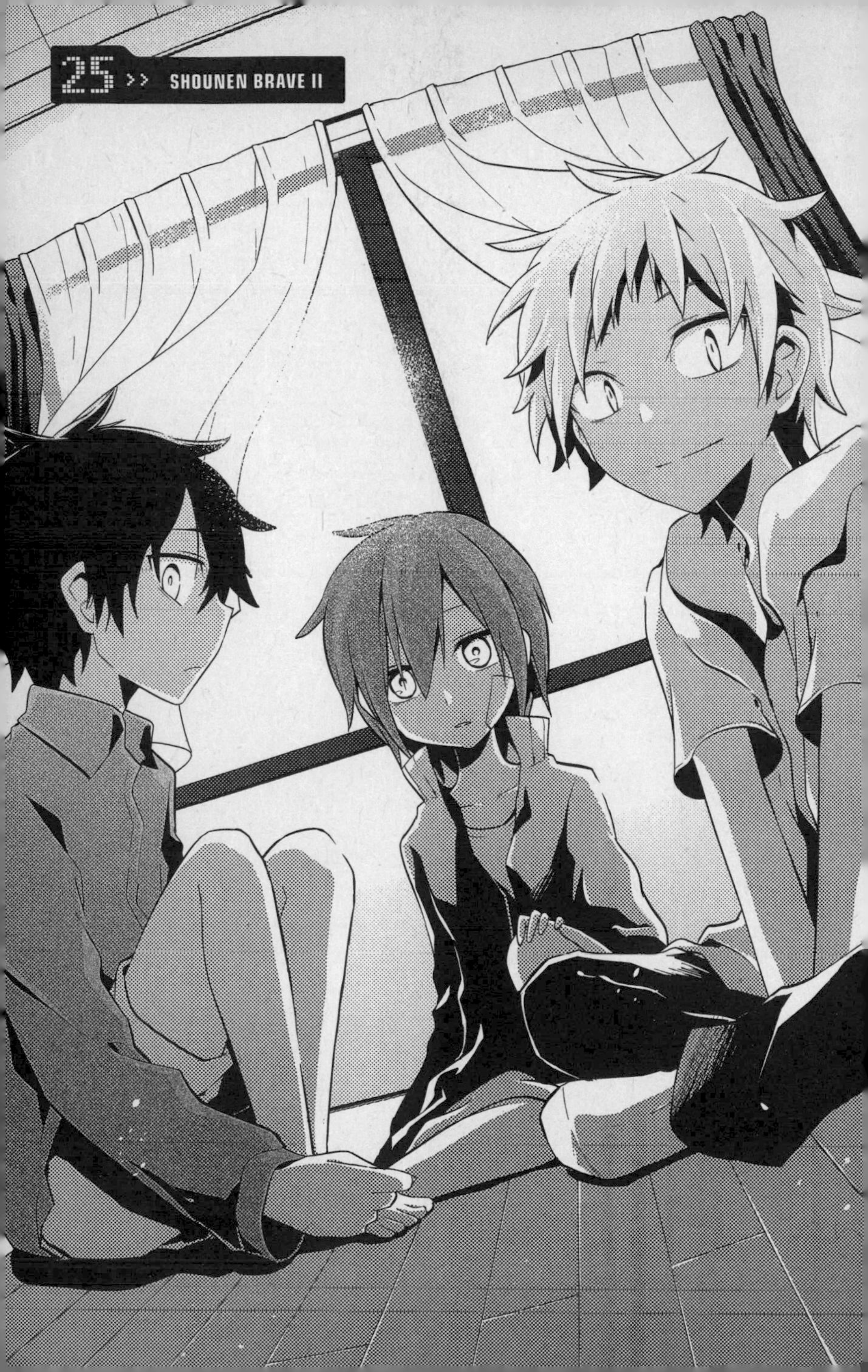

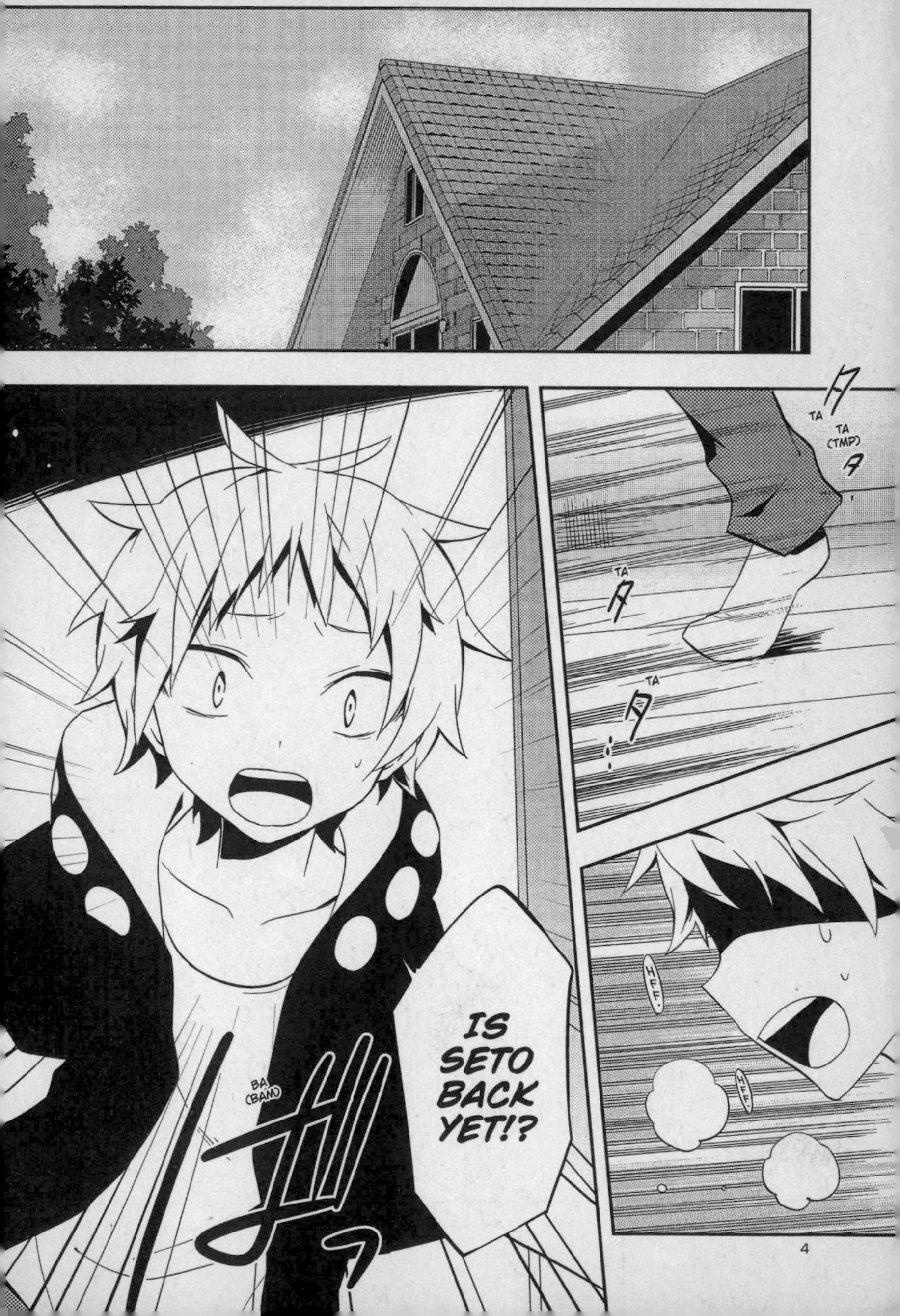
TA
TA (TMP)
TA
TA
HFF.
HFF.
BA (BAM)
IS SETO BACK YET!?

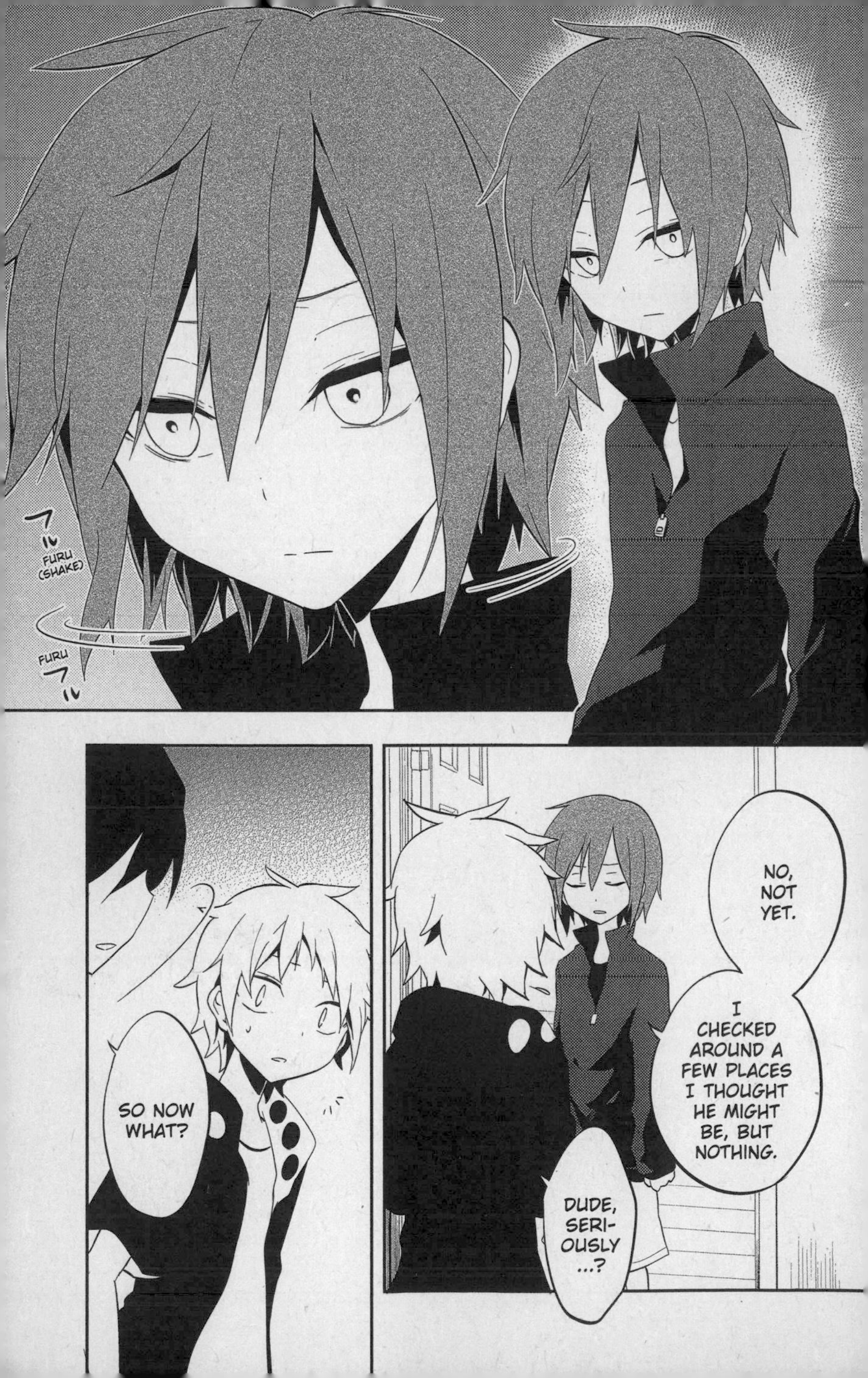
フル
FURU (SHAKE)
FURU
フル
NO, NOT YET.
I CHECKED AROUND A FEW PLACES I THOUGHT HE MIGHT BE, BUT NOTHING.
DUDE, SERI-OUSLY ...?
SO NOW WHAT?

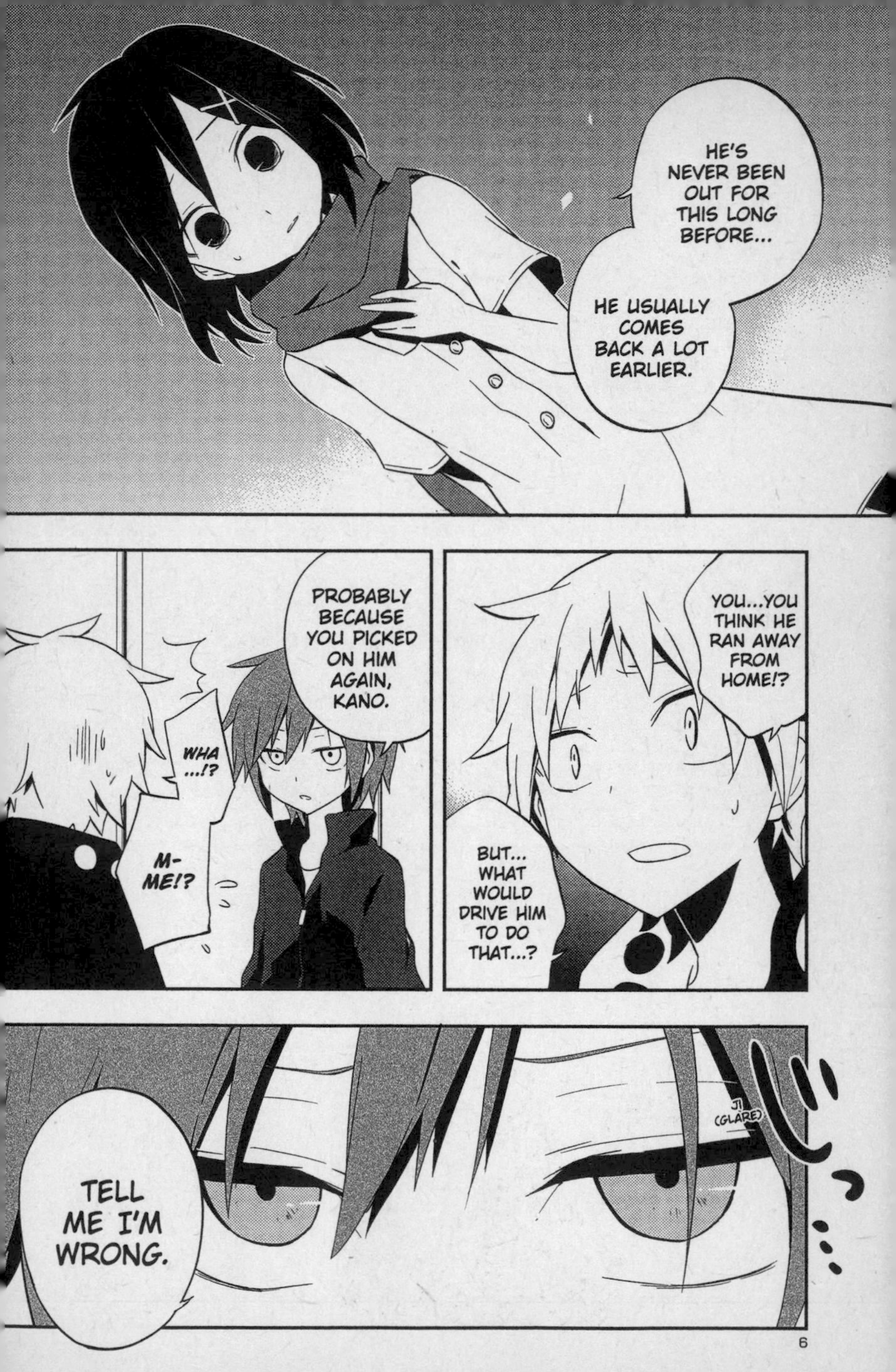
HE'S NEVER BEEN OUT FOR THIS LONG BEFORE...
HE USUALLY COMES BACK A LOT EARLIER.
YOU...YOU THINK HE RAN AWAY FROM HOME!?
BUT... WHAT WOULD DRIVE HIM TO DO THAT...?
PROBABLY BECAUSE YOU PICKED ON HIM AGAIN, KANO.
WHA...!?
M-ME!?
JI (GLARE)
TELL ME I'M WRONG.

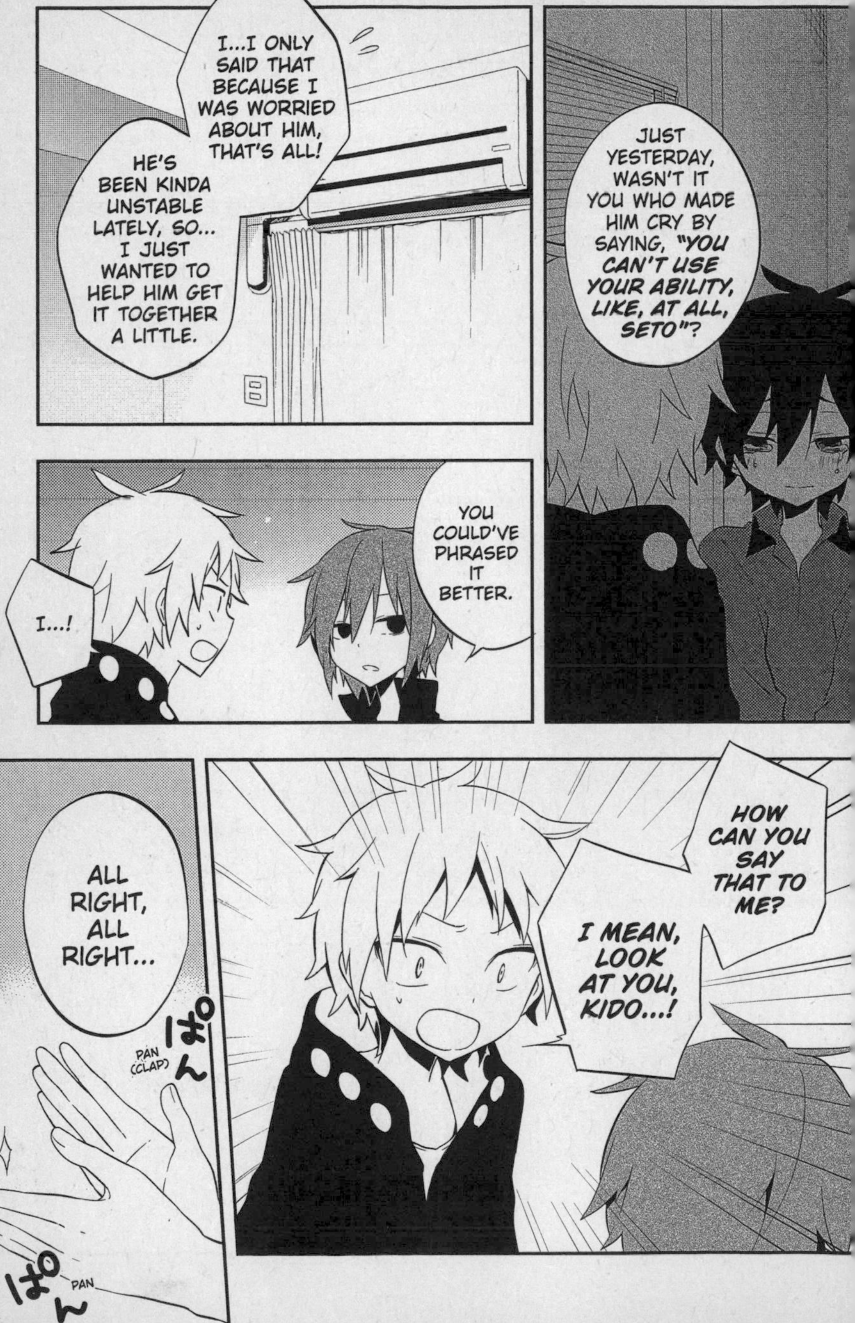
JUST YESTERDAY, WASN'T IT YOU WHO MADE HIM CRY BY SAYING, "YOU CAN'T USE YOUR ABILITY, LIKE, AT ALL, SETO"?
I...I ONLY SAID THAT BECAUSE I WAS WORRIED ABOUT HIM, THAT'S ALL!
HE'S BEEN KINDA UNSTABLE LATELY, SO... I JUST WANTED TO HELP HIM GET IT TOGETHER A LITTLE.
YOU COULD'VE PHRASED IT BETTER.
I...!
HOW CAN YOU SAY THAT TO ME?
I MEAN, LOOK AT YOU, KIDO...!
ALL RIGHT, ALL RIGHT...
ぱん
PAN (CLAP)
ぱん
PAN

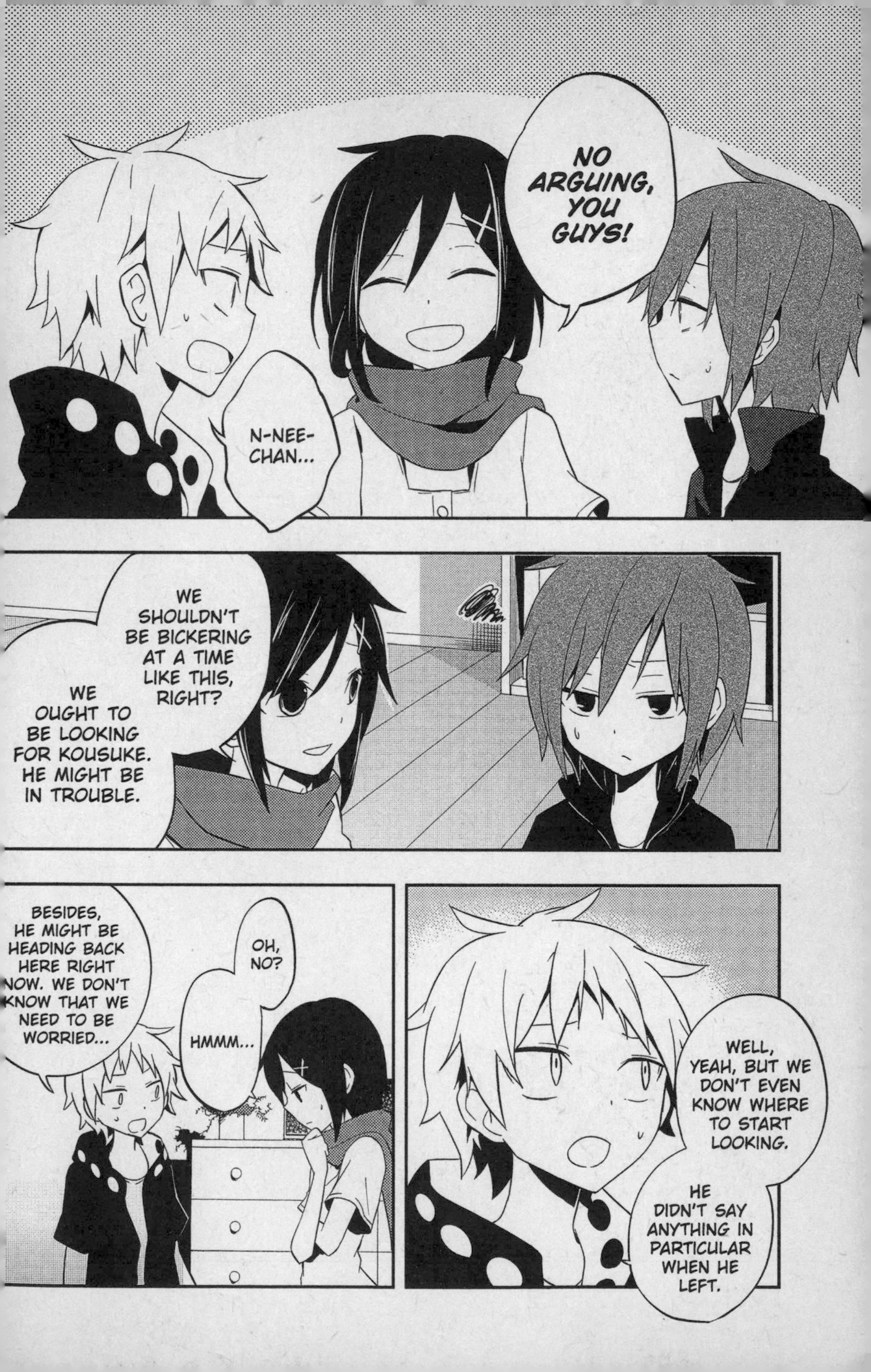
NO ARGUING, YOU GUYS!
N-NEE-CHAN...
WE SHOULDN'T BE BICKERING AT A TIME LIKE THIS, RIGHT?
WE OUGHT TO BE LOOKING FOR KOUSUKE. HE MIGHT BE IN TROUBLE.
WELL, YEAH, BUT WE DON'T EVEN KNOW WHERE TO START LOOKING.
HE DIDN'T SAY ANYTHING IN PARTICULAR WHEN HE LEFT.
BESIDES, HE MIGHT BE HEADING BACK HERE RIGHT NOW. WE DON'T KNOW THAT WE NEED TO BE WORRIED...
OH, NO?
HMMM...

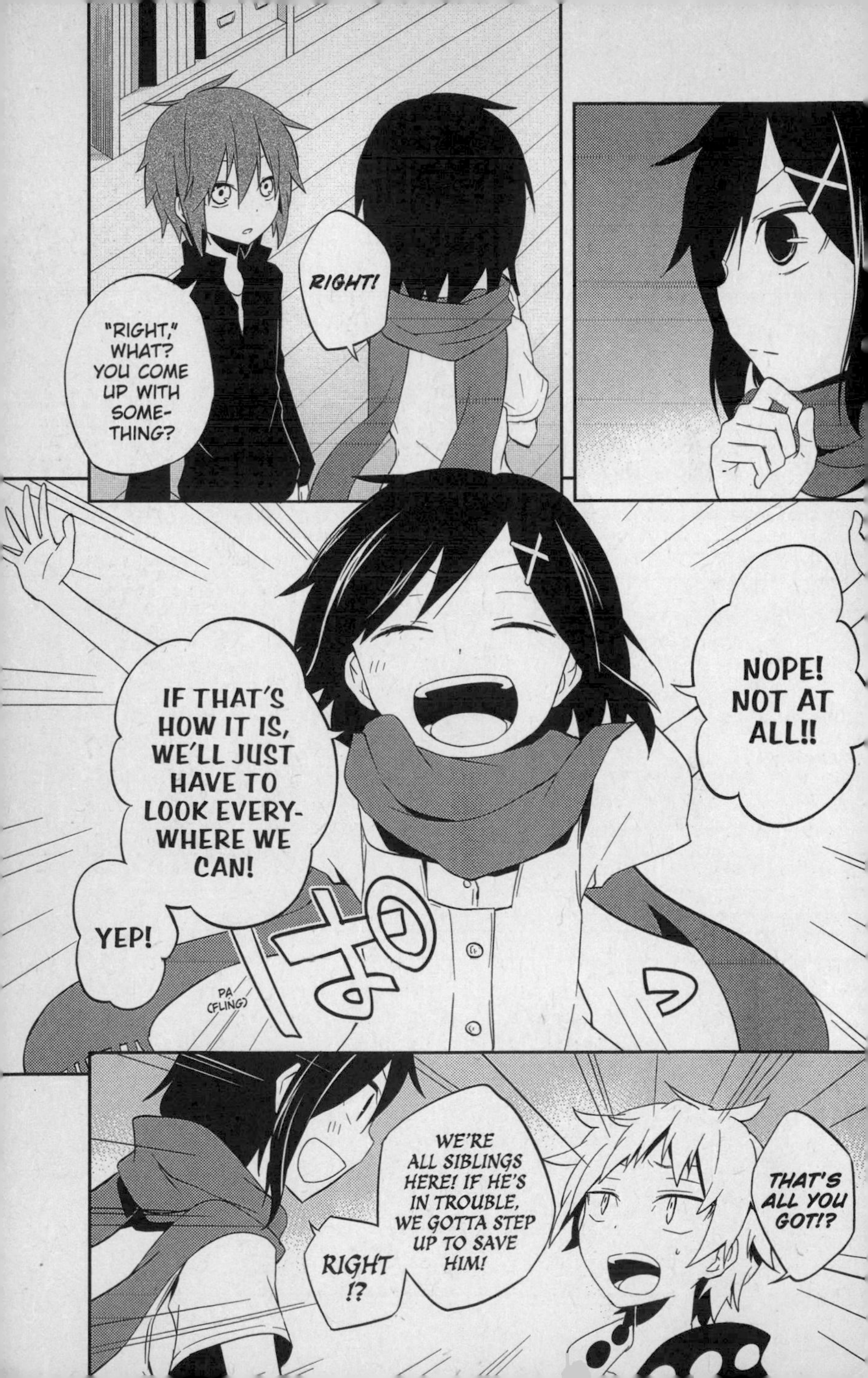
RIGHT!
"RIGHT," WHAT? YOU COME UP WITH SOME-THING?
NOPE! NOT AT ALL!!
IF THAT'S HOW IT IS, WE'LL JUST HAVE TO LOOK EVERY-WHERE WE CAN!
YEP!
PA (FLING)
THAT'S ALL YOU GOT!?
WE'RE ALL SIBLINGS HERE! IF HE'S IN TROUBLE, WE GOTTA STEP UP TO SAVE HIM!
RIGHT !?

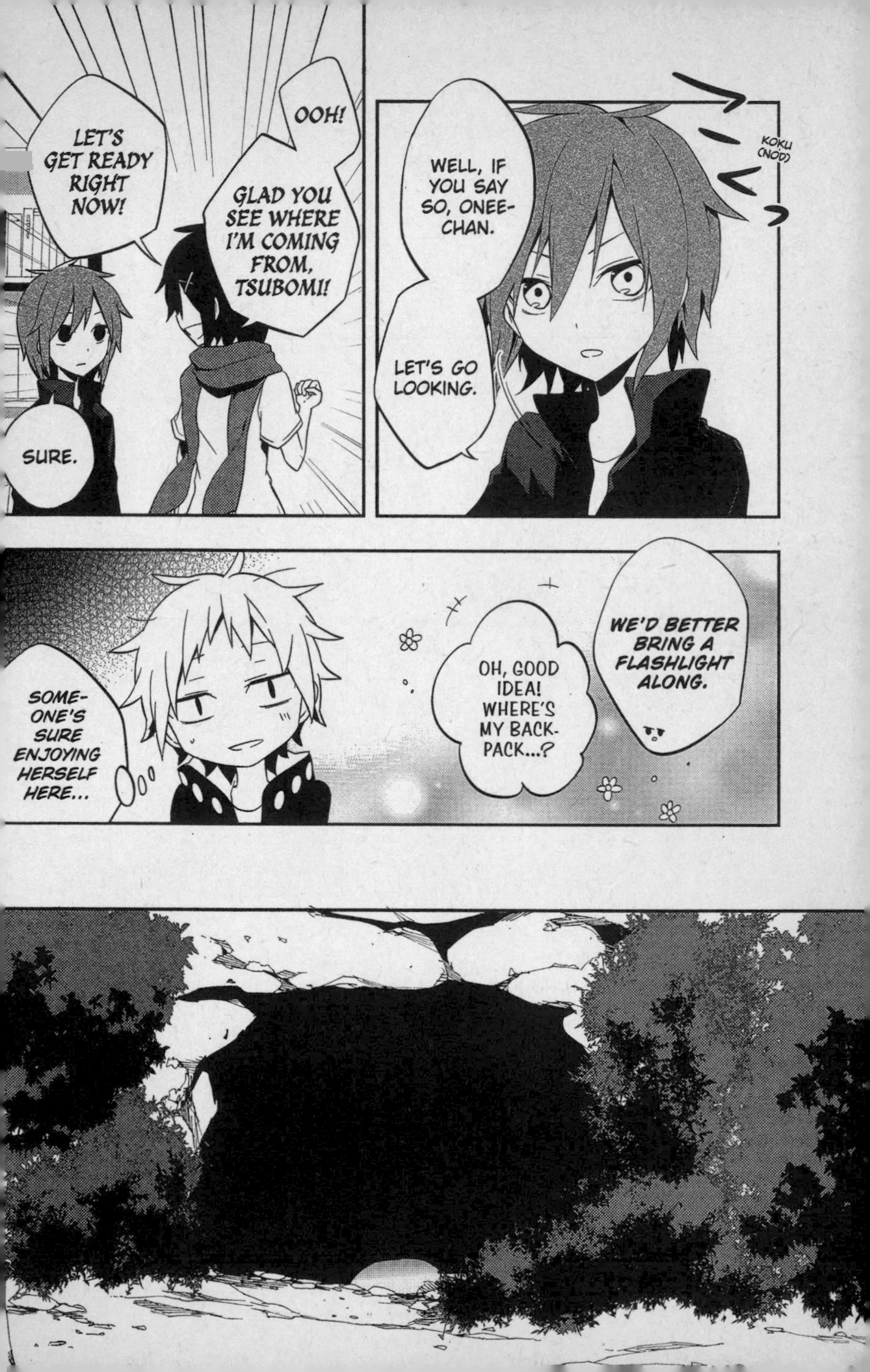
KOKU (NOD)
WELL, IF YOU SAY SO, ONEE-CHAN.
LET'S GO LOOKING.
OOH!
GLAD YOU SEE WHERE I'M COMING FROM, TSUBOMI!
LET'S GET READY RIGHT NOW!
SURE.
WE'D BETTER BRING A FLASHLIGHT ALONG.
OH, GOOD IDEA! WHERE'S MY BACK-PACK...?
SOME-ONE'S SURE ENJOYING HERSELF HERE...

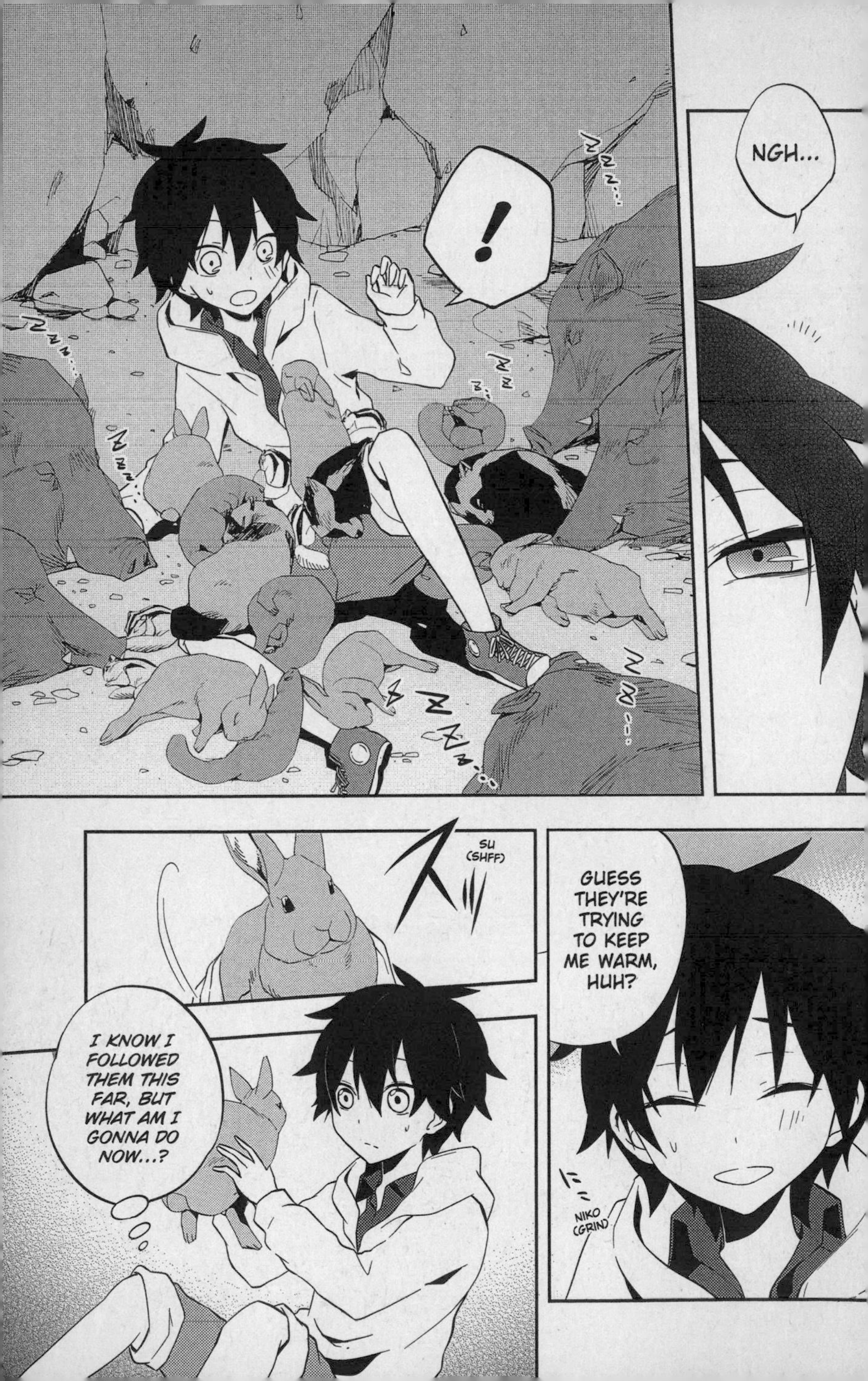
NGH...
!
GUESS THEY'RE TRYING TO KEEP ME WARM, HUH?
NIKO (GRIN)
SU (SHFF)
I KNOW I FOLLOWED THEM THIS FAR, BUT WHAT AM I GONNA DO NOW...?

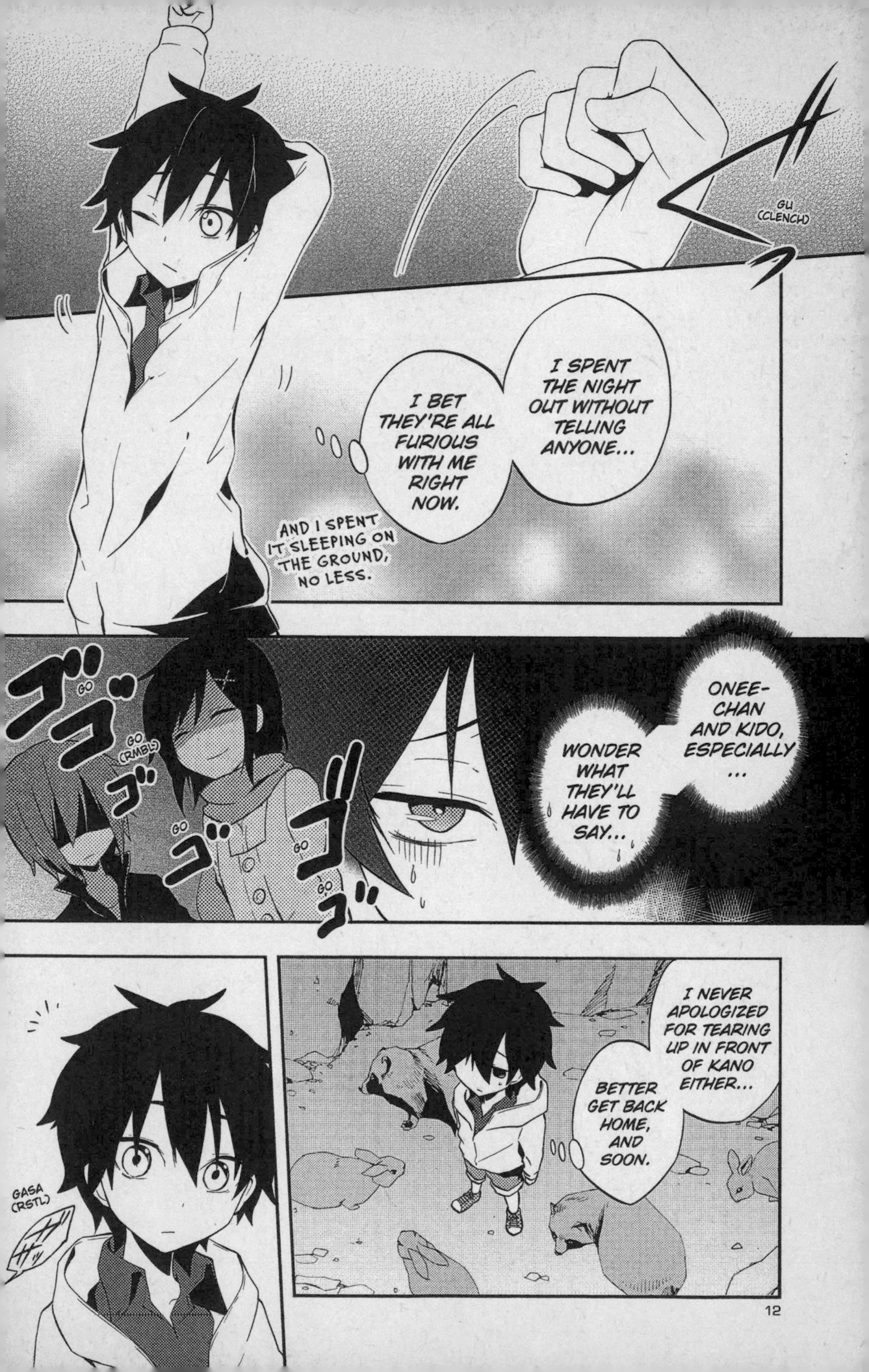
GU (CLENCH)
I SPENT THE NIGHT OUT WITHOUT TELLING ANYONE...
I BET THEY'RE ALL FURIOUS WITH ME RIGHT NOW.
AND I SPENT IT SLEEPING ON THE GROUND, NO LESS.
ONEE-CHAN AND KIDO, ESPECIALLY...
WONDER WHAT THEY'LL HAVE TO SAY...
GO
GO
GO
GO (RMBL)
GO
I NEVER APOLOGIZED FOR TEARING UP IN FRONT OF KANO EITHER...
BETTER GET BACK HOME, AND SOON.
GASA (RSTL)

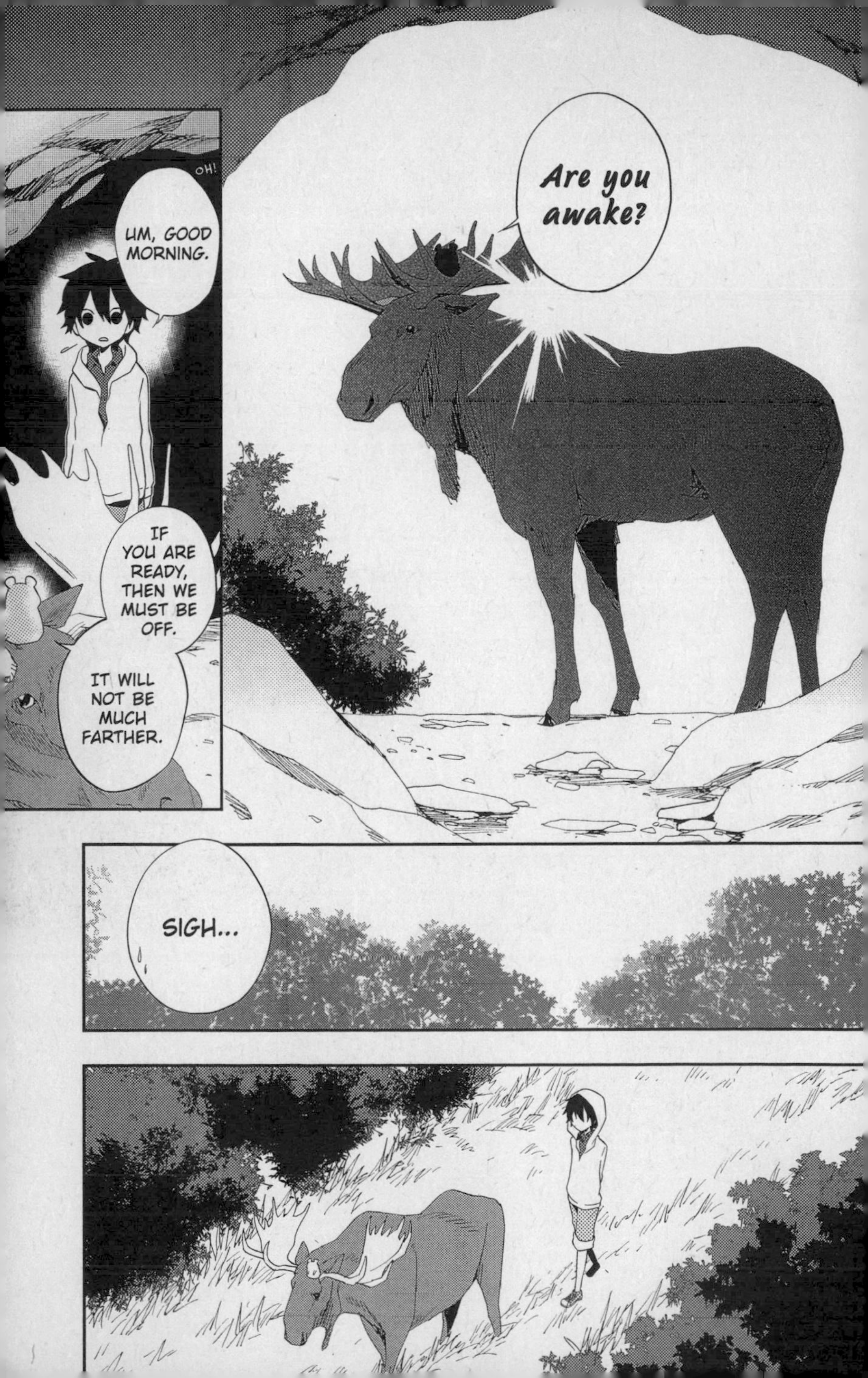
Are you awake?
OH!
UM, GOOD MORNING.
IF YOU ARE READY, THEN WE MUST BE OFF.
IT WILL NOT BE MUCH FARTHER.
SIGH...

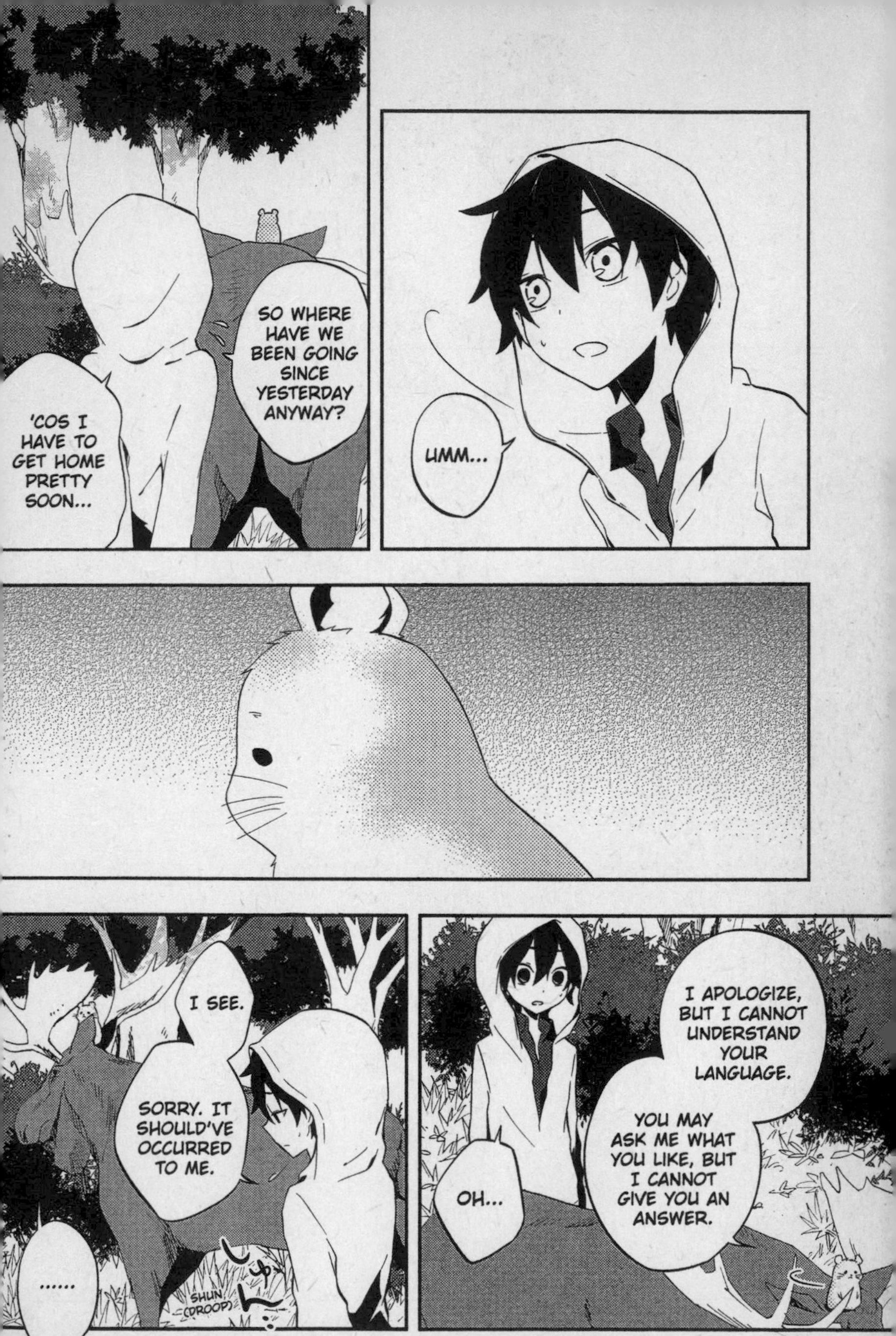
UMM...
SO WHERE HAVE WE BEEN GOING SINCE YESTERDAY ANYWAY?
'COS I HAVE TO GET HOME PRETTY SOON...
I APOLOGIZE, BUT I CANNOT UNDERSTAND YOUR LANGUAGE.
YOU MAY ASK ME WHAT YOU LIKE, BUT I CANNOT GIVE YOU AN ANSWER.
OH...
I SEE.
SORRY. IT SHOULD'VE OCCURRED TO ME.
SHUN (DROOP)
......

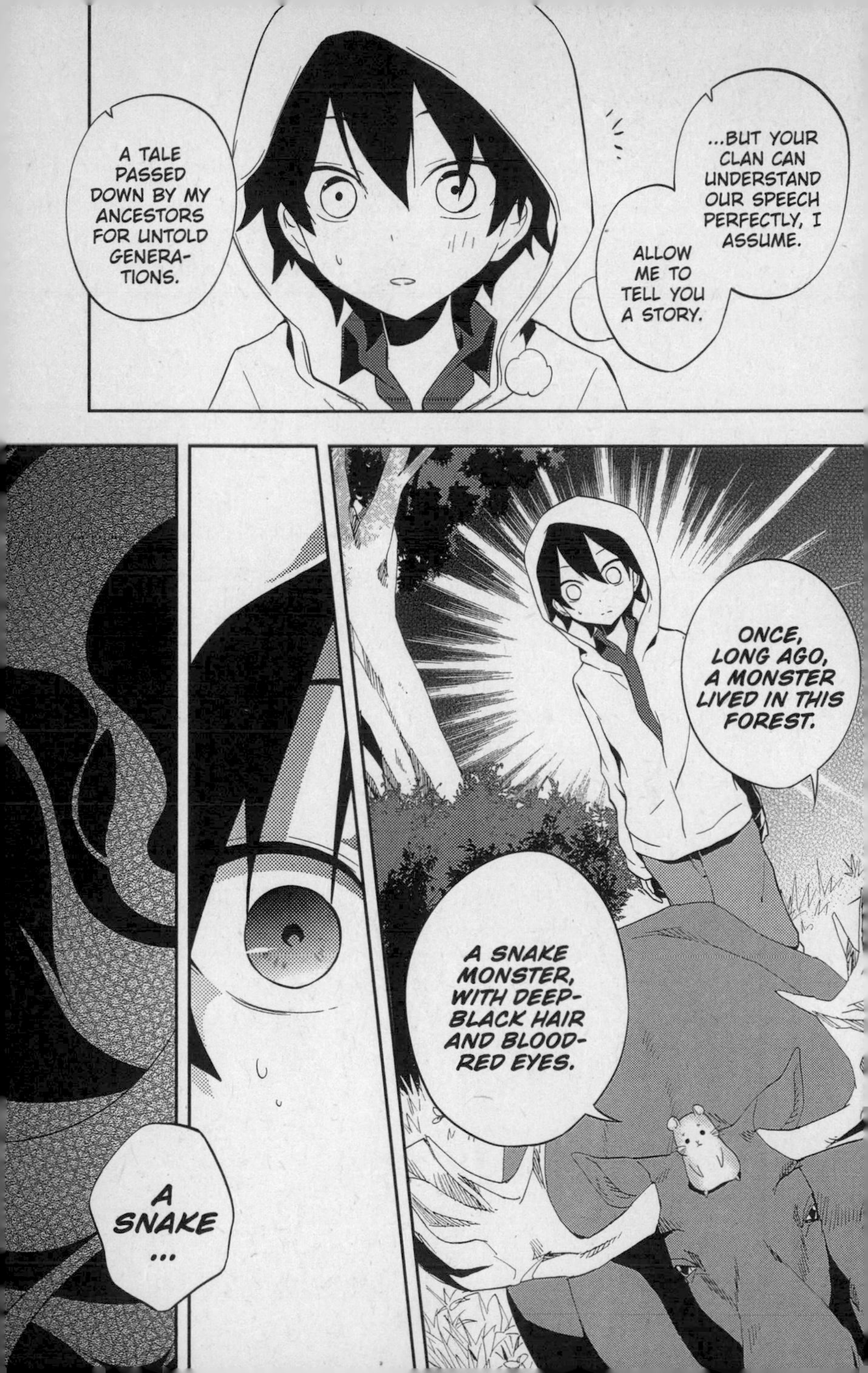
...BUT YOUR CLAN CAN UNDERSTAND OUR SPEECH PERFECTLY, I ASSUME.
ALLOW ME TO TELL YOU A STORY.
A TALE PASSED DOWN BY MY ANCESTORS FOR UNTOLD GENERATIONS.
ONCE, LONG AGO, A MONSTER LIVED IN THIS FOREST.
A SNAKE MONSTER, WITH DEEP-BLACK HAIR AND BLOOD-RED EYES.
A SNAKE...

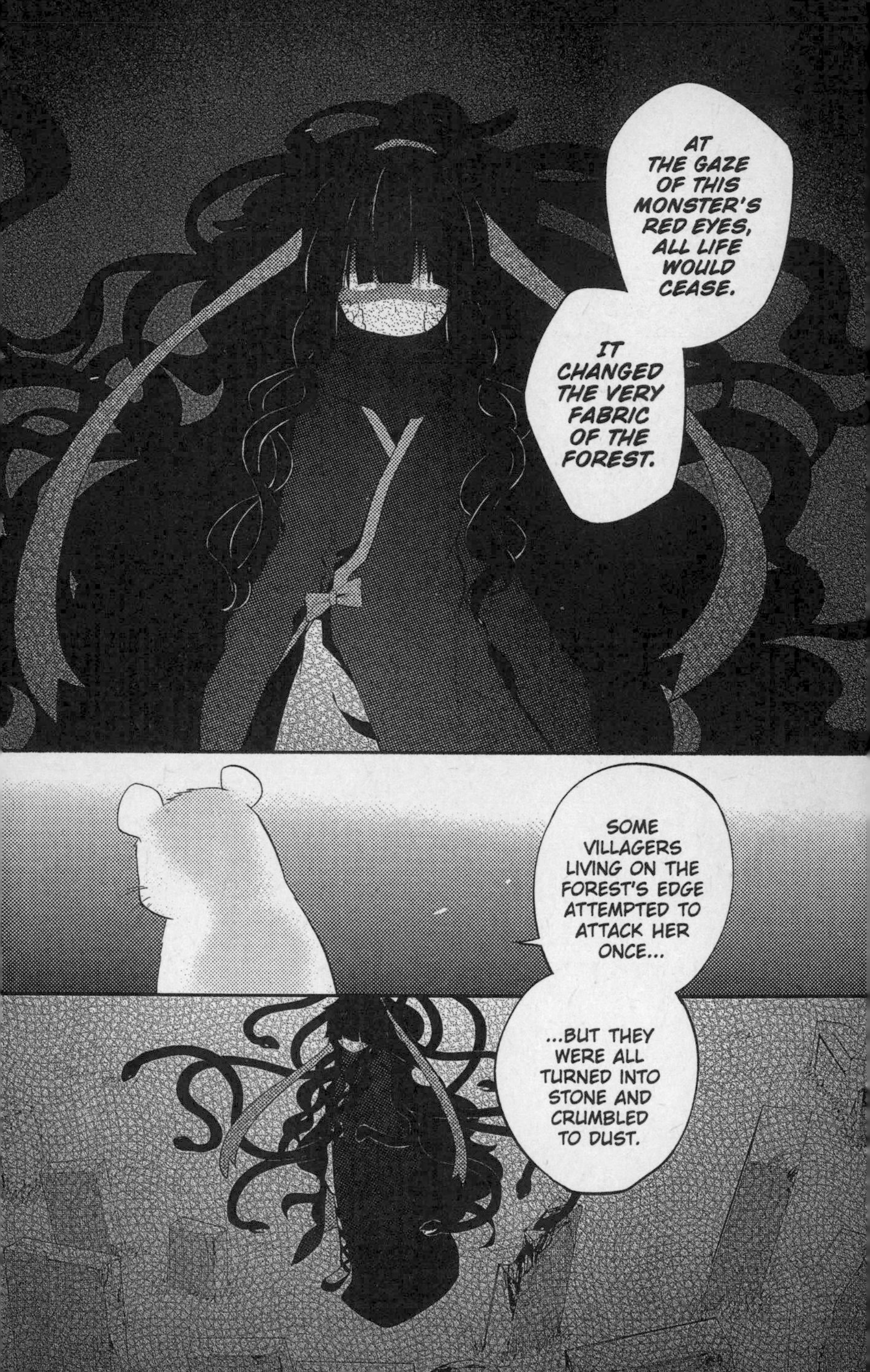
AT THE GAZE OF THIS MONSTER'S RED EYES, ALL LIFE WOULD CEASE.
IT CHANGED THE VERY FABRIC OF THE FOREST.
SOME VILLAGERS LIVING ON THE FOREST'S EDGE ATTEMPTED TO ATTACK HER ONCE...
...BUT THEY WERE ALL TURNED INTO STONE AND CRUMBLED TO DUST.

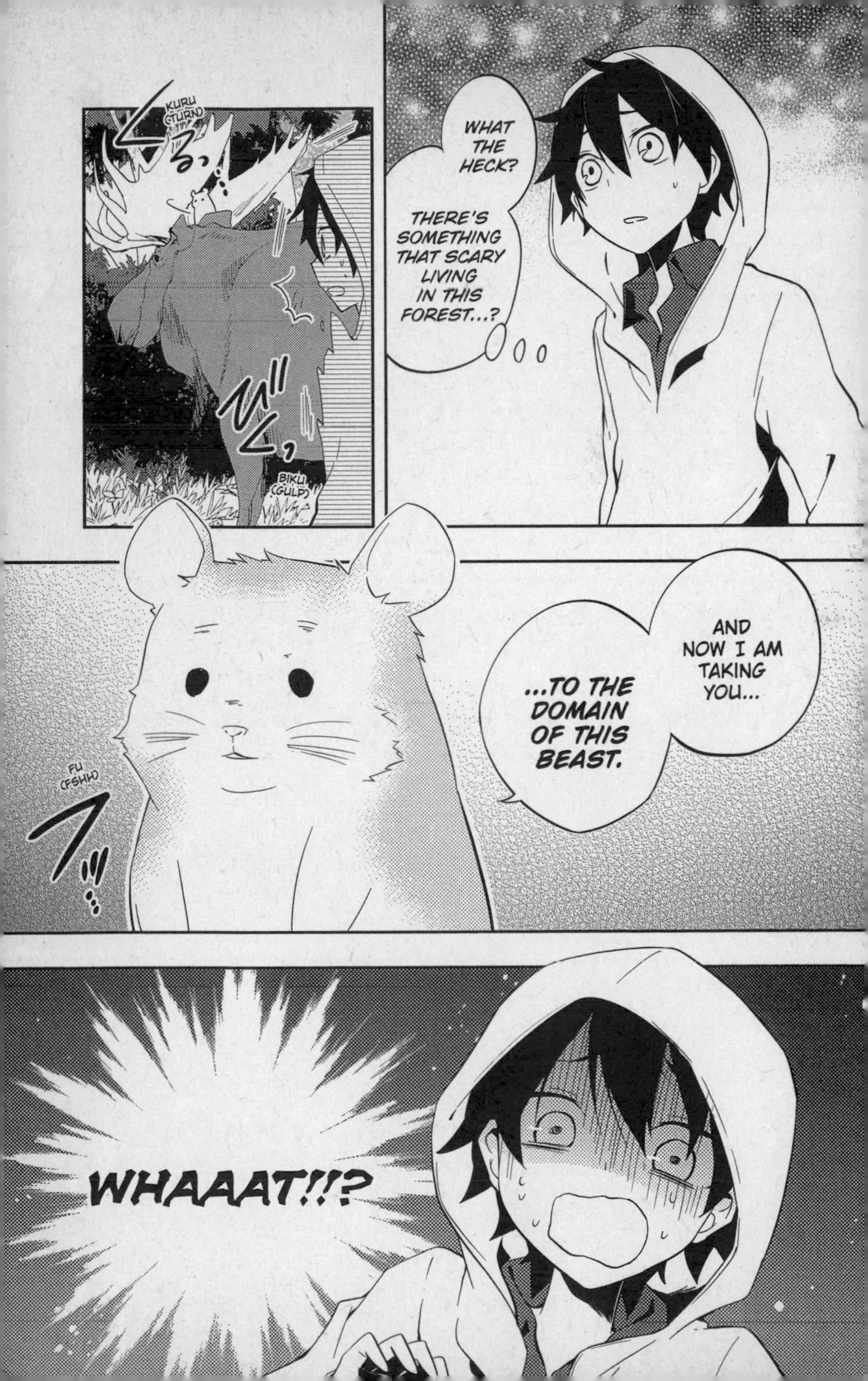
WHAT THE HECK?
THERE'S SOMETHING THAT SCARY LIVING IN THIS FOREST...?
KURU (TURN)
BIKU (GULP)
AND NOW I AM TAKING YOU...
...TO THE DOMAIN OF THIS BEAST.
FU (FSHH)
WHAAAT!!?

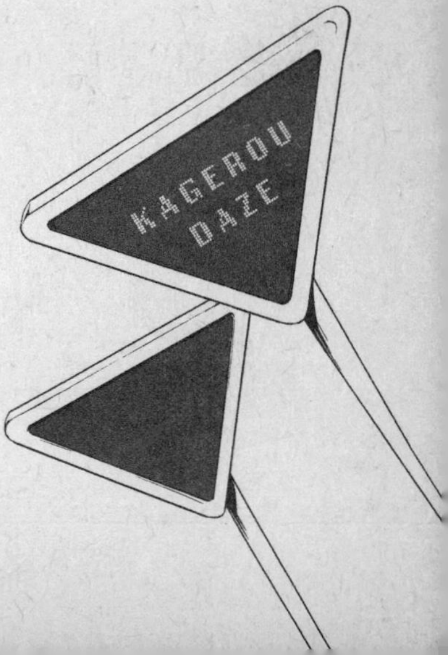
KAGEROU
DAZE

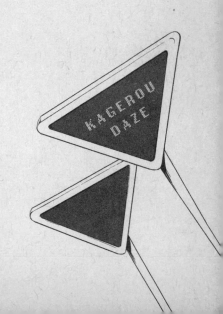

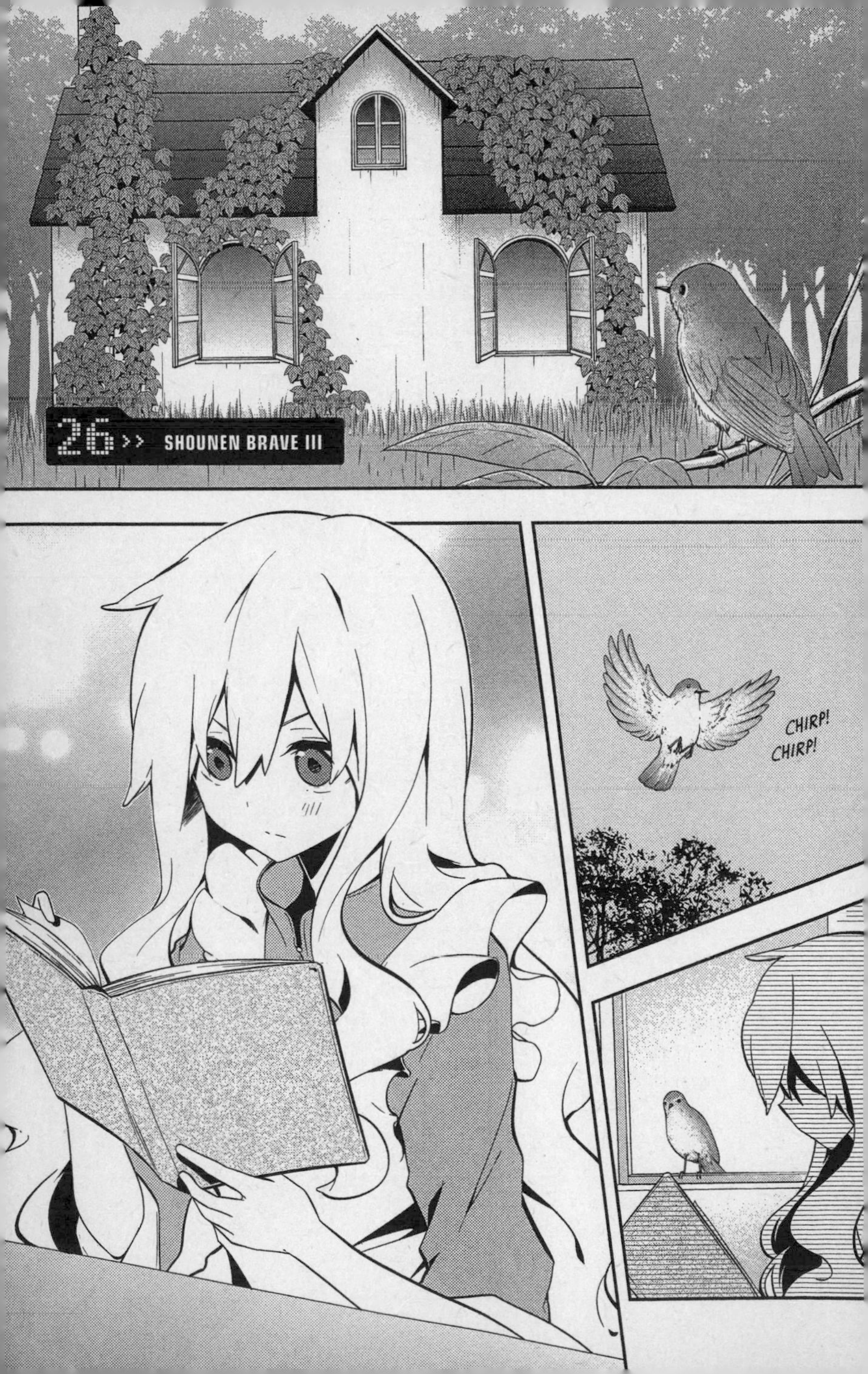
26 >> SHOUNEN BRAVE III
CHIRP! CHIRP!

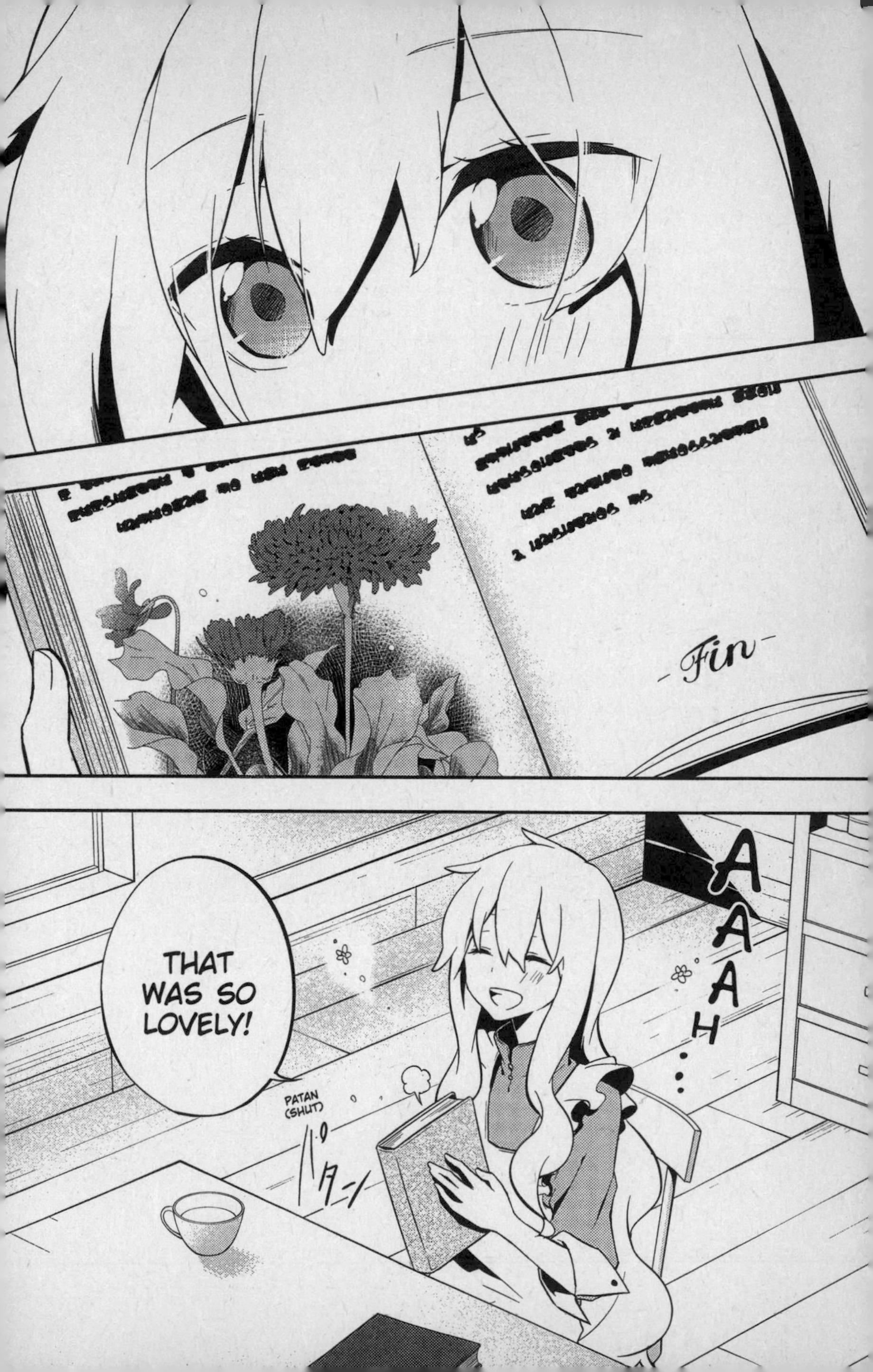

Fin
AAAAH...
THAT WAS SO LOVELY!
PATAN (SHUT)

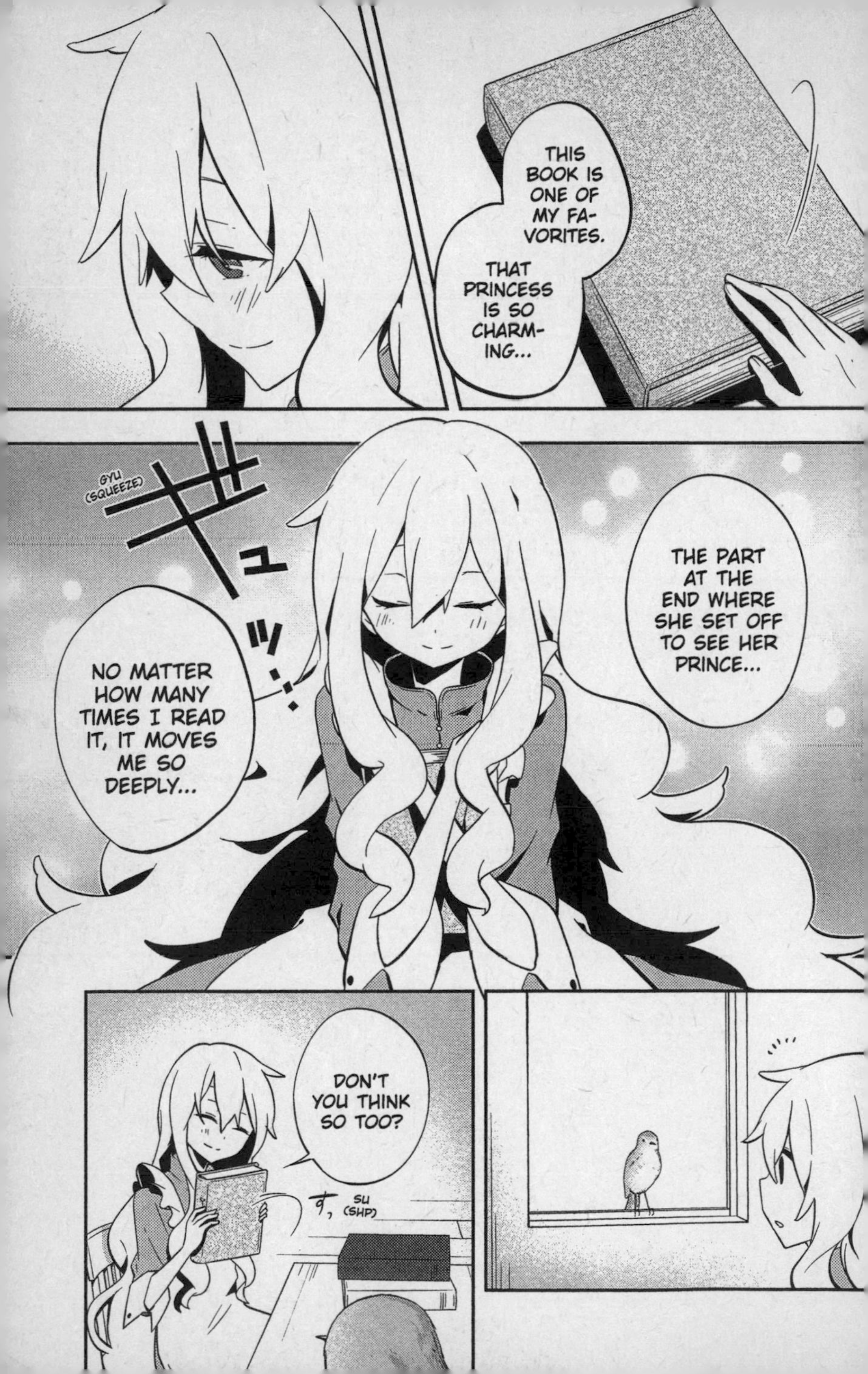
THIS BOOK IS ONE OF MY FAVORITES.
THAT PRINCESS IS SO CHARMING...
THE PART AT THE END WHERE SHE SET OFF TO SEE HER PRINCE...
ギュッ
GYU (SQUEEZE)
NO MATTER HOW MANY TIMES I READ IT, IT MOVES ME SO DEEPLY...
DON'T YOU THINK SO TOO?
す,
SU (SHP)

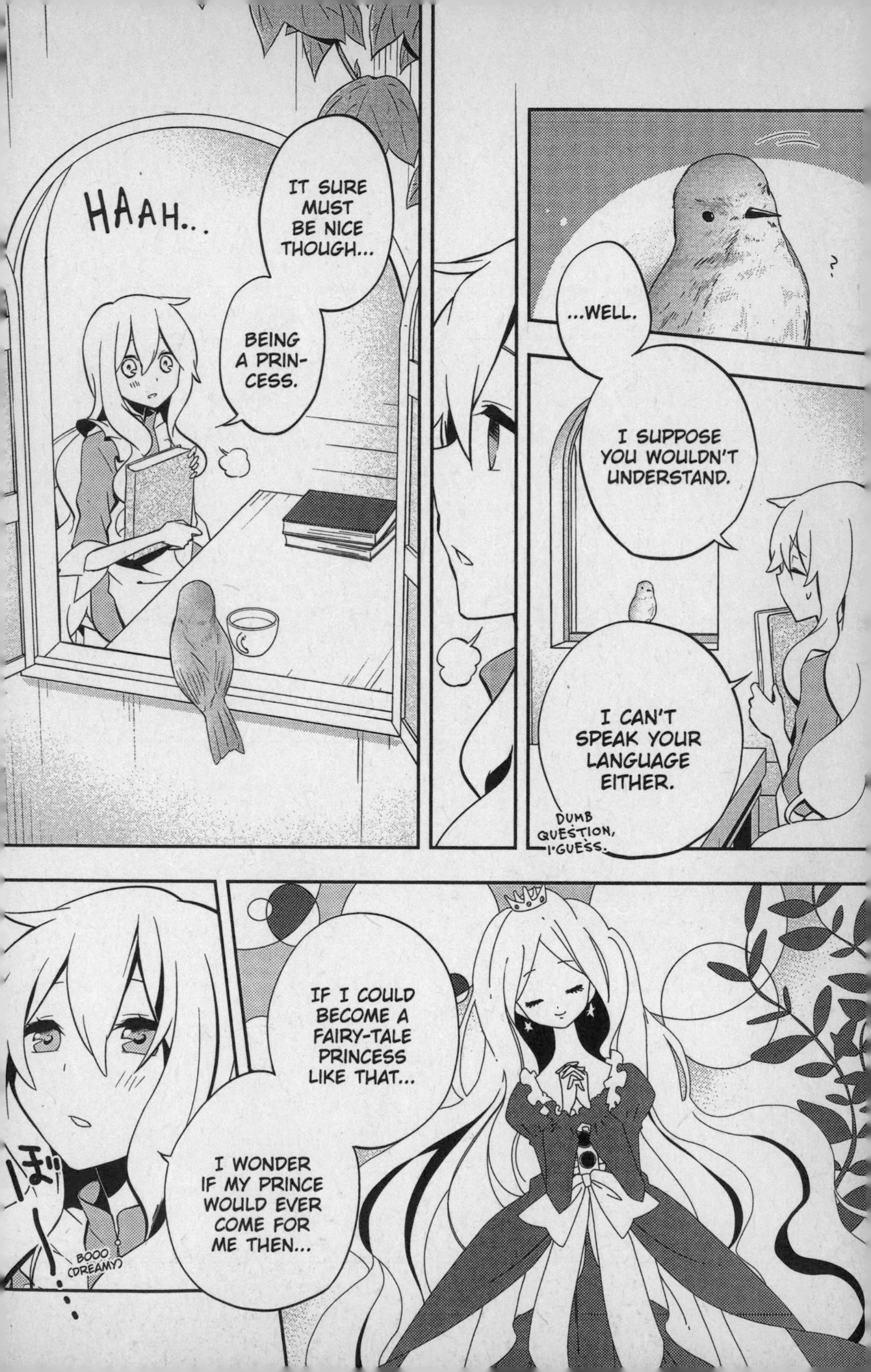
...WELL.
I SUPPOSE YOU WOULDN'T UNDERSTAND.
I CAN'T SPEAK YOUR LANGUAGE EITHER.
DUMB QUESTION, I GUESS.
HAAH...
IT SURE MUST BE NICE THOUGH...
BEING A PRINCESS.
IF I COULD BECOME A FAIRY-TALE PRINCESS LIKE THAT...
I WONDER IF MY PRINCE WOULD EVER COME FOR ME THEN...
BOOO (DREAMY)

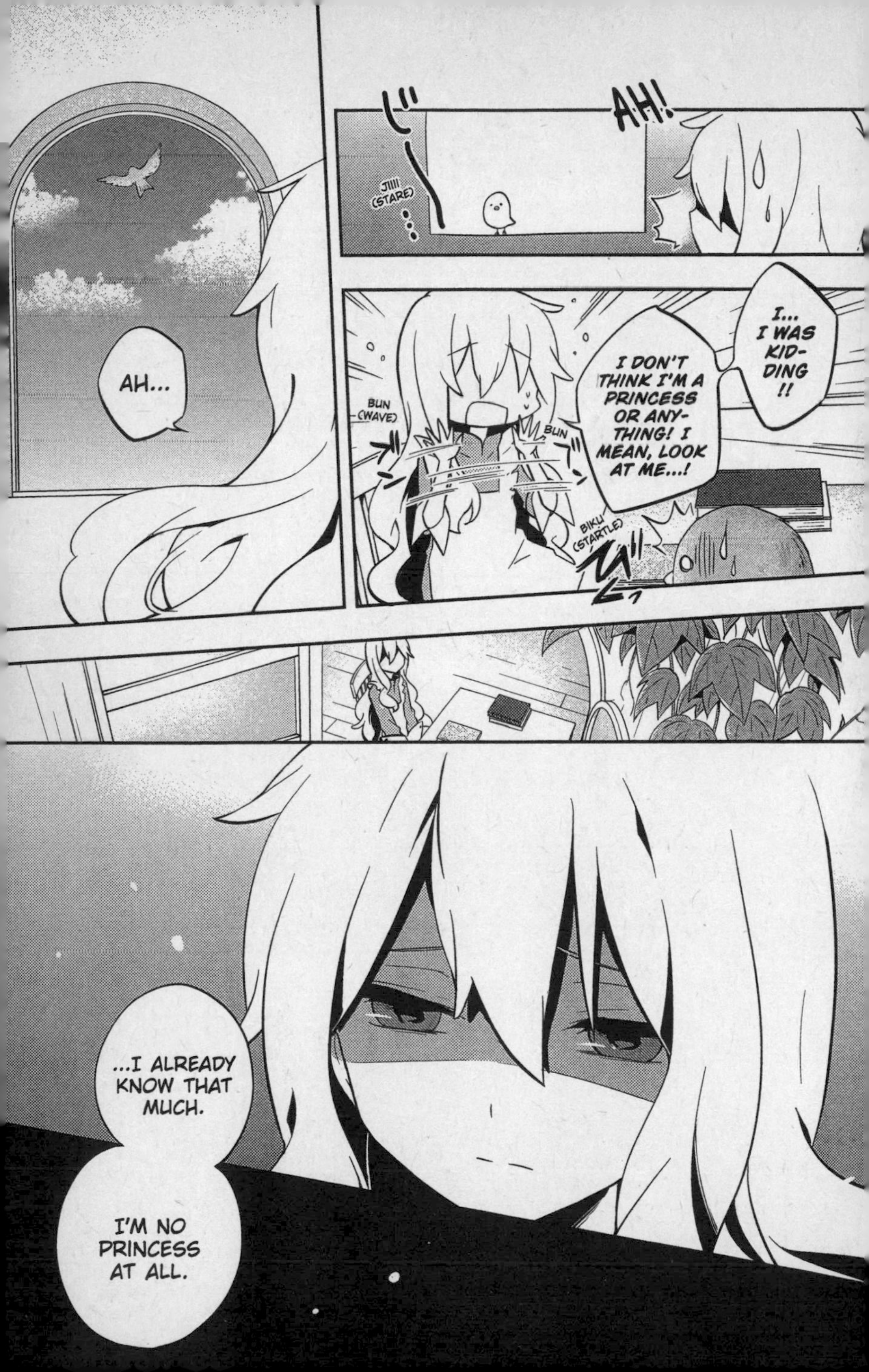
AH!
じー
JIIII (STARE)
I... I WAS KID-DING!!
I DON'T THINK I'M A PRINCESS OR ANY-THING! I MEAN, LOOK AT ME...!
BIKU (STARTLE)
BUN
BUN (WAVE)
AH...
...I ALREADY KNOW THAT MUCH.
I'M NO PRINCESS AT ALL.

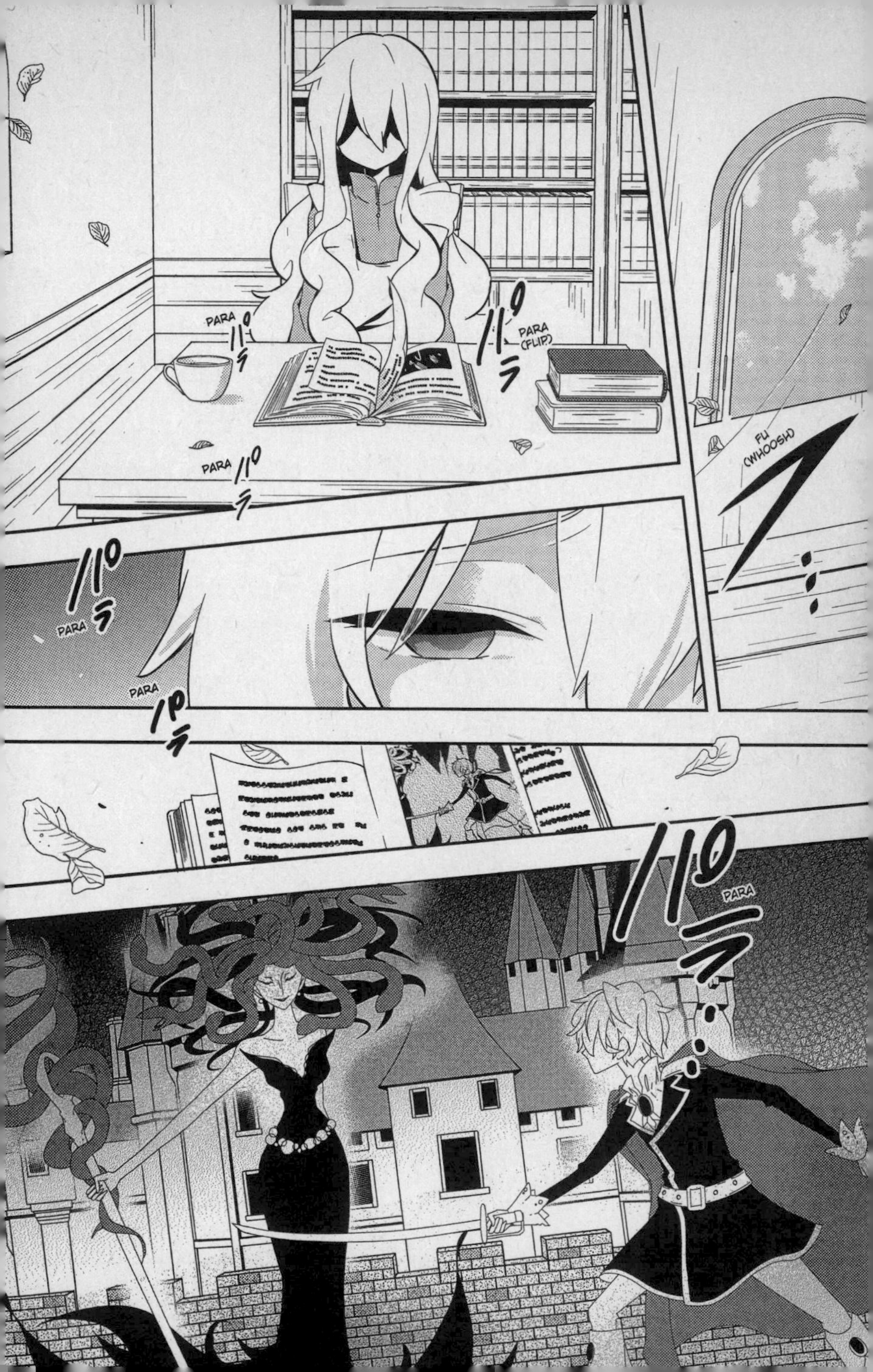
FU (WHOOSH)
...
PARA (FLIP)
PARA
PARA
PARA
PARA
PARA
...

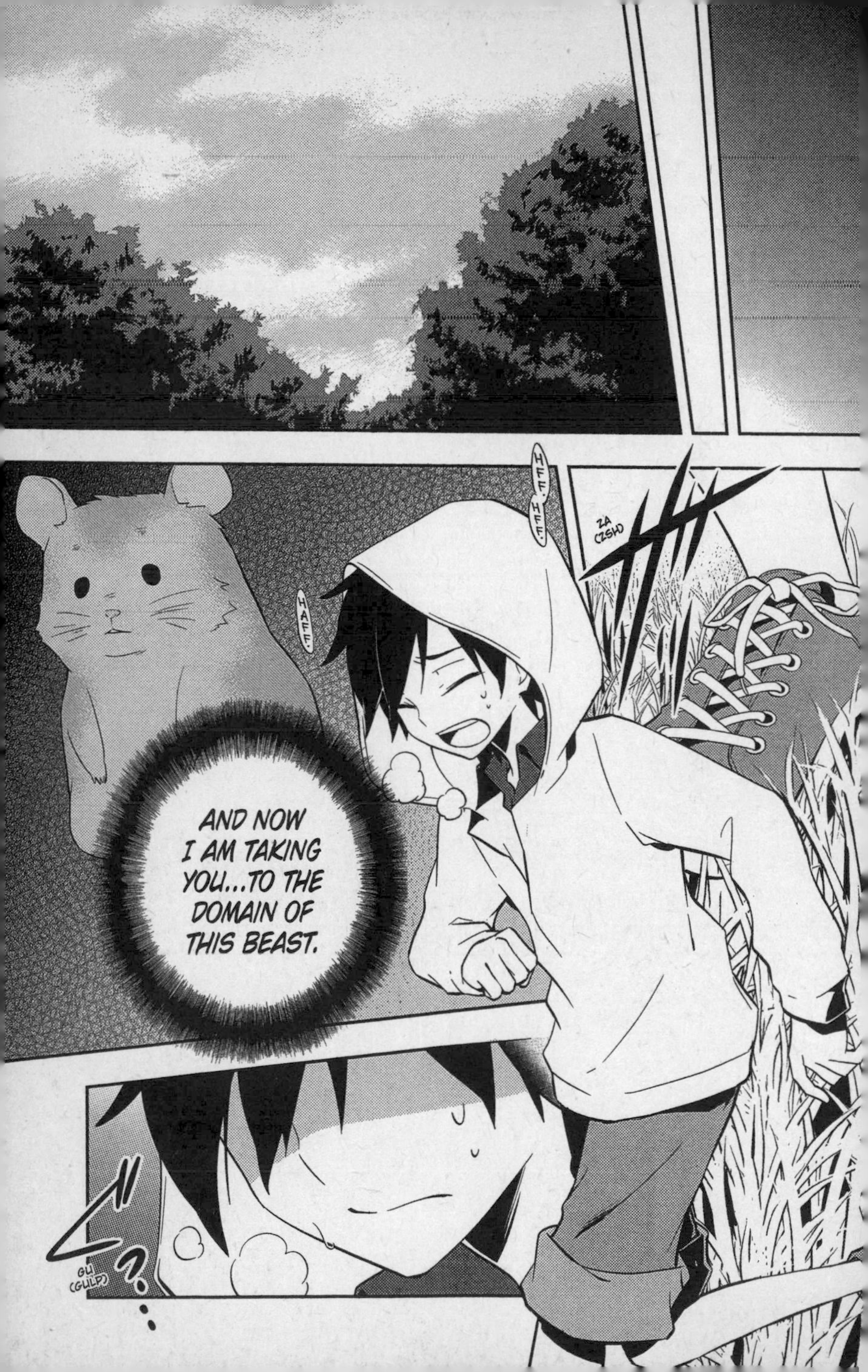
ZA (ZSH)
HFF. HFF.
HAFF.
AND NOW I AM TAKING YOU...TO THE DOMAIN OF THIS BEAST.
GU (GULP)

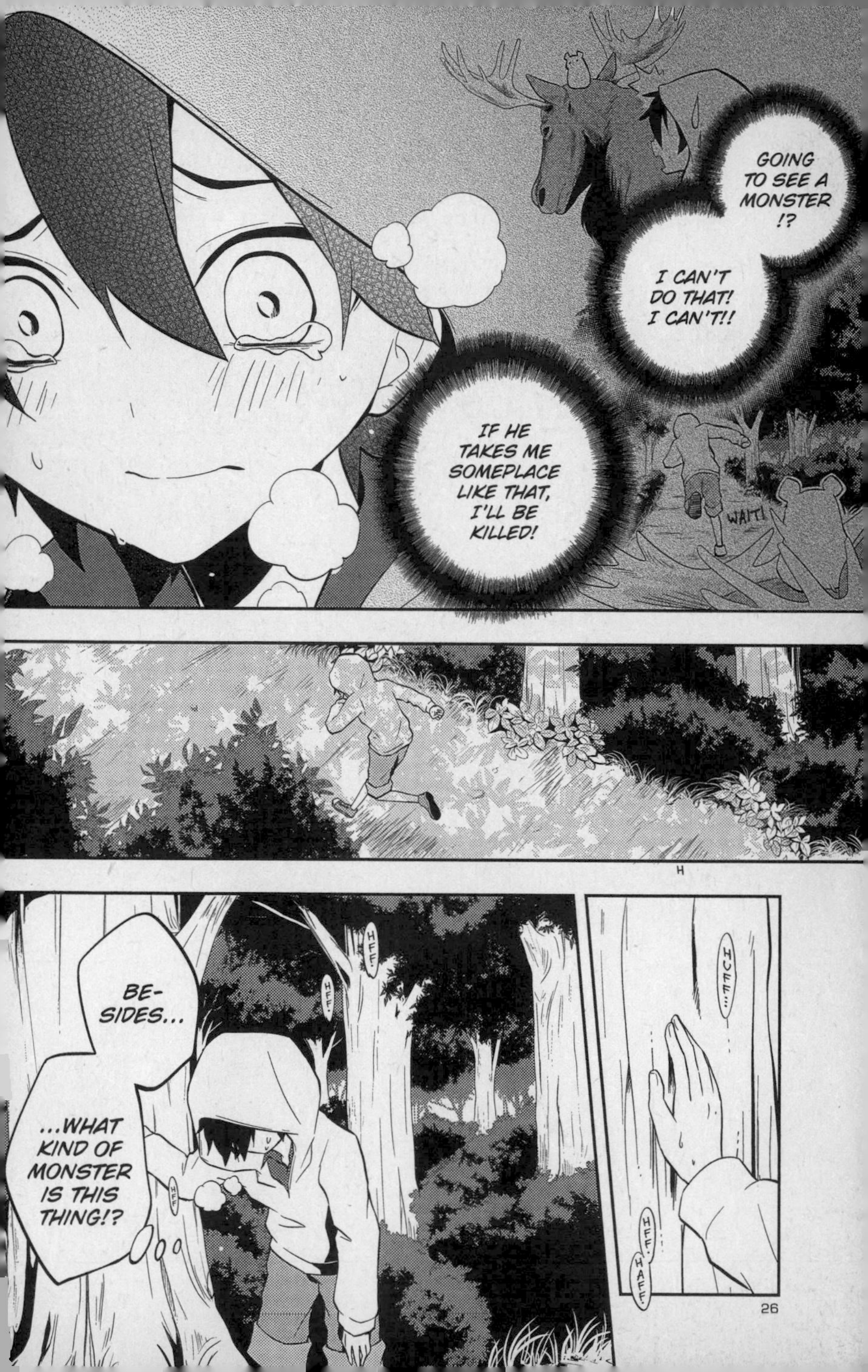
GOING TO SEE A MONSTER!?
I CAN'T DO THAT! I CAN'T!!
IF HE TAKES ME SOMEPLACE LIKE THAT, I'LL BE KILLED!
WAIT!
HUFF...
HFF.
HAFF.
HFF.
HFF.
BE-SIDES...
...WHAT KIND OF MONSTER IS THIS THING!?
HFF

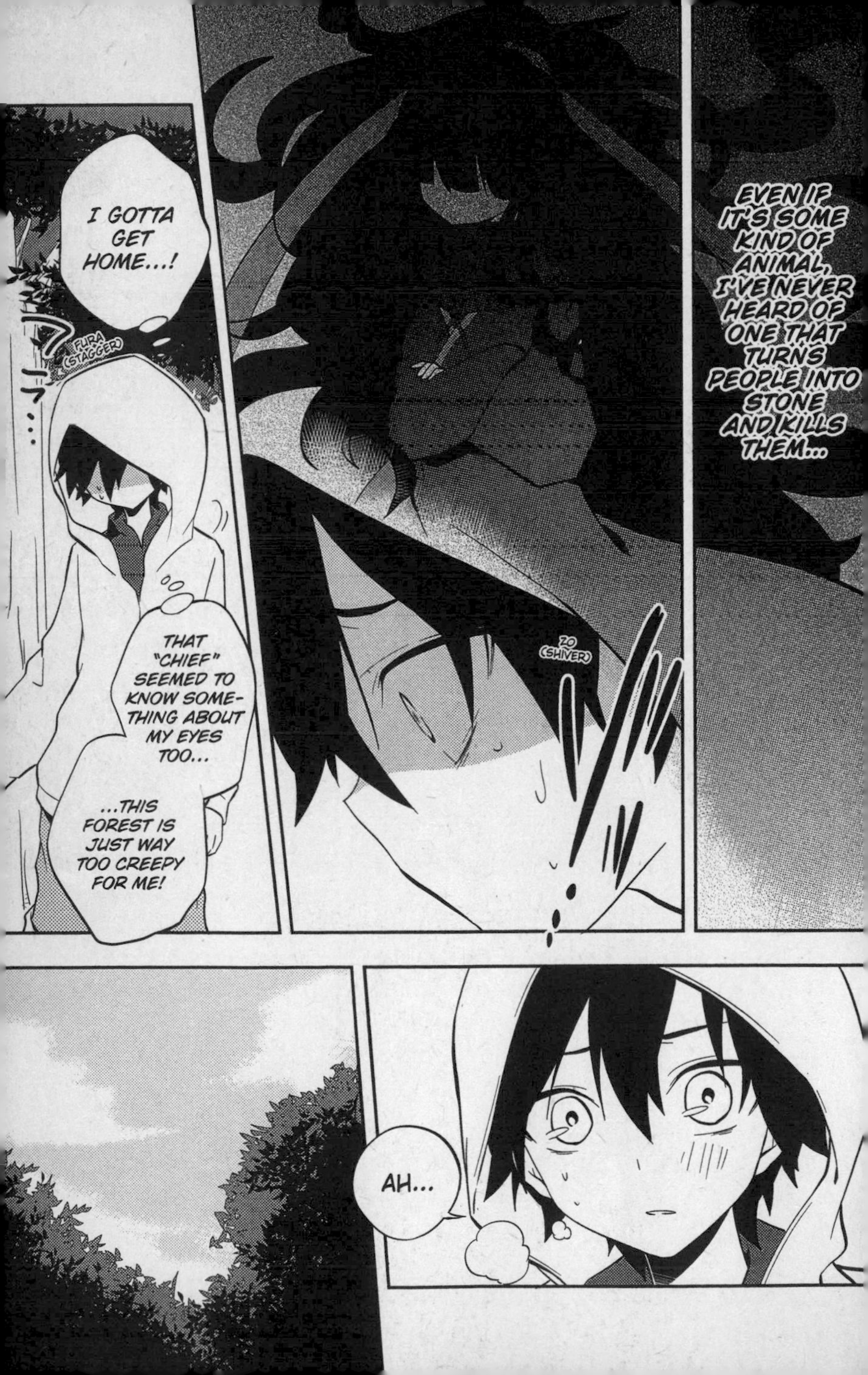
EVEN IF IT'S SOME KIND OF ANIMAL, I'VE NEVER HEARD OF ONE THAT TURNS PEOPLE INTO STONE AND KILLS THEM...
ZO (SHIVER)
I GOTTA GET HOME...!
FURA (STAGGER)
THAT "CHIEF" SEEMED TO KNOW SOME-THING ABOUT MY EYES TOO...
...THIS FOREST IS JUST WAY TOO CREEPY FOR ME!
AH...

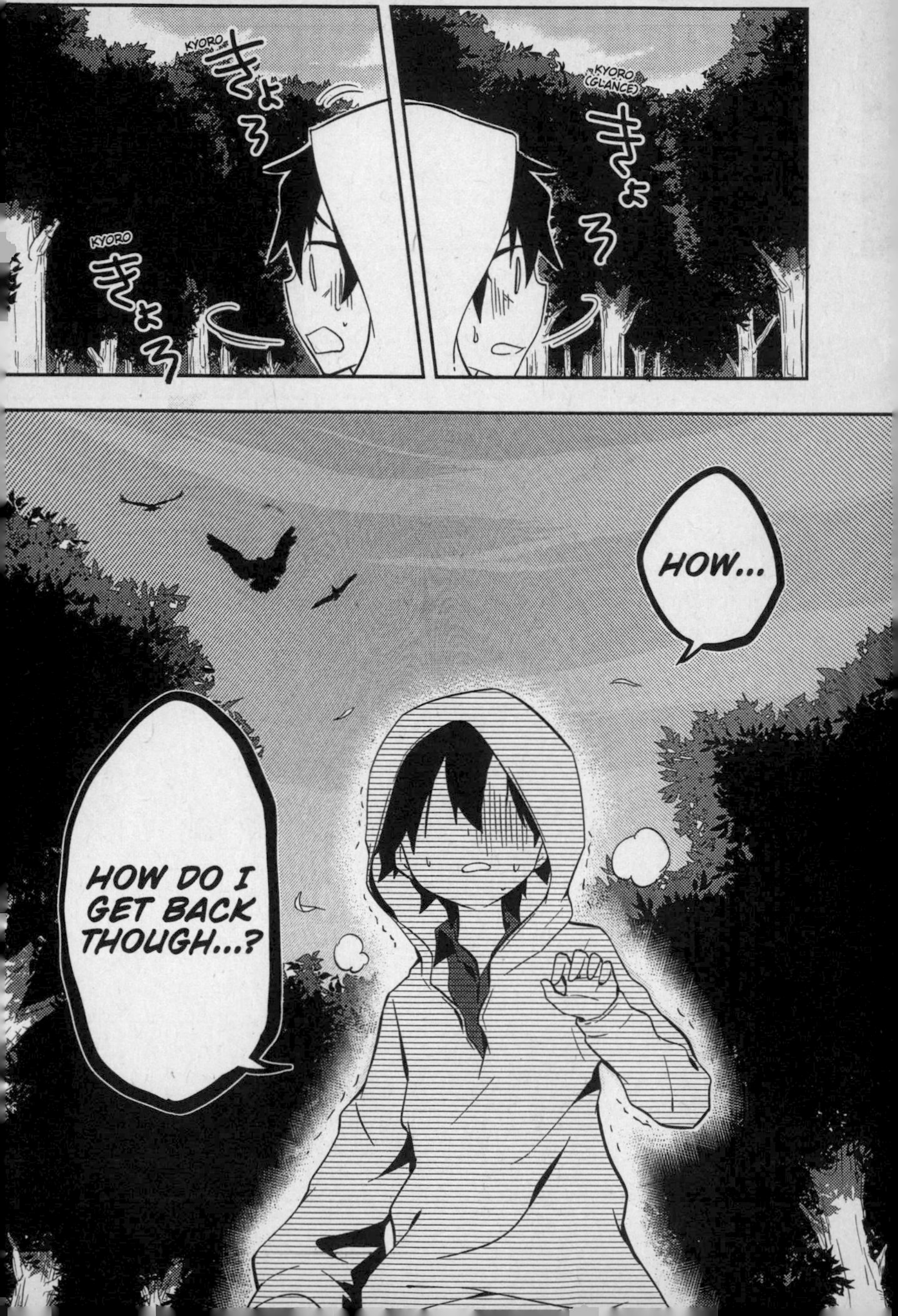
KYORO (GLANCE)
きょろ
KYORO
きょろ
KYORO
きょろ
HOW...
HOW DO I GET BACK THOUGH...?

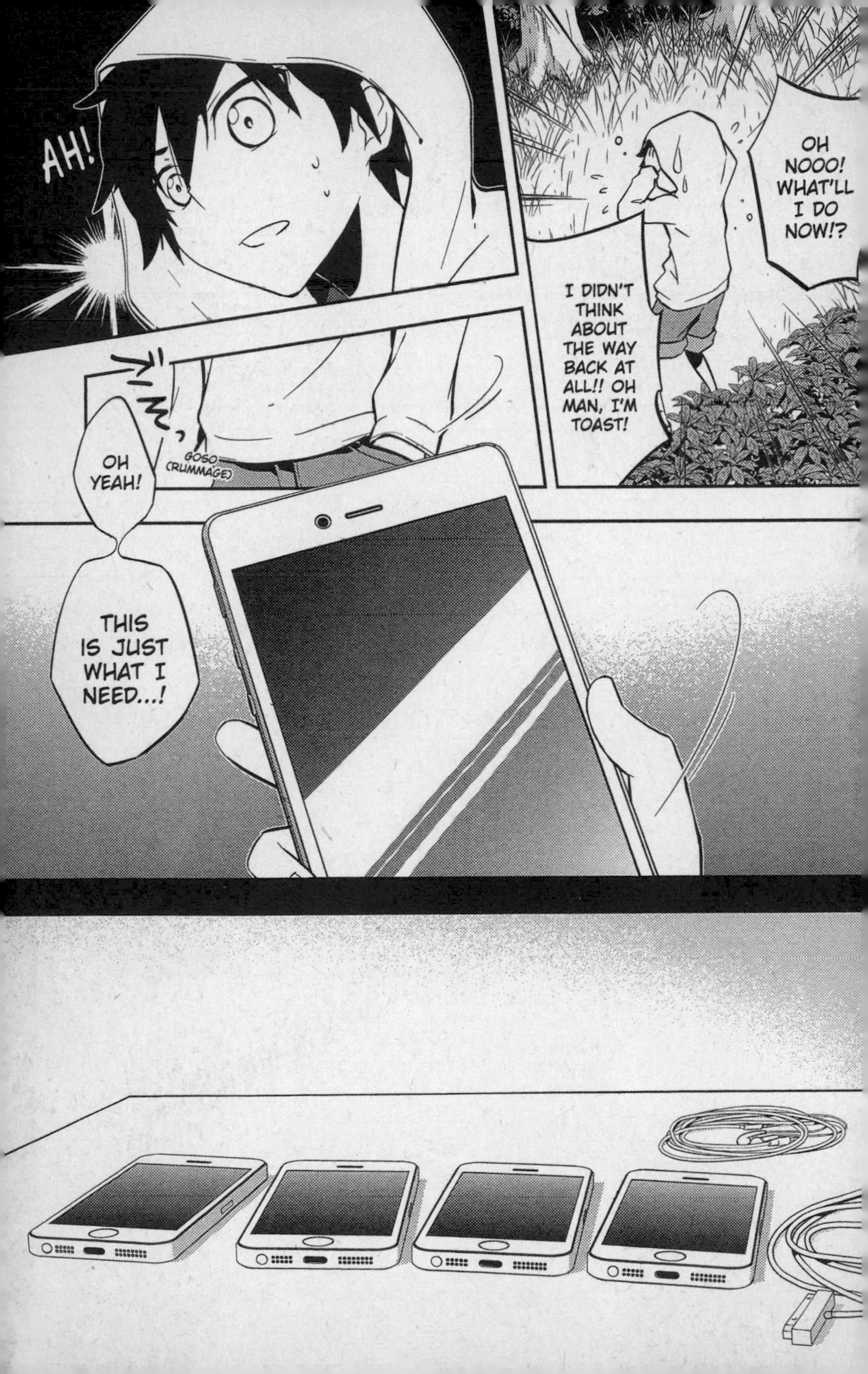
OH NOOO! WHAT'LL I DO NOW!?
I DIDN'T THINK ABOUT THE WAY BACK AT ALL!! OH MAN, I'M TOAST!
AH!
GOSO (RUMMAGE)
OH YEAH!
THIS IS JUST WHAT I NEED...!

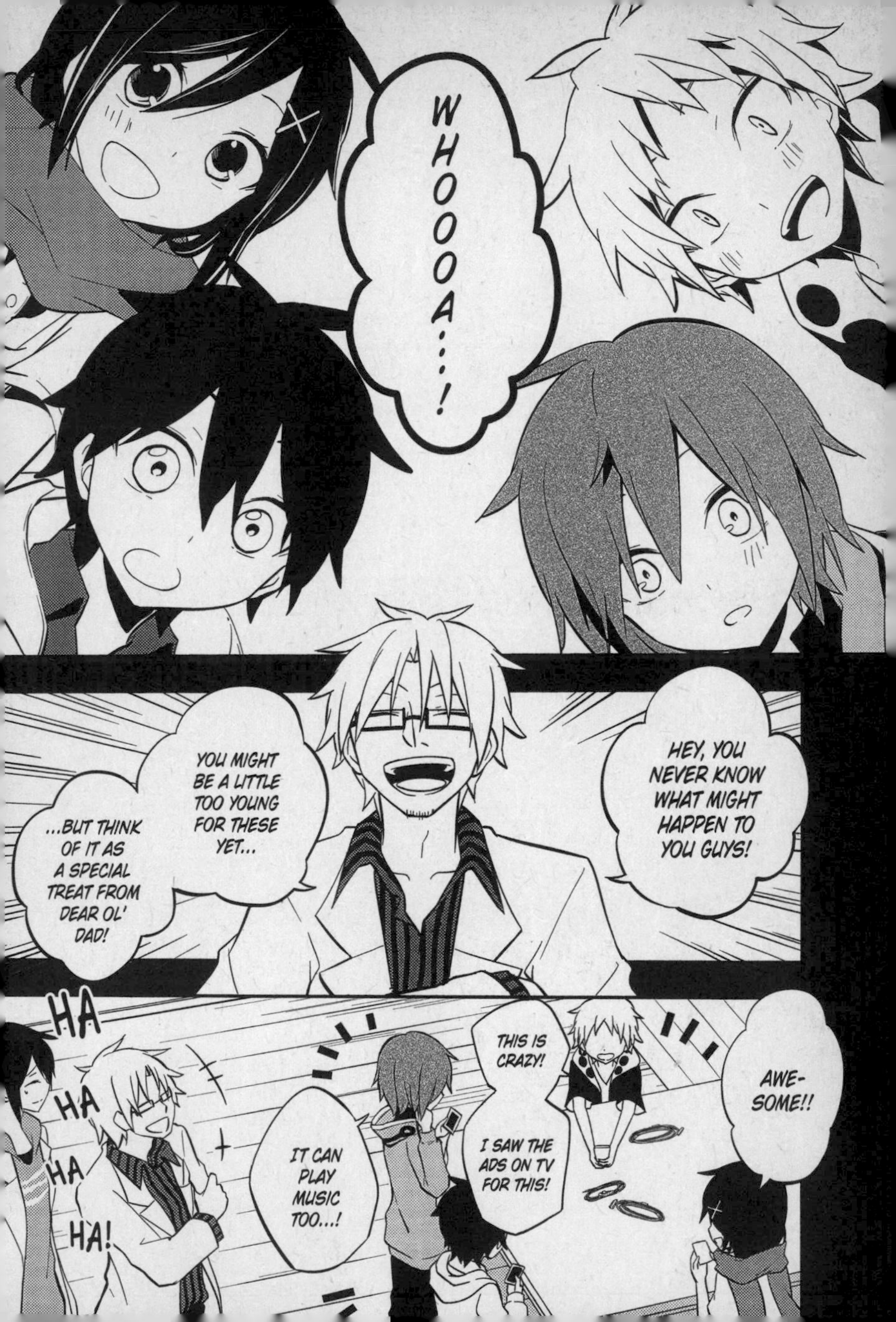
WHOOOA...!
HEY, YOU NEVER KNOW WHAT MIGHT HAPPEN TO YOU GUYS!
YOU MIGHT BE A LITTLE TOO YOUNG FOR THESE YET...
...BUT THINK OF IT AS A SPECIAL TREAT FROM DEAR OL' DAD!
AWE-SOME!!
THIS IS CRAZY!
I SAW THE ADS ON TV FOR THIS!
IT CAN PLAY MUSIC TOO...!
HA HA HA HA!

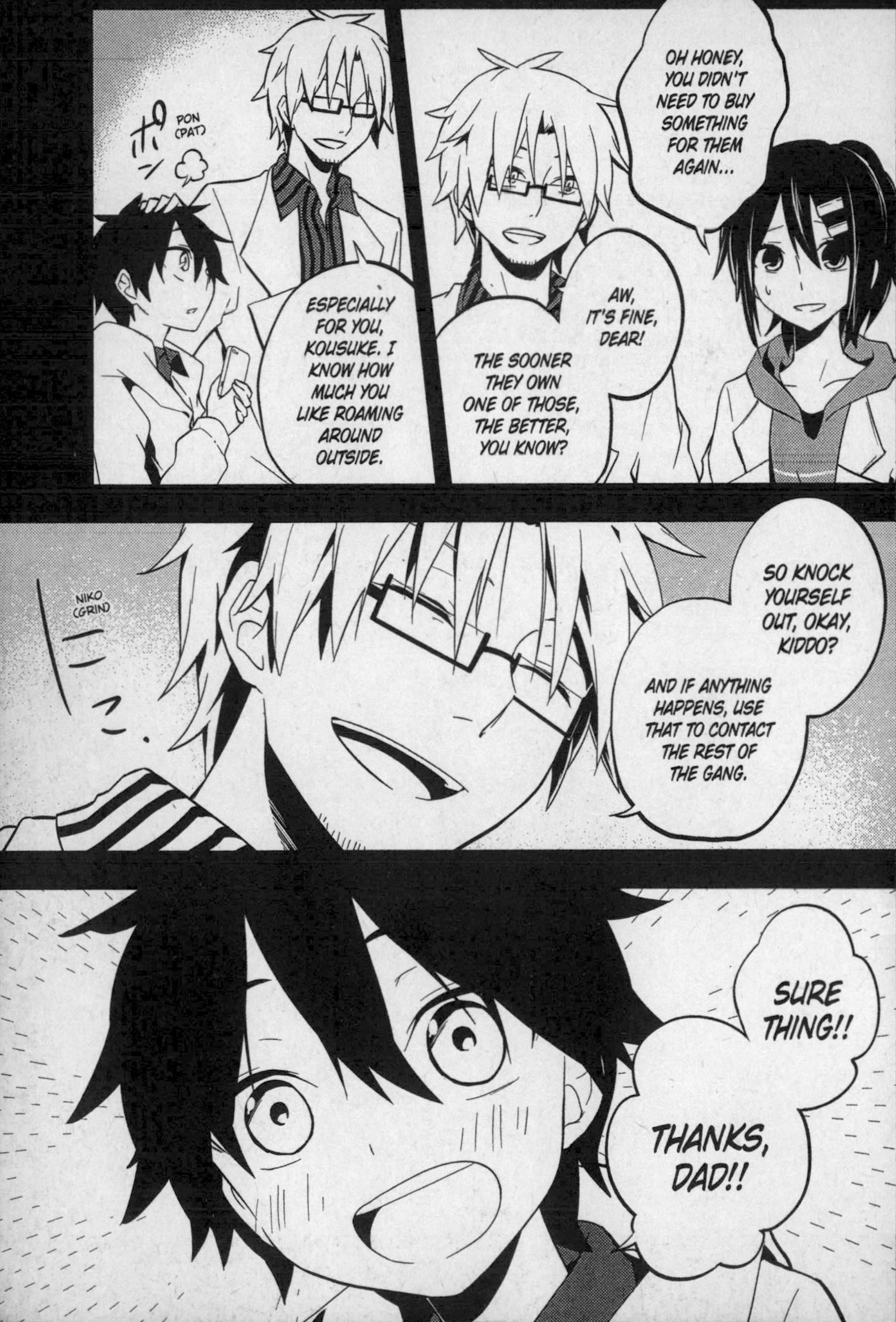
OH HONEY, YOU DIDN'T NEED TO BUY SOMETHING FOR THEM AGAIN...
AW, IT'S FINE, DEAR!
THE SOONER THEY OWN ONE OF THOSE, THE BETTER, YOU KNOW?
PON (PAT)
ESPECIALLY FOR YOU, KOUSUKE. I KNOW HOW MUCH YOU LIKE ROAMING AROUND OUTSIDE.
SO KNOCK YOURSELF OUT, OKAY, KIDDO?
AND IF ANYTHING HAPPENS, USE THAT TO CONTACT THE REST OF THE GANG.
NIKO (GRIN)
SURE THING!!
THANKS, DAD!!

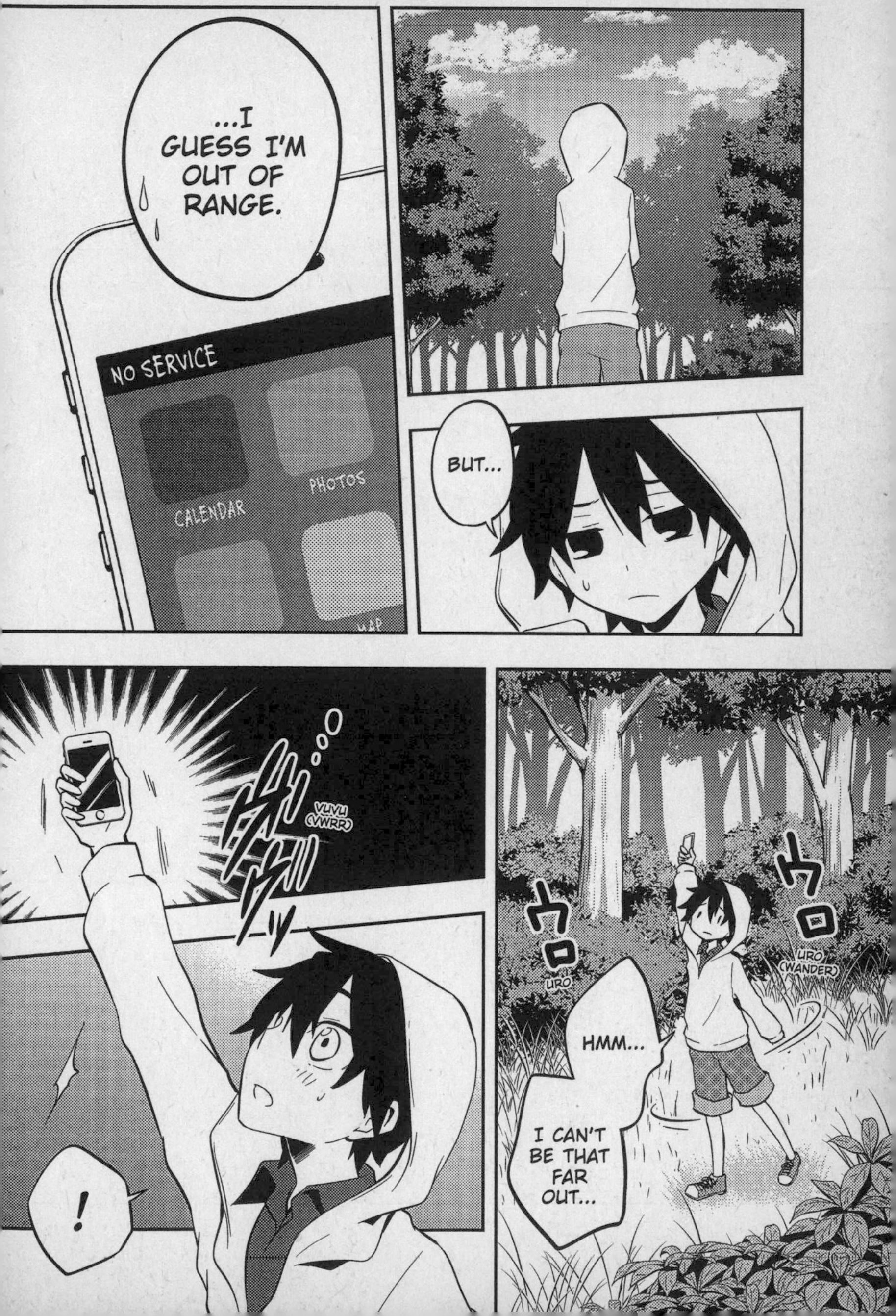
BUT...
...I GUESS I'M OUT OF RANGE.
NO SERVICE
PHOTOS
CALENDAR
MAP
ウロ
URO (WANDER)
ウロ
URO
HMM...
I CAN'T BE THAT FAR OUT...
VUVU (VWRR)
!

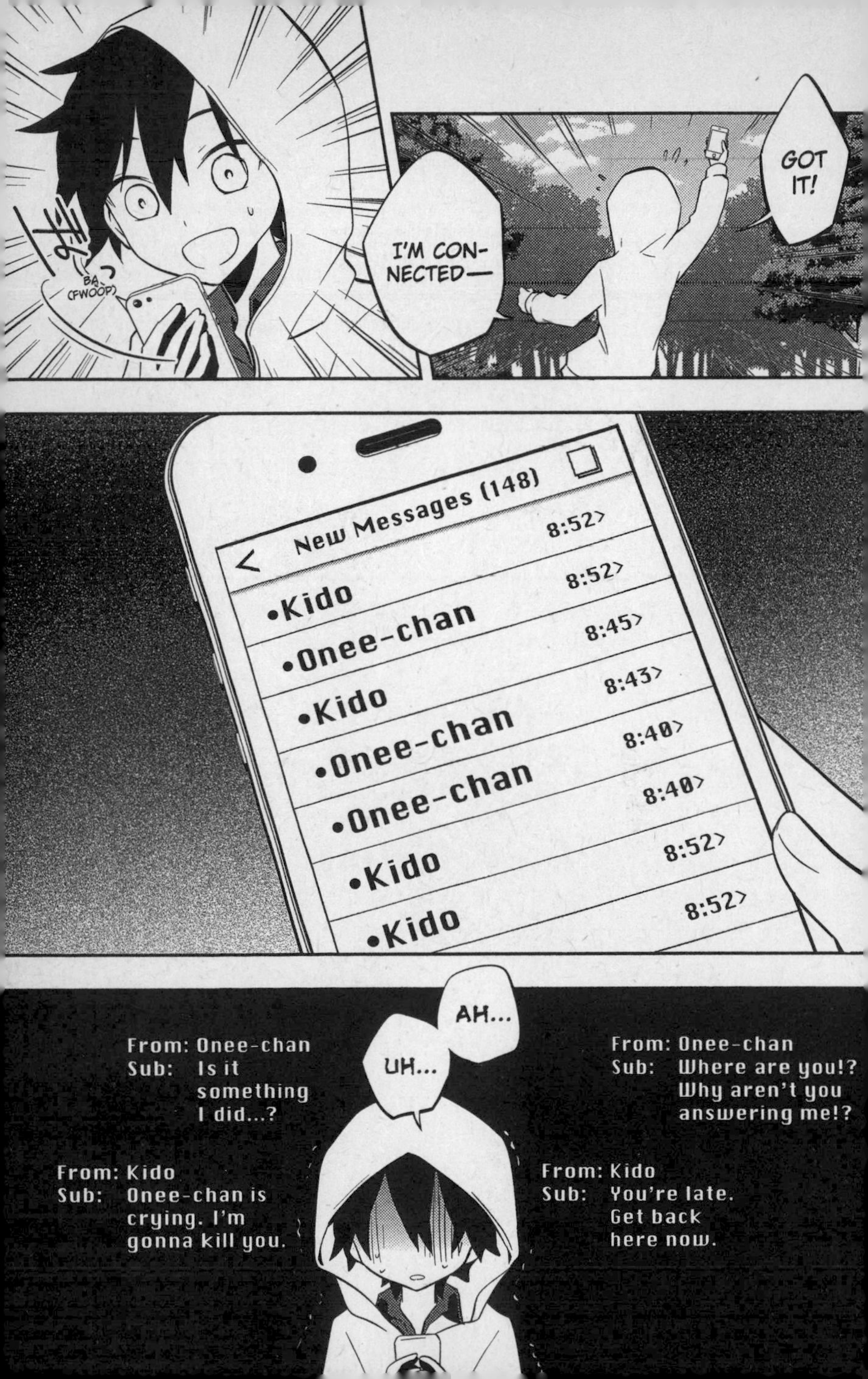
GOT IT!
I'M CON-NECTED—
BA (FWOOP)
New Messages (148)
•Kido 8:52>
•Onee-chan 8:52>
•Kido 8:45>
•Onee-chan 8:43>
•Onee-chan 8:40>
•Kido 8:40>
•Kido 8:52>
8:52>
AH...
UH...
From: Onee-chan Sub: Where are you!? Why aren't you answering me!?
From: Onee-chan Sub: Is it something I did...?
From: Kido Sub: You're late. Get back here now.
From: Kido Sub: Onee-chan is crying. I'm gonna kill you.

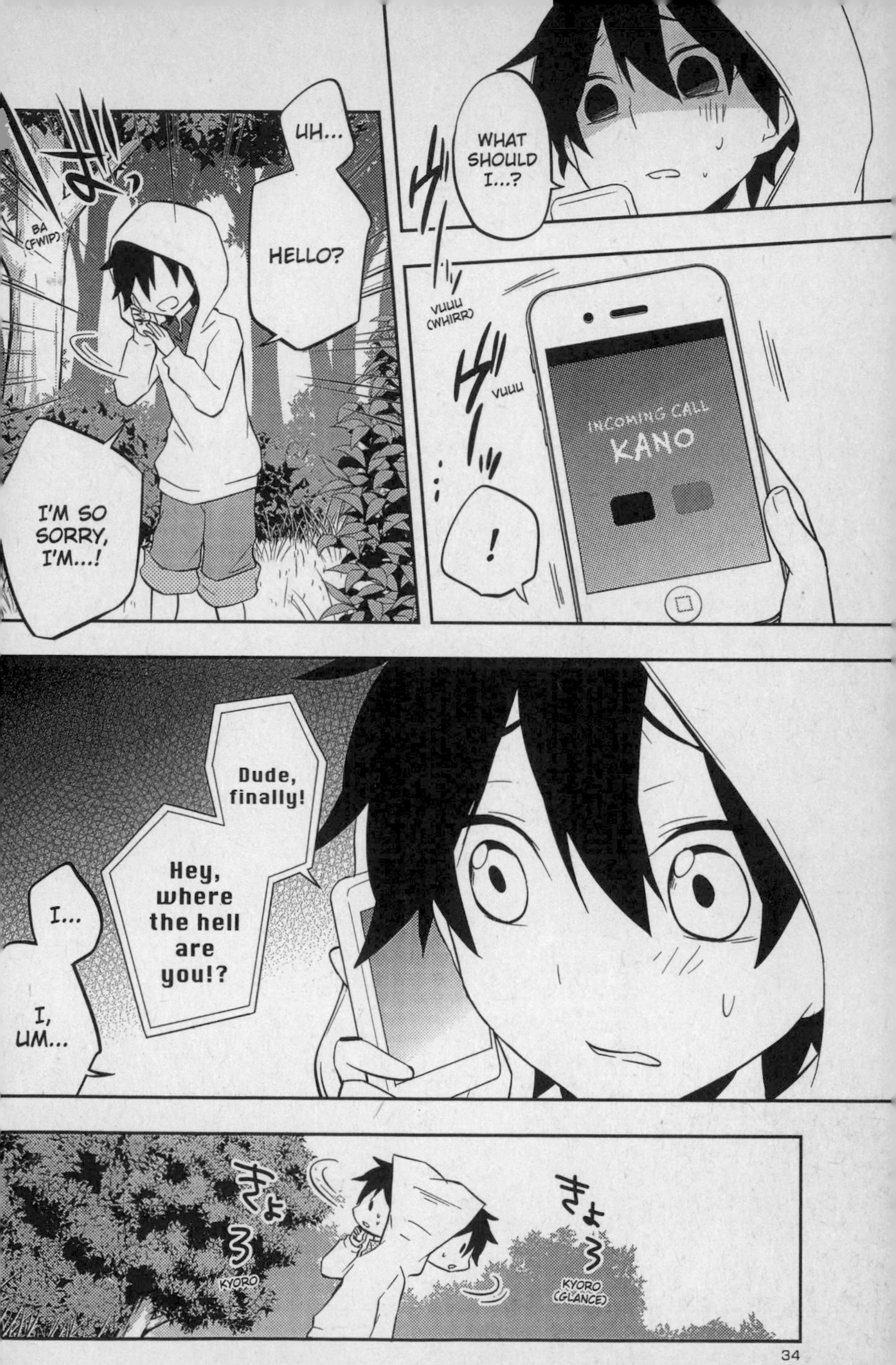
WHAT SHOULD I...?
VUUU (WHIRR)
VUUU
INCOMING CALL
KANO
!
BA (FWIP)
UH...
HELLO?
I'M SO SORRY, I'M...!
Dude, finally!
Hey, where the hell are you!?
I...
I, UM...
きょろ
KYORO (GLANCE)
きょろ
KYORO

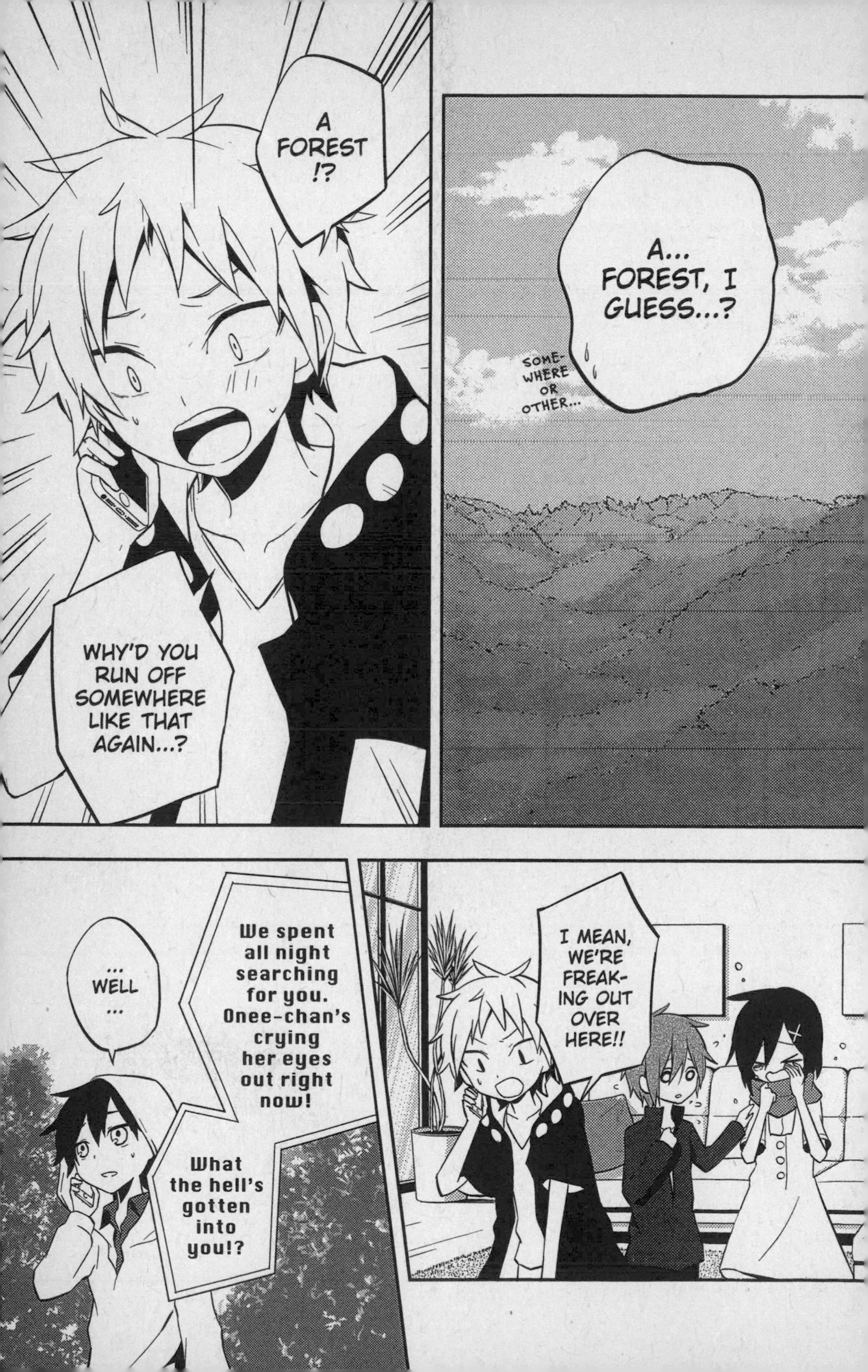
A... FOREST, I GUESS...?
SOME-WHERE OR OTHER...
A FOREST !?
WHY'D YOU RUN OFF SOMEWHERE LIKE THAT AGAIN...?
I MEAN, WE'RE FREAK-ING OUT OVER HERE!!
We spent all night searching for you. Onee-chan's crying her eyes out right now!
What the hell's gotten into you!?
... WELL ...

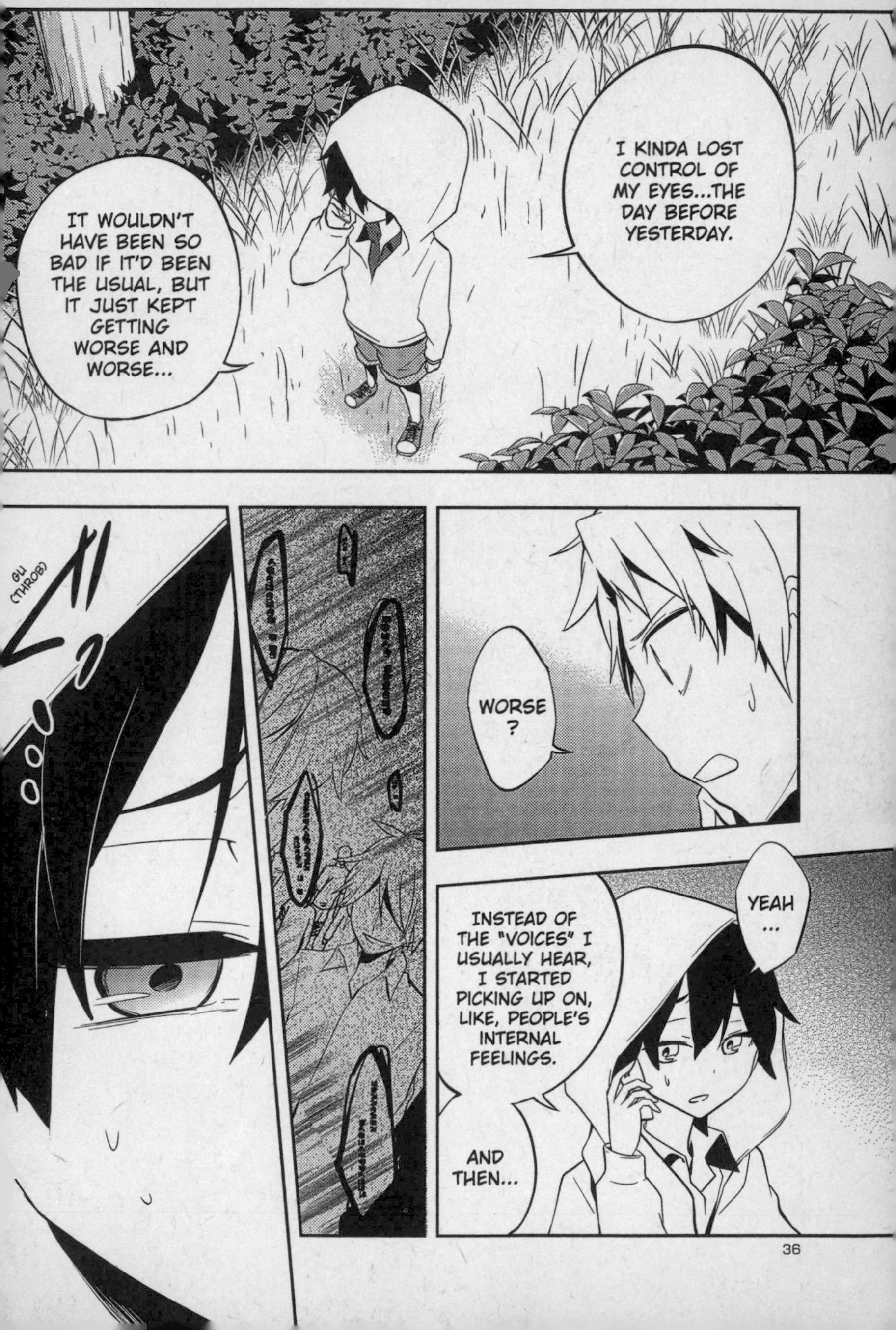
I KINDA LOST CONTROL OF MY EYES...THE DAY BEFORE YESTERDAY.
IT WOULDN'T HAVE BEEN SO BAD IF IT'D BEEN THE USUAL, BUT IT JUST KEPT GETTING WORSE AND WORSE...
WORSE?
YEAH...
INSTEAD OF THE "VOICES" I USUALLY HEAR, I STARTED PICKING UP ON, LIKE, PEOPLE'S INTERNAL FEELINGS.
AND THEN...
GU (THROB)

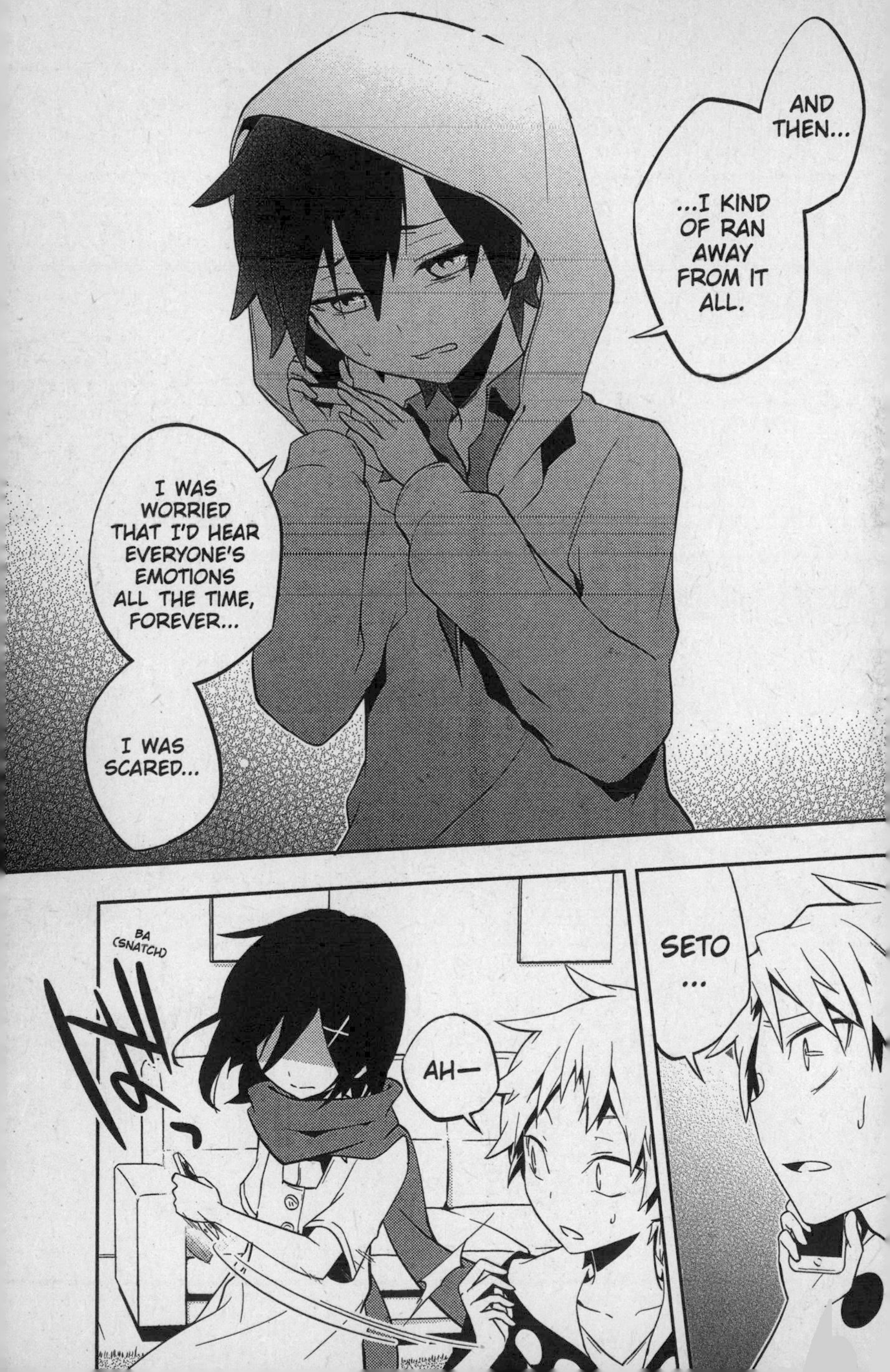
AND THEN...
...I KIND OF RAN AWAY FROM IT ALL.
I WAS WORRIED THAT I'D HEAR EVERYONE'S EMOTIONS ALL THE TIME, FOREVER...
I WAS SCARED...
SETO ...
BA (SNATCH)
AH—

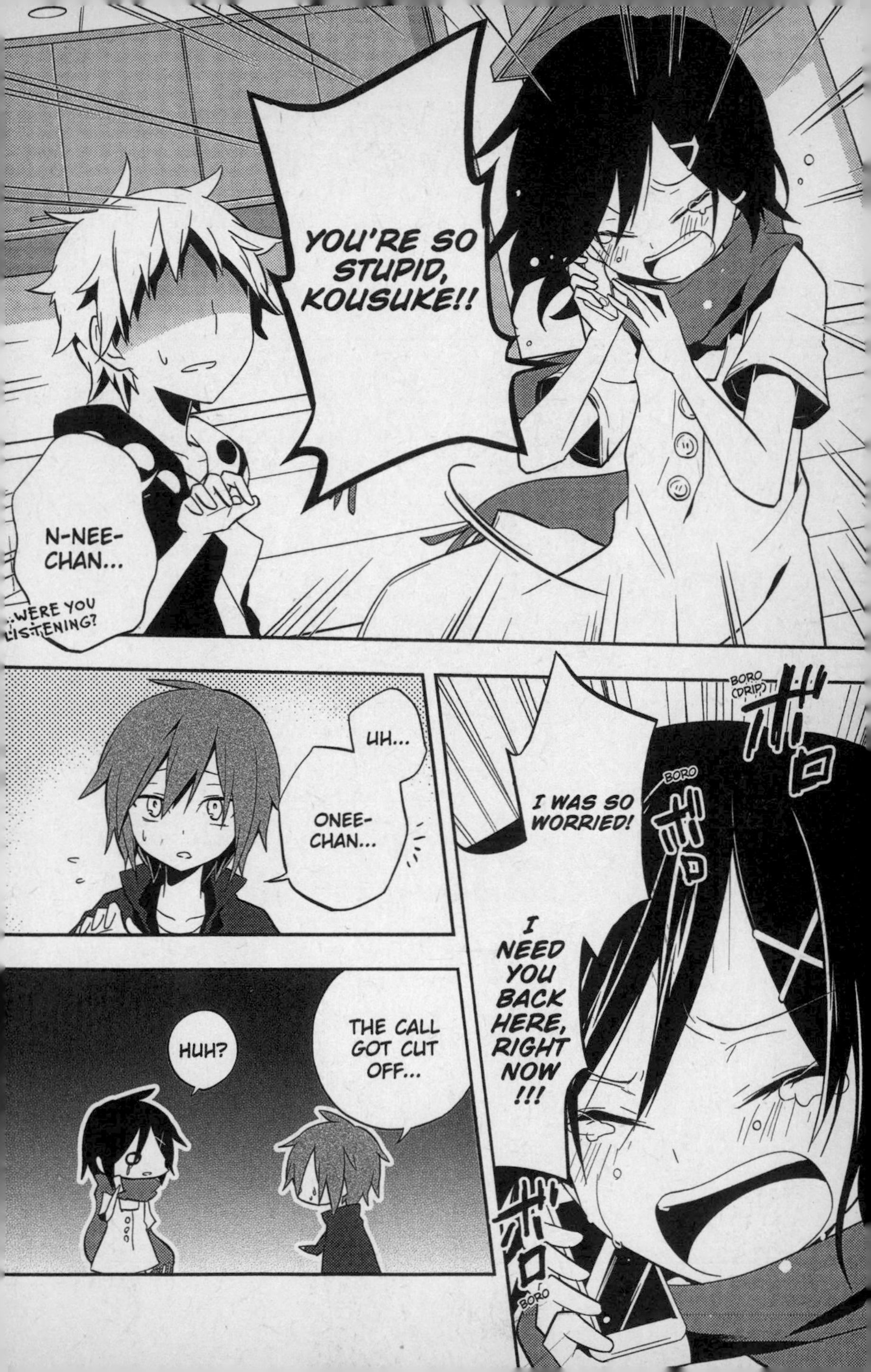
YOU'RE SO STUPID, KOUSUKE!!
N-NEE-CHAN...
...WERE YOU LISTENING?
BORO (DRIP)
BORO
I WAS SO WORRIED!
I NEED YOU BACK HERE, RIGHT NOW!!!
BORO
UH...
ONEE-CHAN...
THE CALL GOT CUT OFF...
HUH?

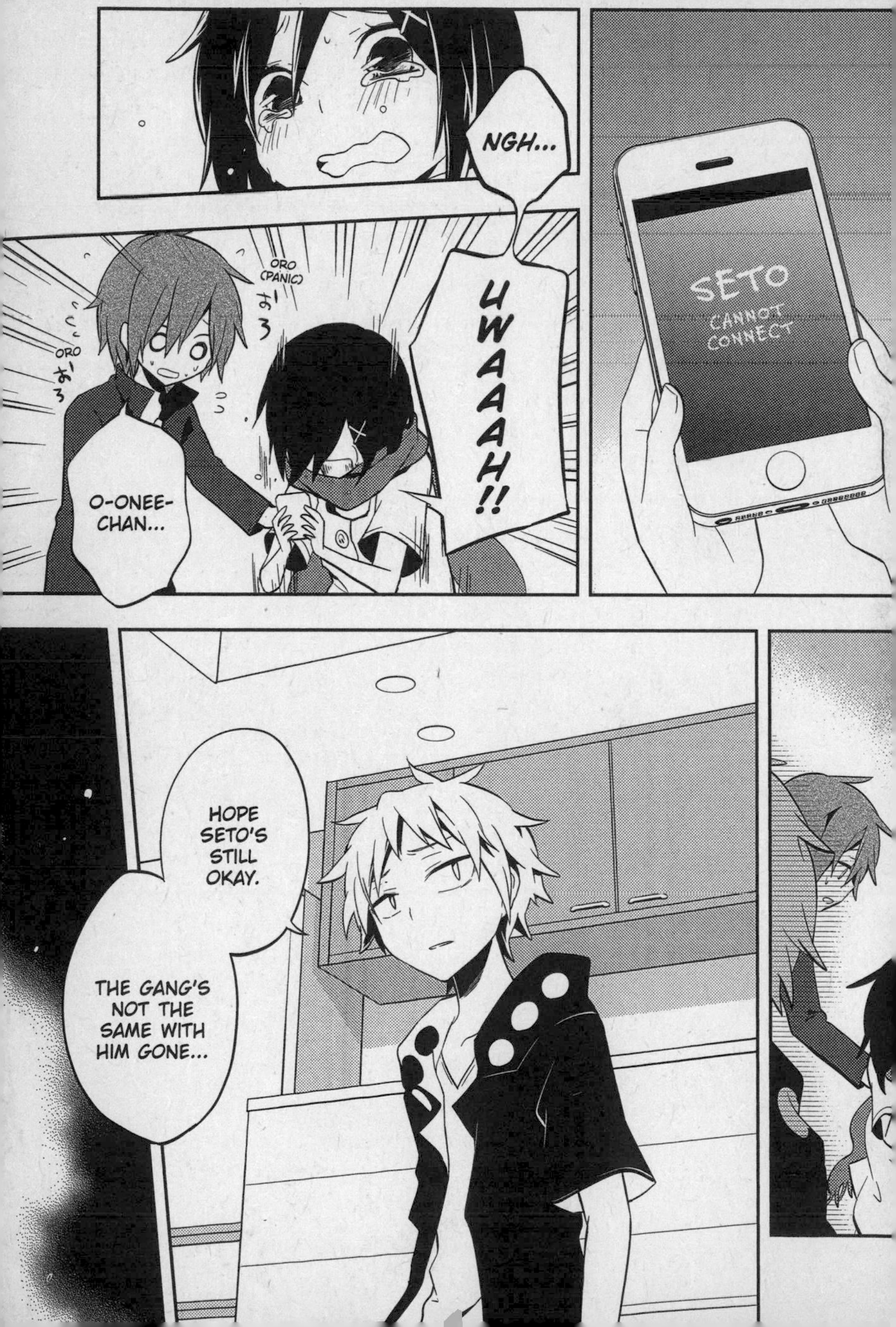
SETO
CANNOT CONNECT
NGH...
UWAAAAH!!
ORO (PANIC)
おろ
ORO
おろ
O-ONEE-CHAN...
HOPE SETO'S STILL OKAY.
THE GANG'S NOT THE SAME WITH HIM GONE...

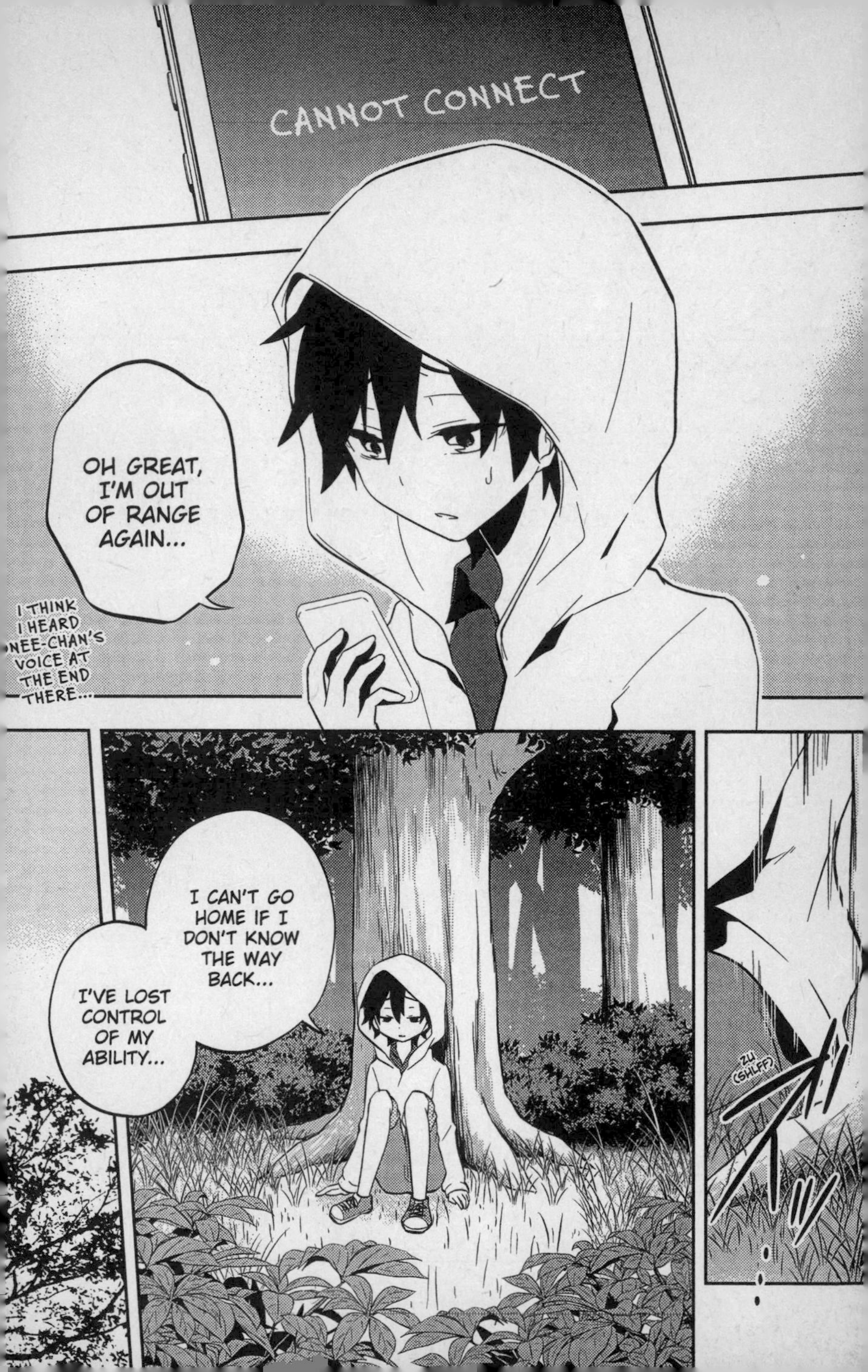
CANNOT CONNECT
OH GREAT, I'M OUT OF RANGE AGAIN...
I THINK I HEARD NEE-CHAN'S VOICE AT THE END THERE...
ZU (SHLFF)
...
I CAN'T GO HOME IF I DON'T KNOW THE WAY BACK...
I'VE LOST CONTROL OF MY ABILITY...

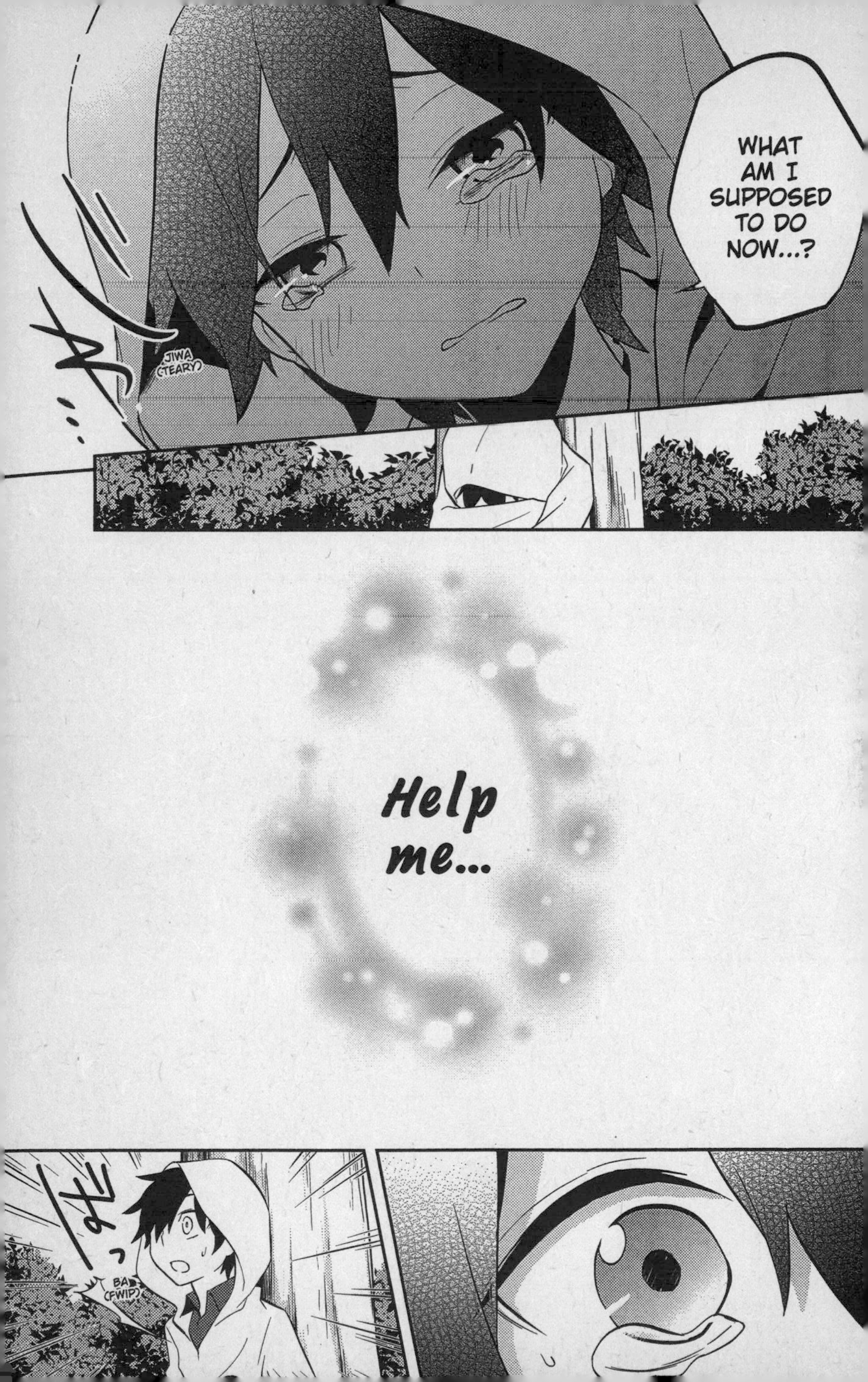
WHAT AM I SUPPOSED TO DO NOW...?
JIWA (TEARY)
Help me...
BA (FWIP)

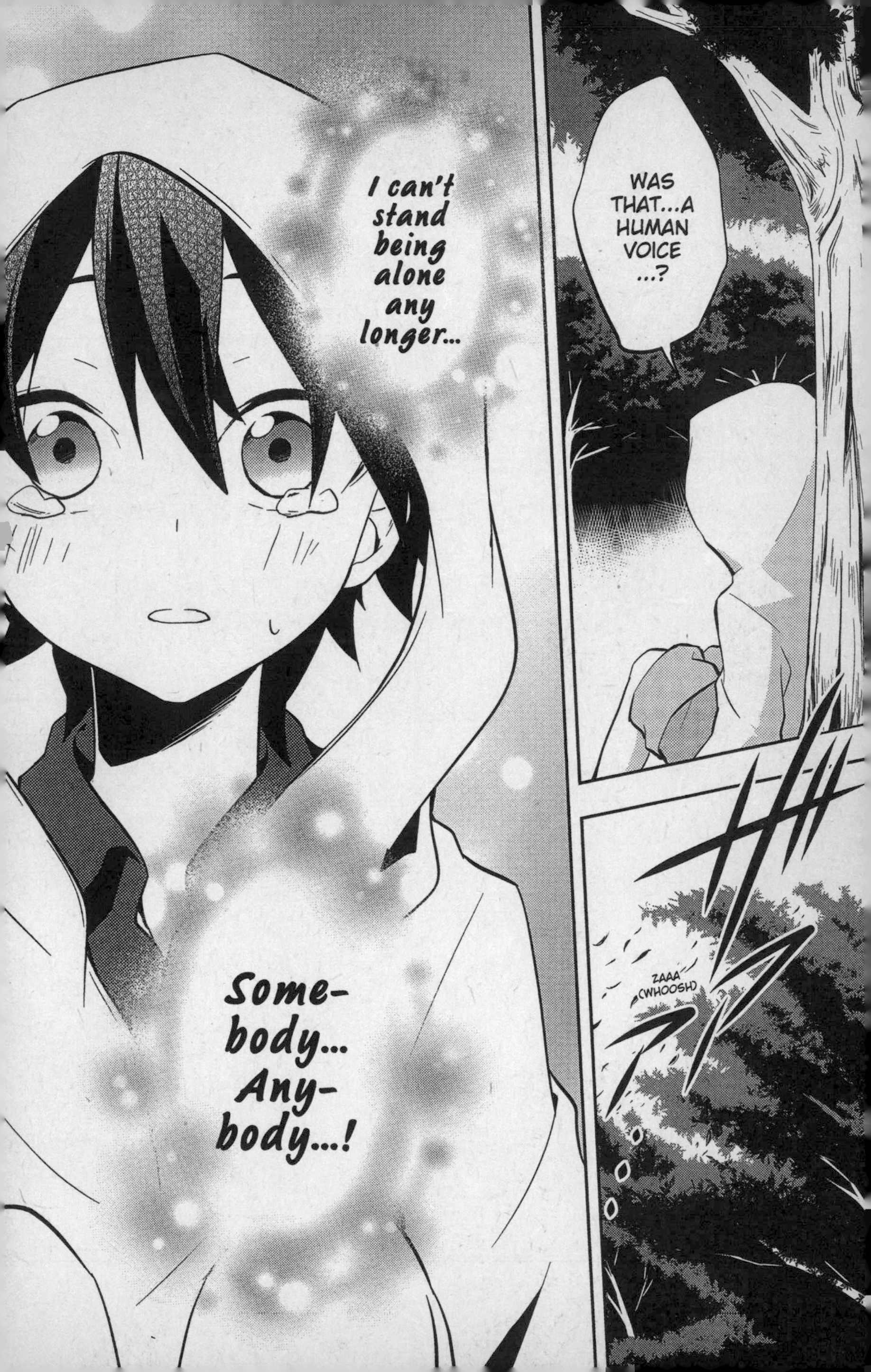
WAS THAT...A HUMAN VOICE ...?
ZAAA (WHOOSH)
I can't stand being alone any longer...
Some-body... Any-body...!

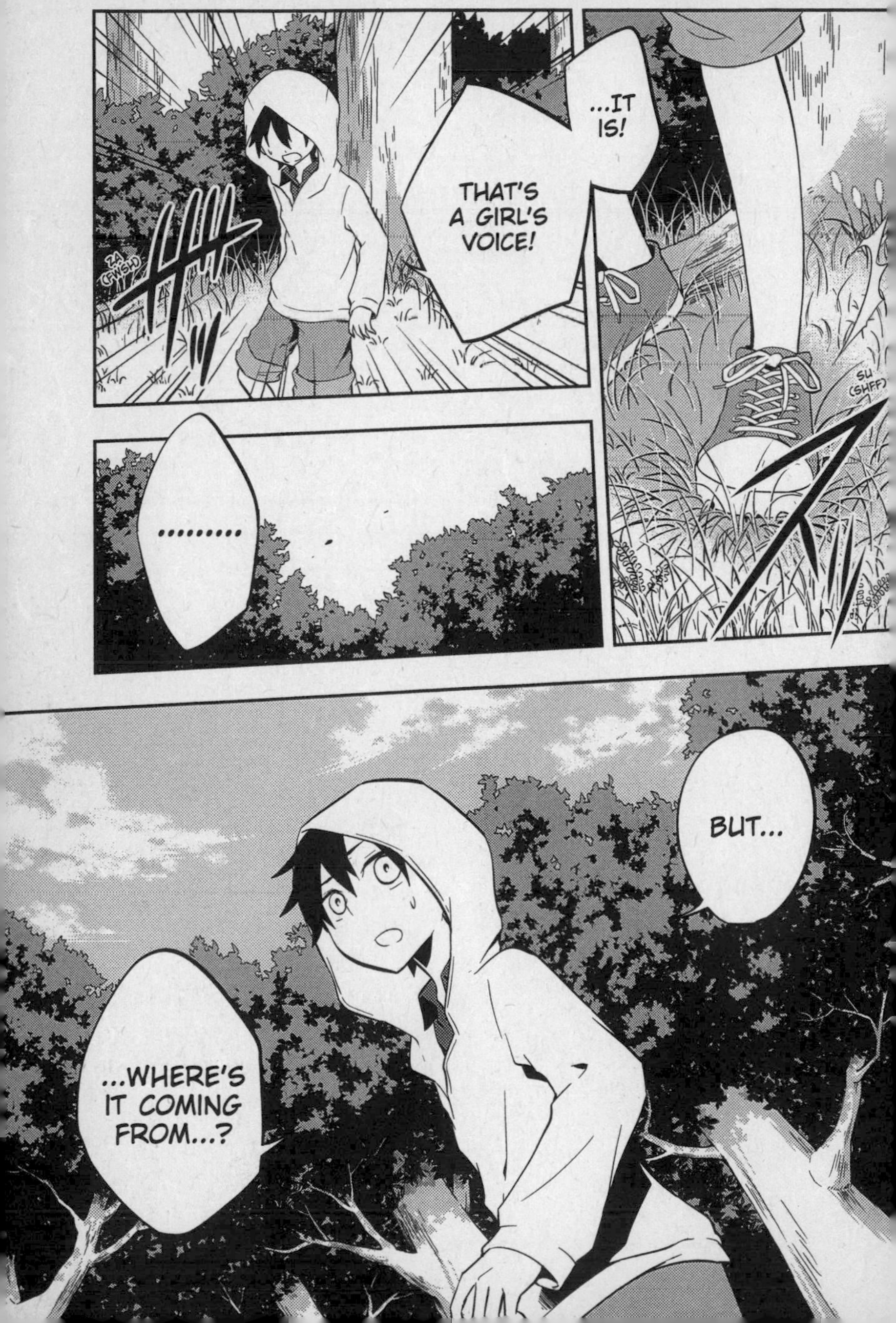
SU (SHFF)
...IT IS!
THAT'S A GIRL'S VOICE!
ZA (FWSH)
....
BUT...
...WHERE'S IT COMING FROM...?

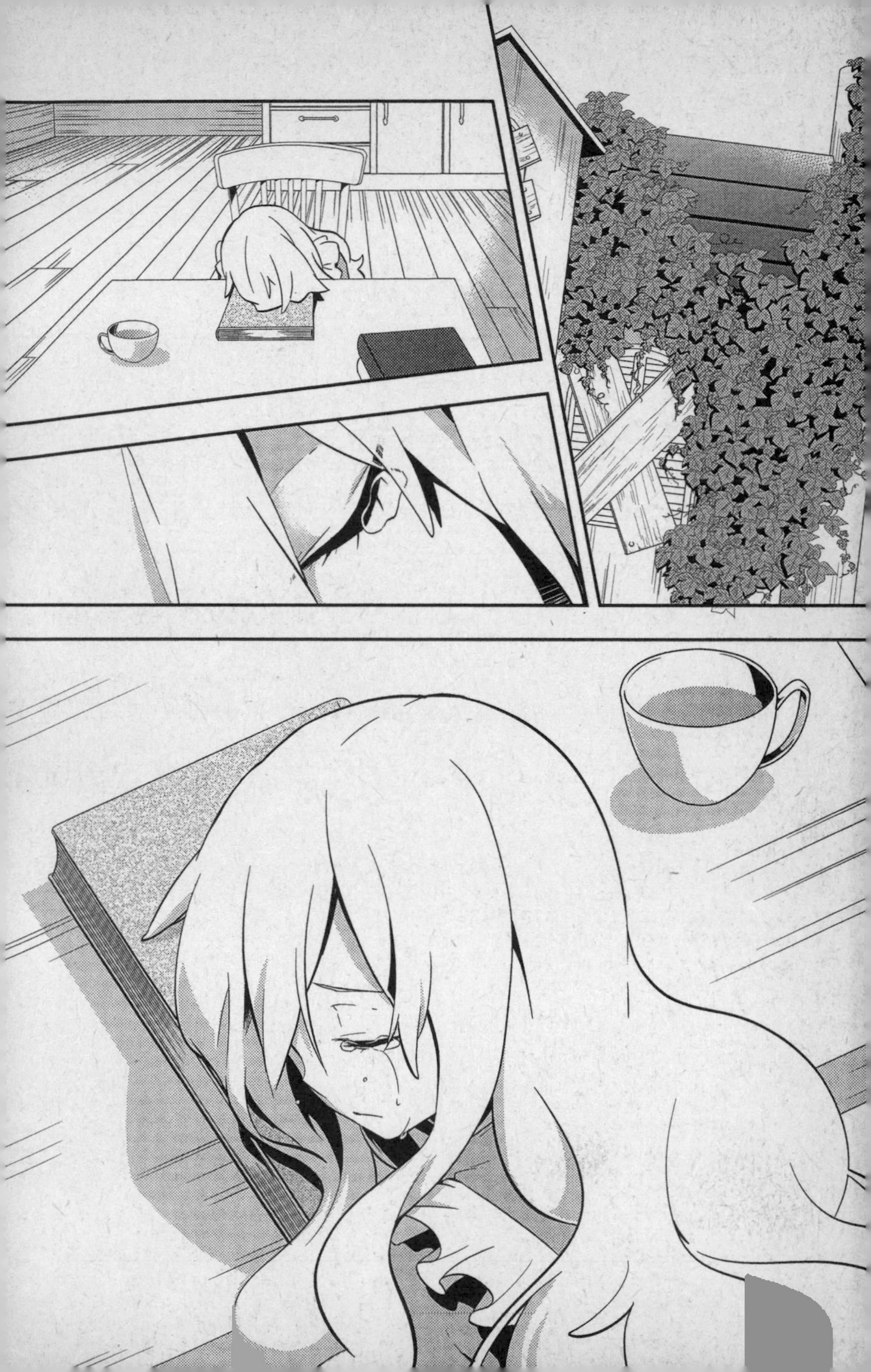

"YOU MUST NEVER GO OUTSIDE UNTIL YOU'RE GROWN UP."

THAT WAS THE SOLE PROMISE...

...I MADE WITH MY MOTHER.

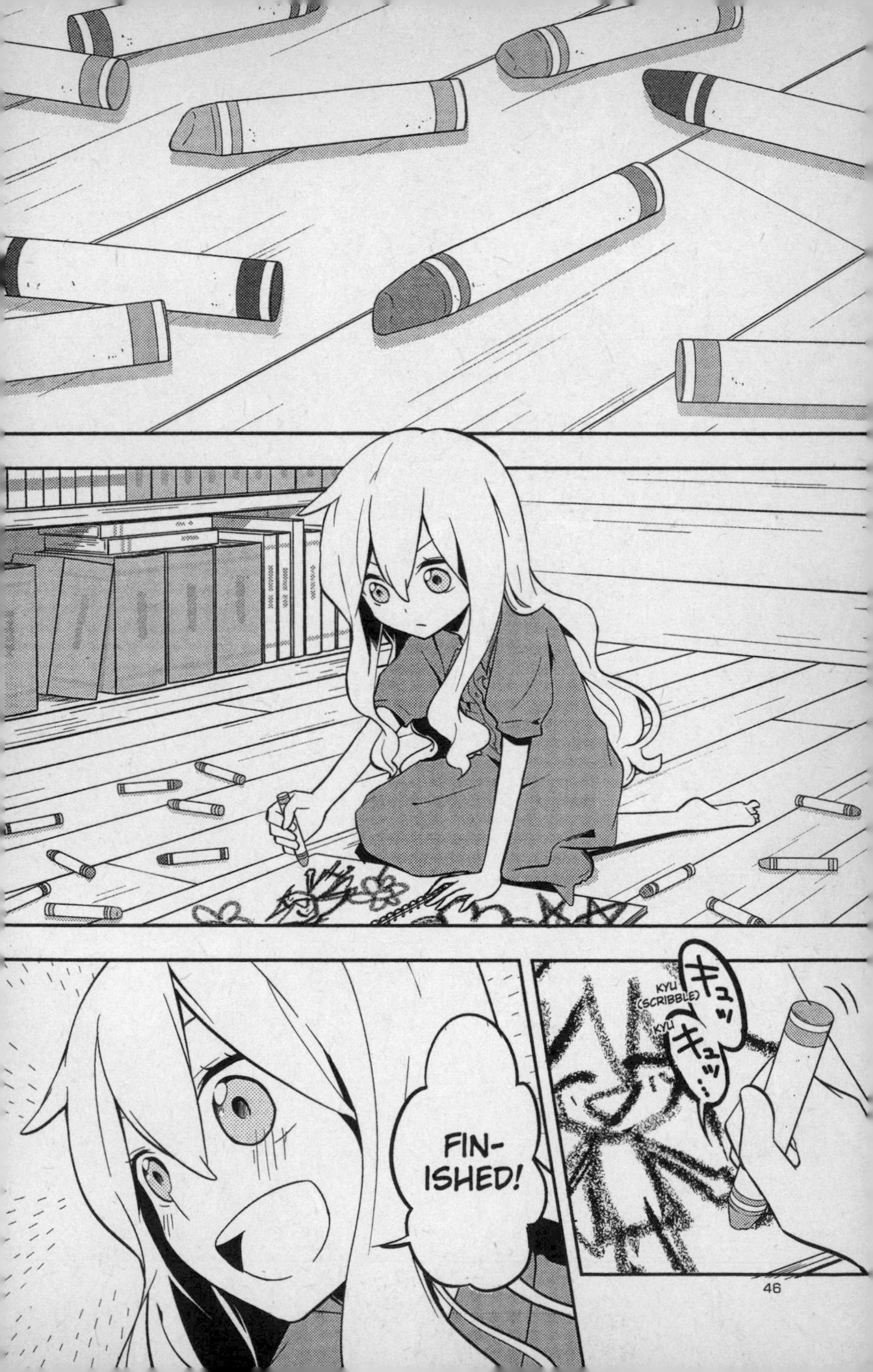
キュッ
KYU (SCRIBBLE)
キュッ…
KYU
FIN-ISHED!

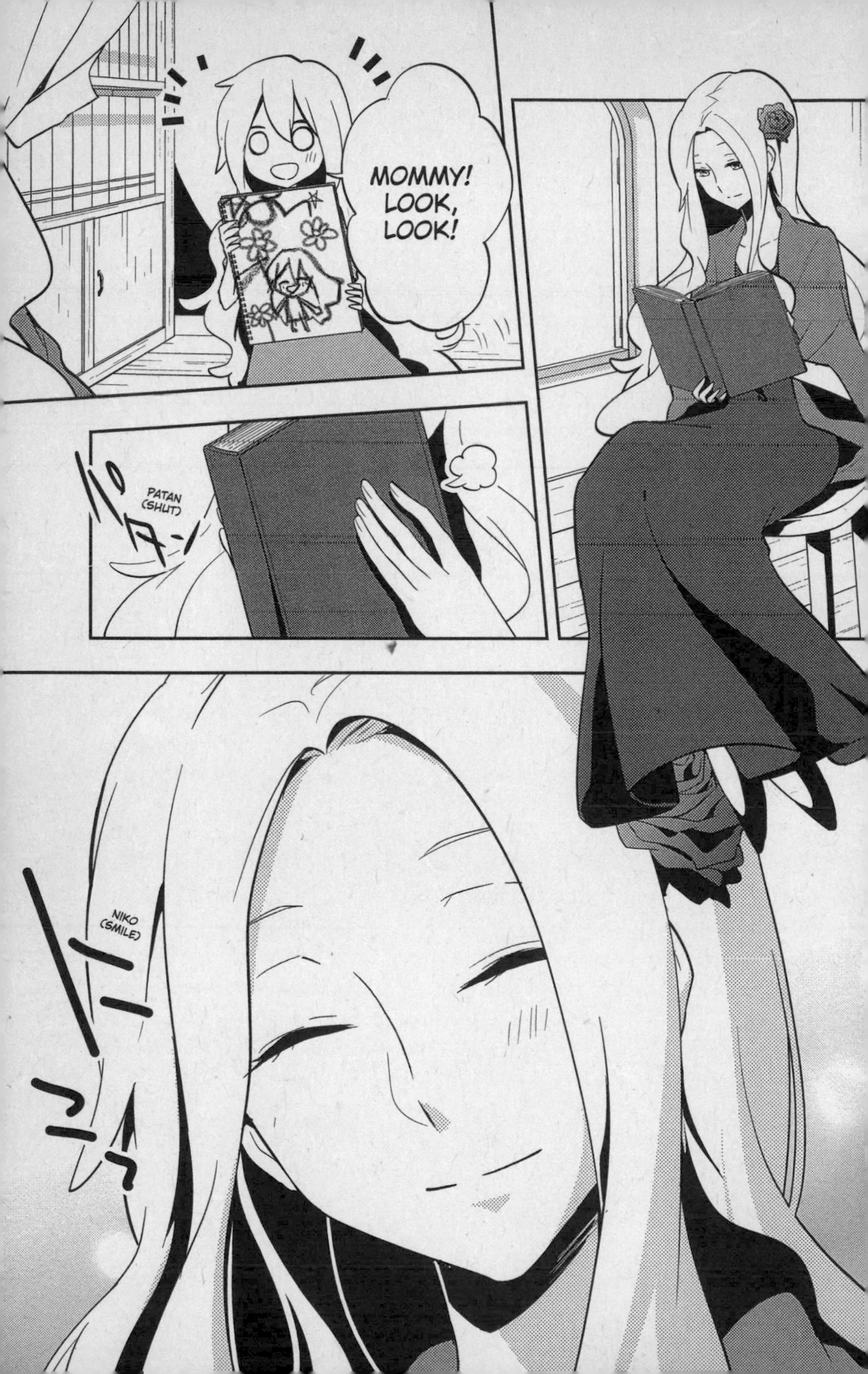
MOMMY! LOOK, LOOK!
PATAN (SHUT)
NIKO (SMILE)

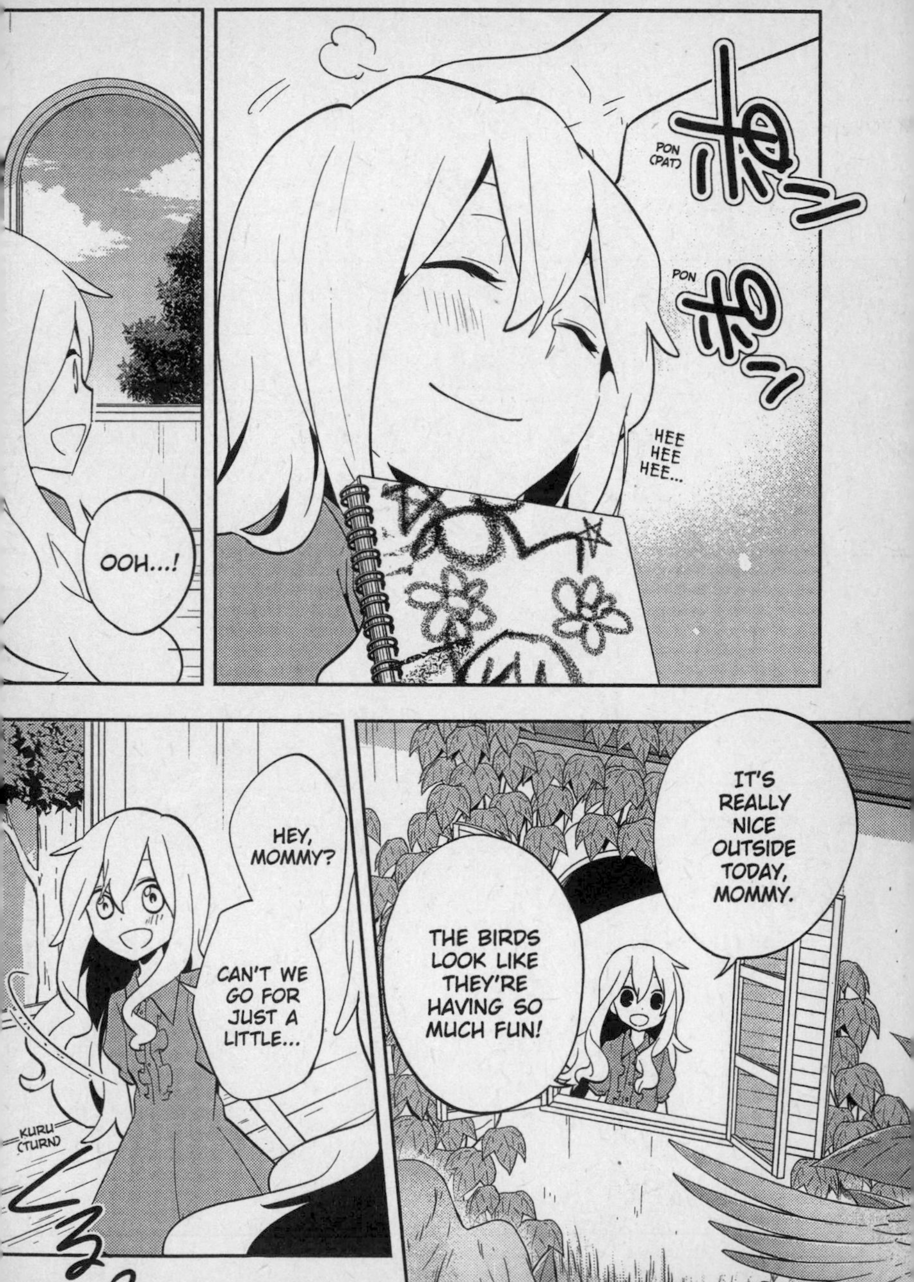
PON (PAT)
PON
HEE HEE HEE...
OOH...!
IT'S REALLY NICE OUTSIDE TODAY, MOMMY.
THE BIRDS LOOK LIKE THEY'RE HAVING SO MUCH FUN!
HEY, MOMMY?
CAN'T WE GO FOR JUST A LITTLE...
KURU (TURN)

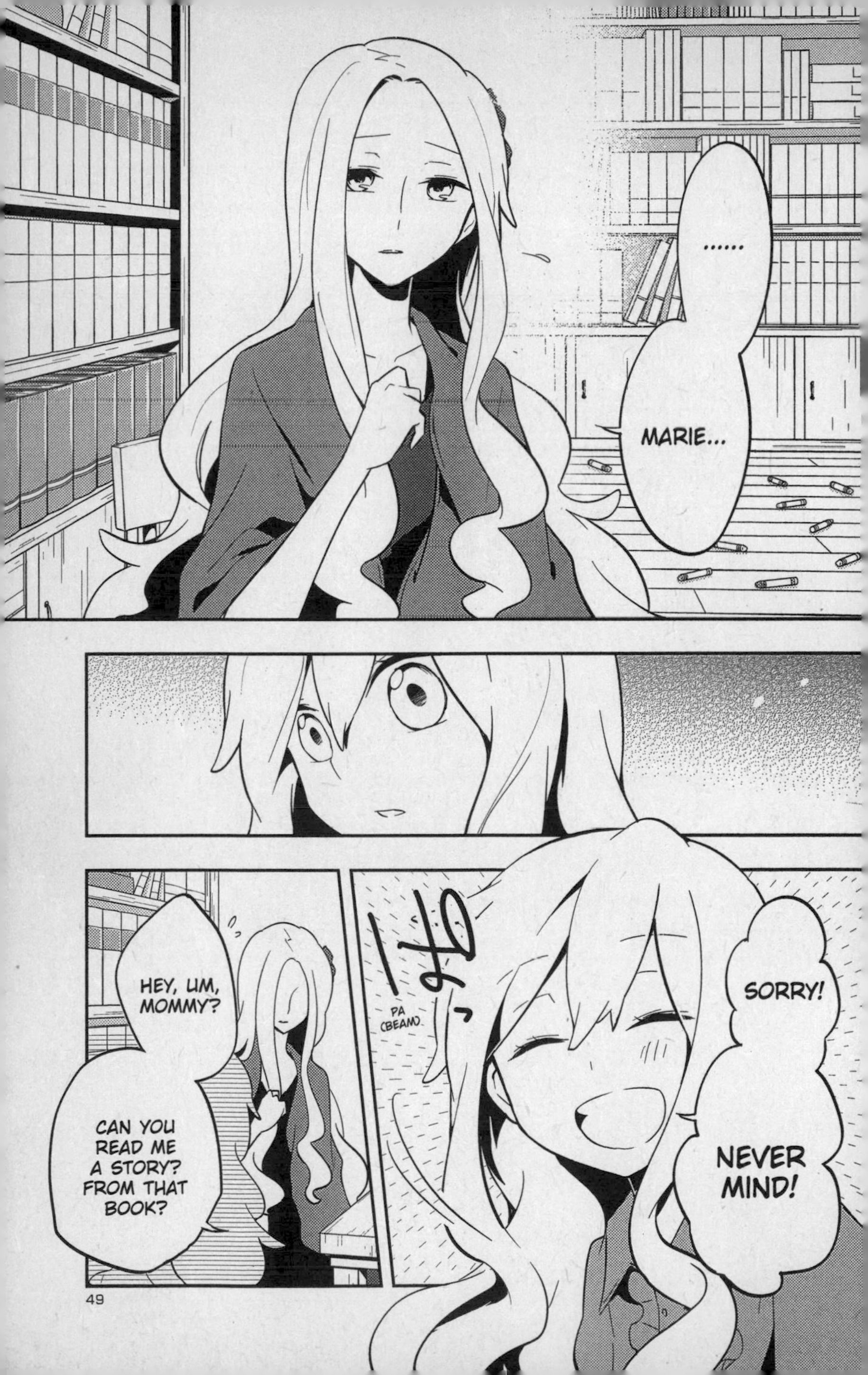
......
MARIE...
SORRY!
PA (BEAM)
NEVER MIND!
HEY, UM, MOMMY?
CAN YOU READ ME A STORY? FROM THAT BOOK?

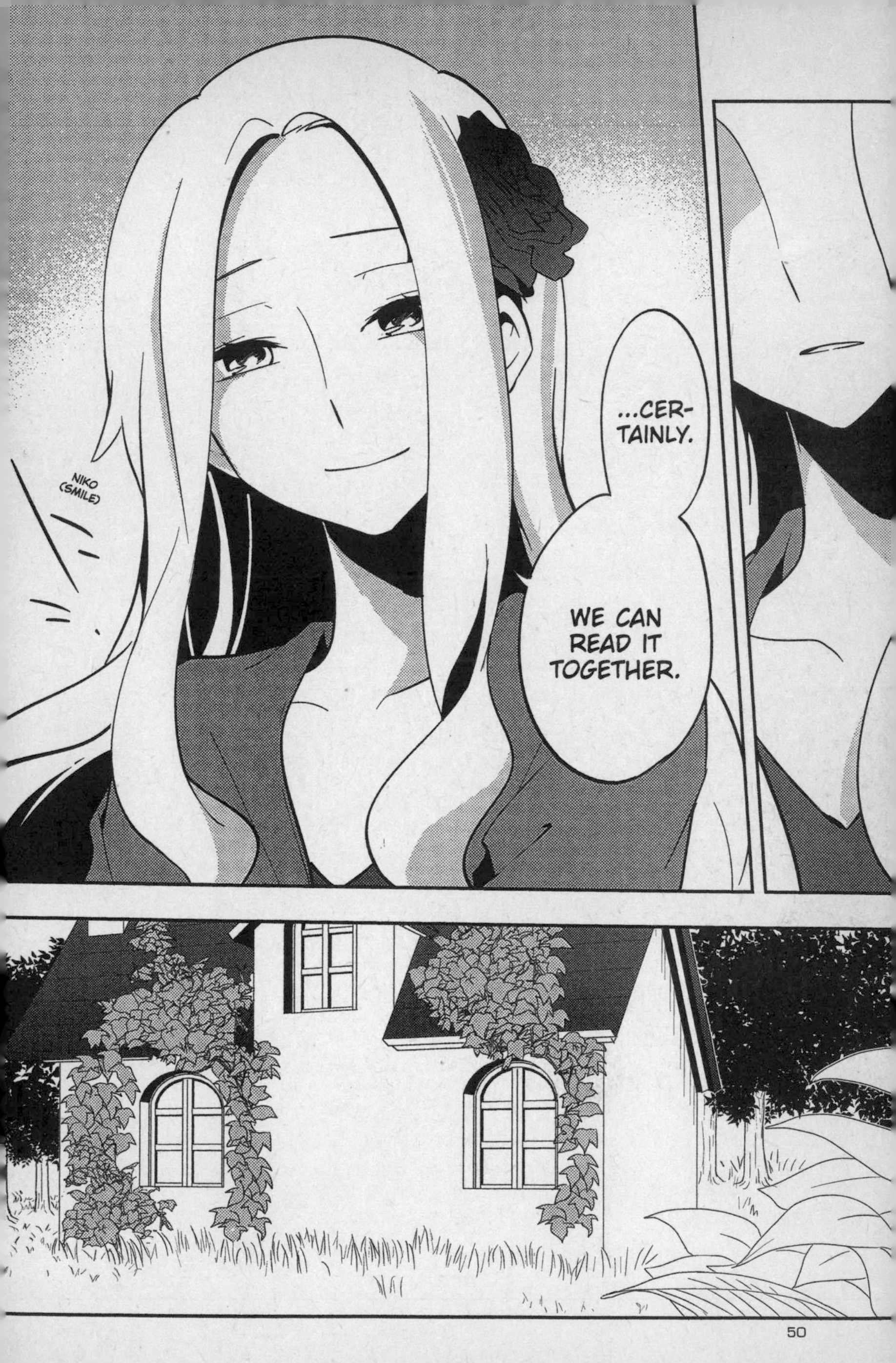
...CER-
TAINLY.
WE CAN
READ IT
TOGETHER.
NIKO
(SMILE)

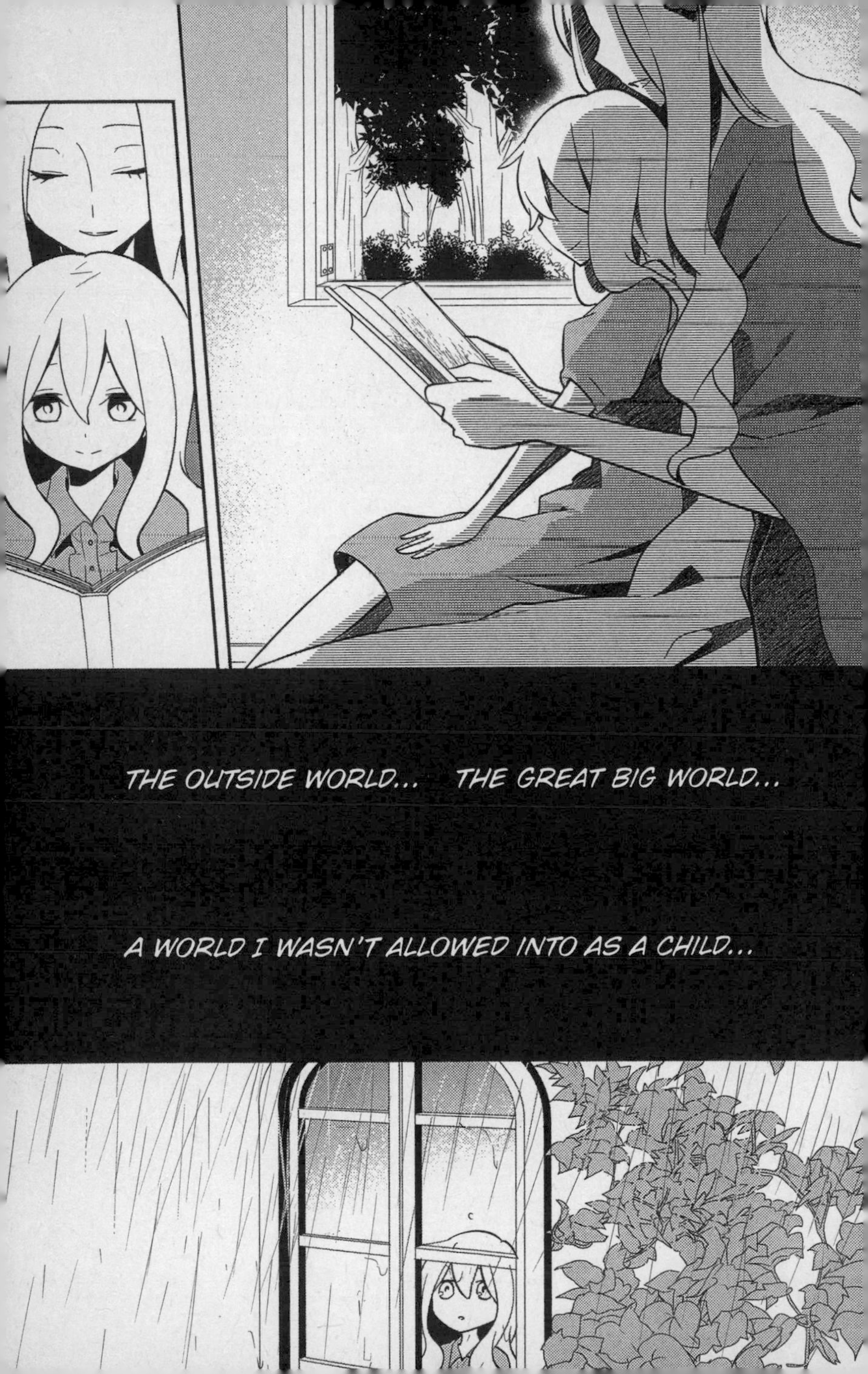
THE OUTSIDE WORLD... THE GREAT BIG WORLD...
A WORLD I WASN'T ALLOWED INTO AS A CHILD...

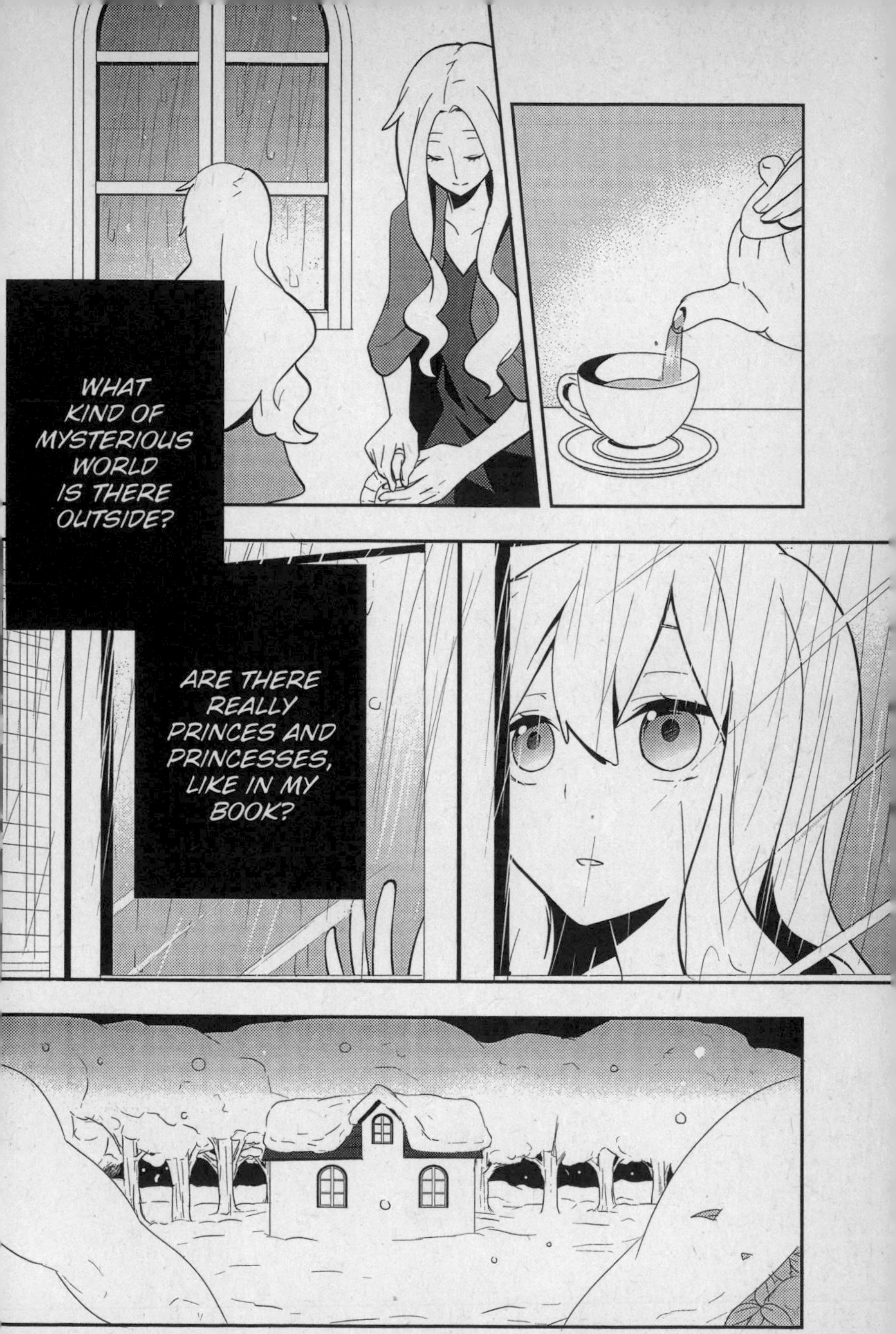
WHAT KIND OF MYSTERIOUS WORLD IS THERE OUTSIDE?
ARE THERE REALLY PRINCES AND PRINCESSES, LIKE IN MY BOOK?

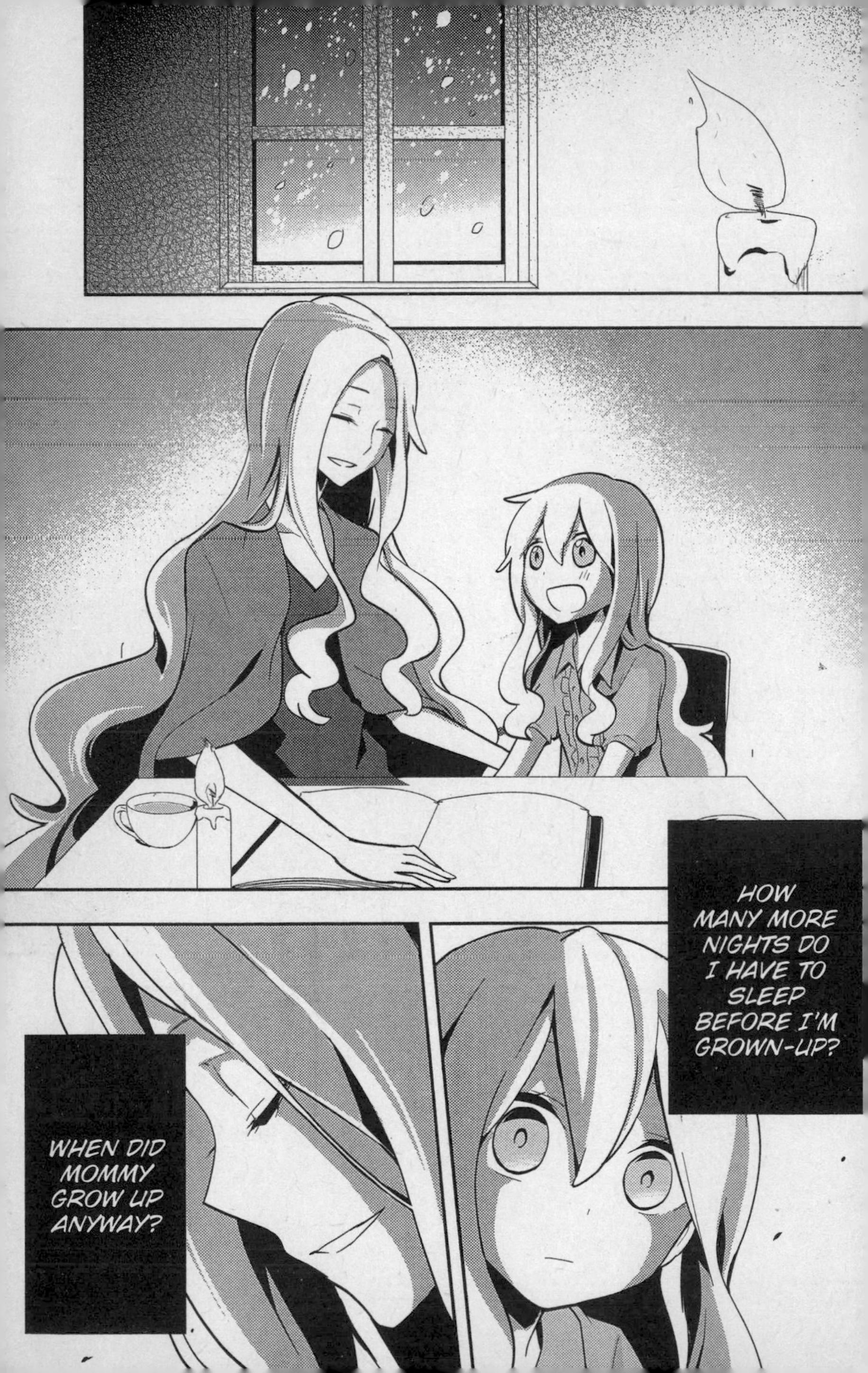
HOW MANY MORE NIGHTS DO I HAVE TO SLEEP BEFORE I'M GROWN-UP?
WHEN DID MOMMY GROW UP ANYWAY?

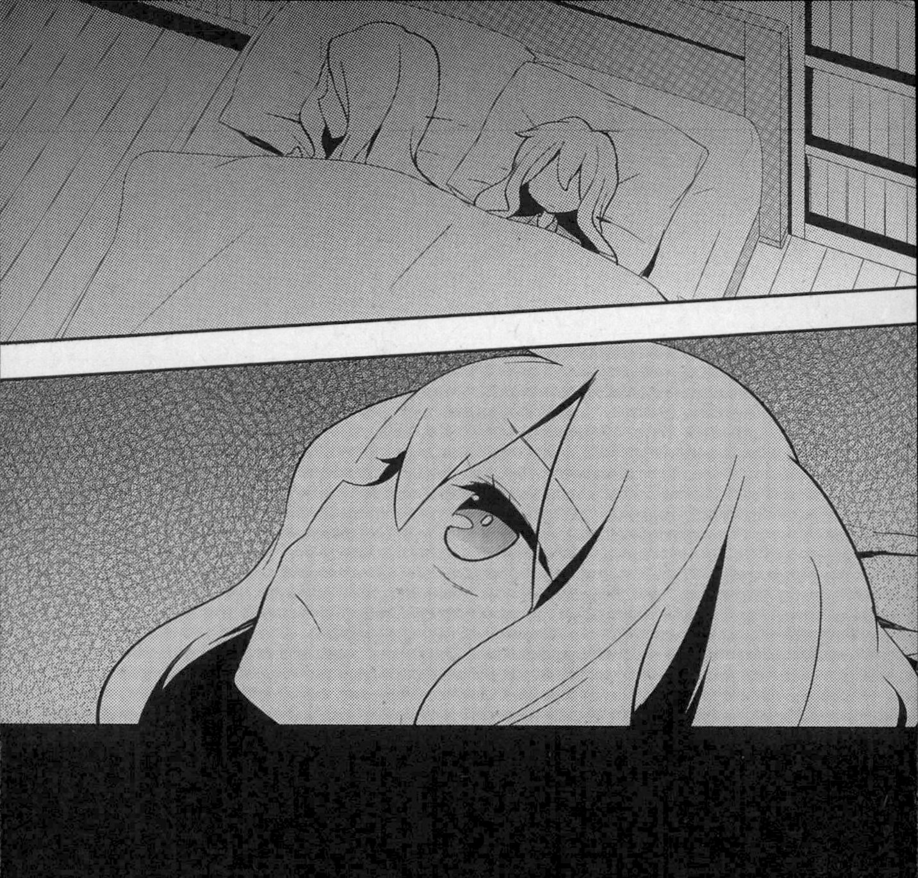

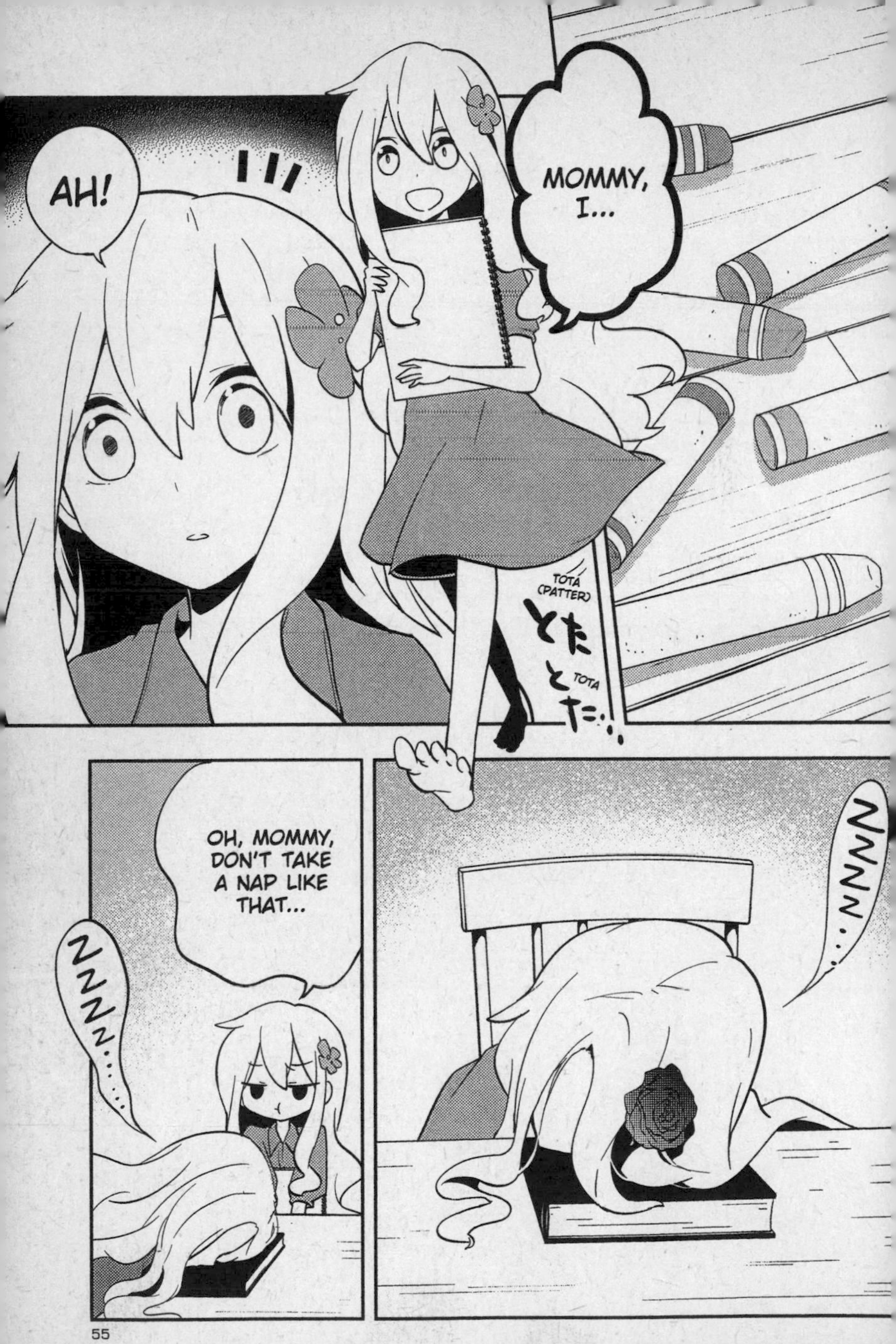
MOMMY, I...
AH!
TOTA (PATTER)
とたとた
TOTA
ZZZZ...
OH, MOMMY, DON'T TAKE A NAP LIKE THAT...
ZZZZ...

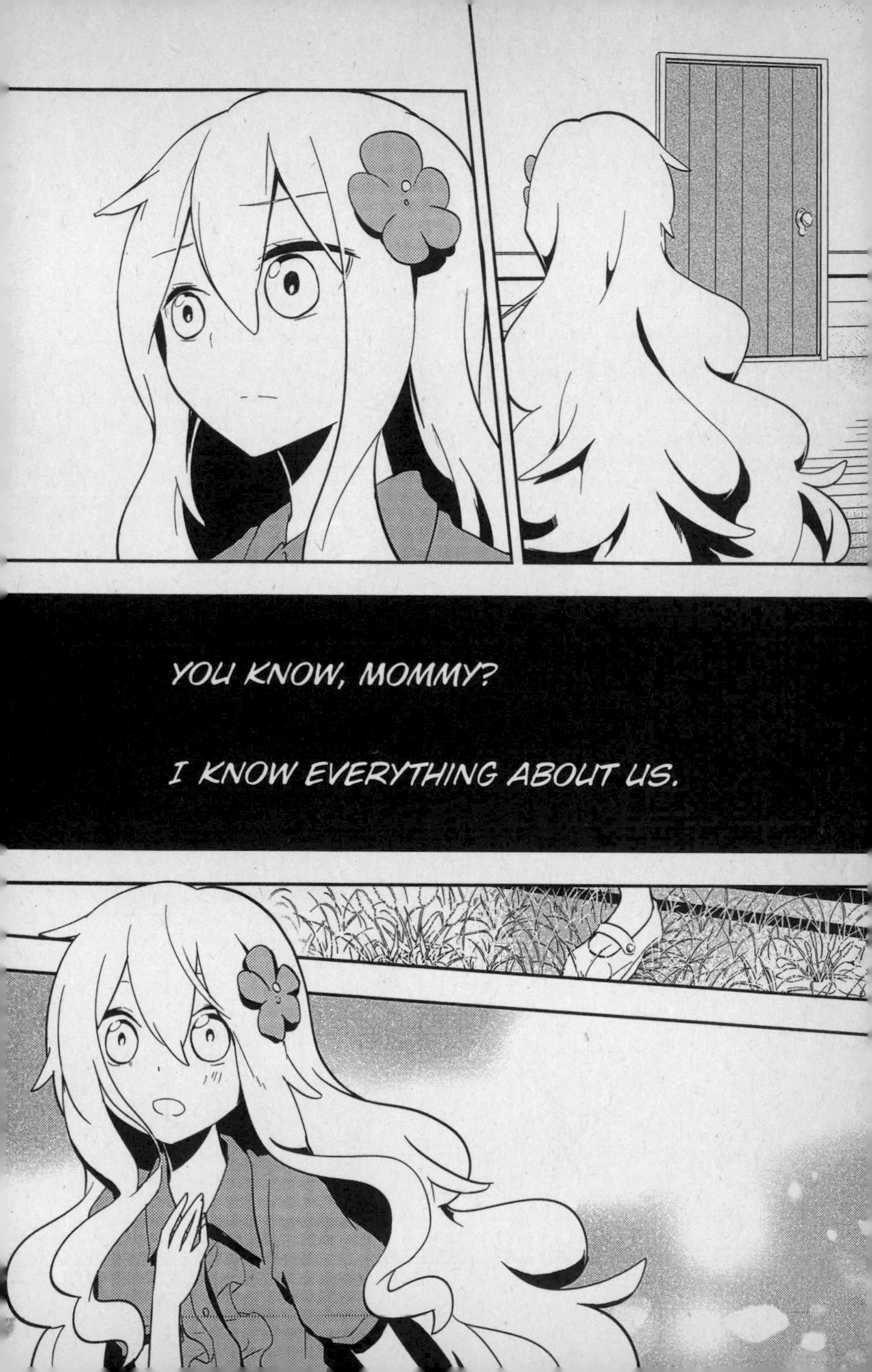
YOU KNOW, MOMMY?
I KNOW EVERYTHING ABOUT US.

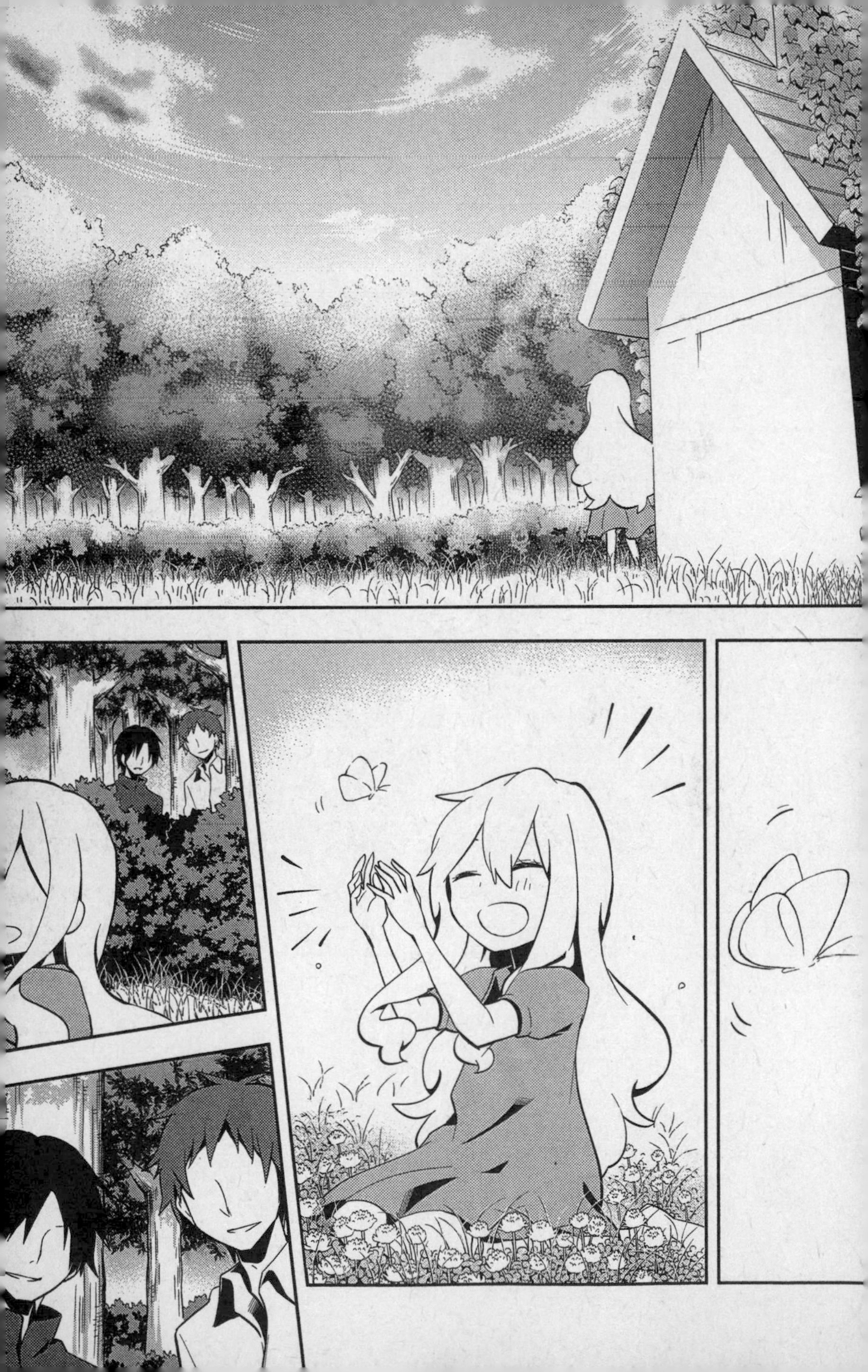

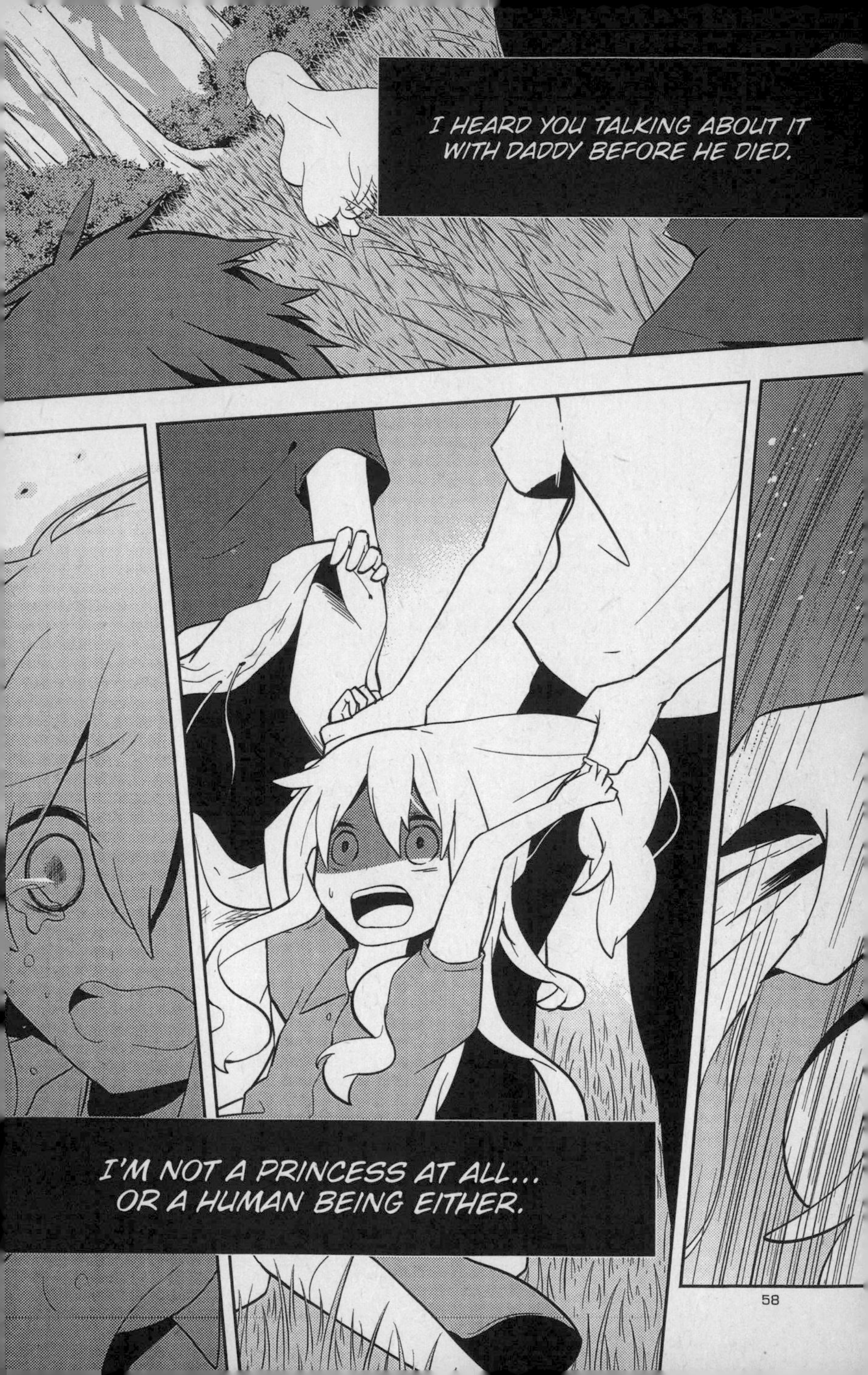
I HEARD YOU TALKING ABOUT IT WITH DADDY BEFORE HE DIED.
I'M NOT A PRINCESS AT ALL... OR A HUMAN BEING EITHER.

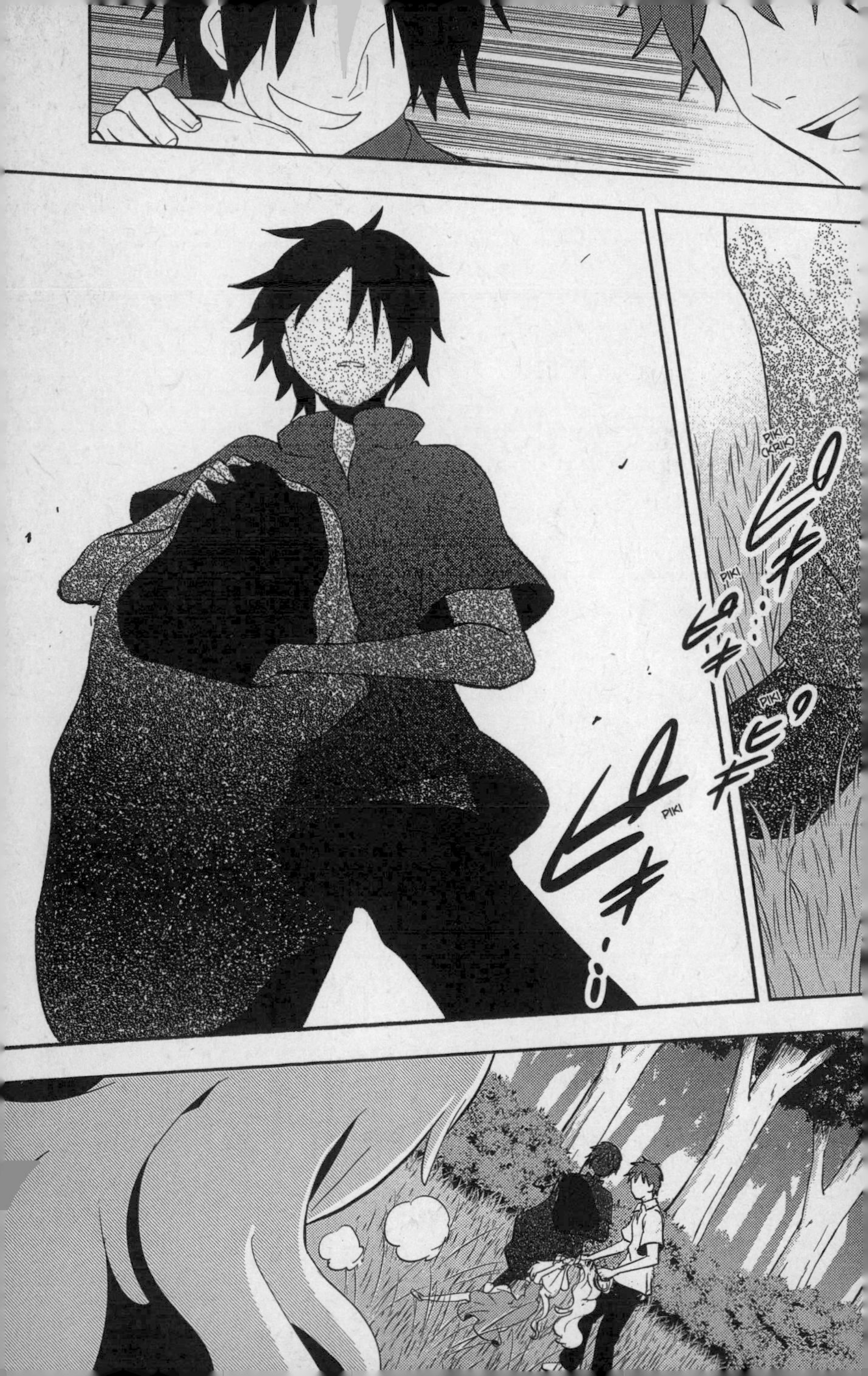
ピキ…
PIKI (KRIK)
ピキ
PIKI
ピキ
PIKI
ピキ…
PIKI

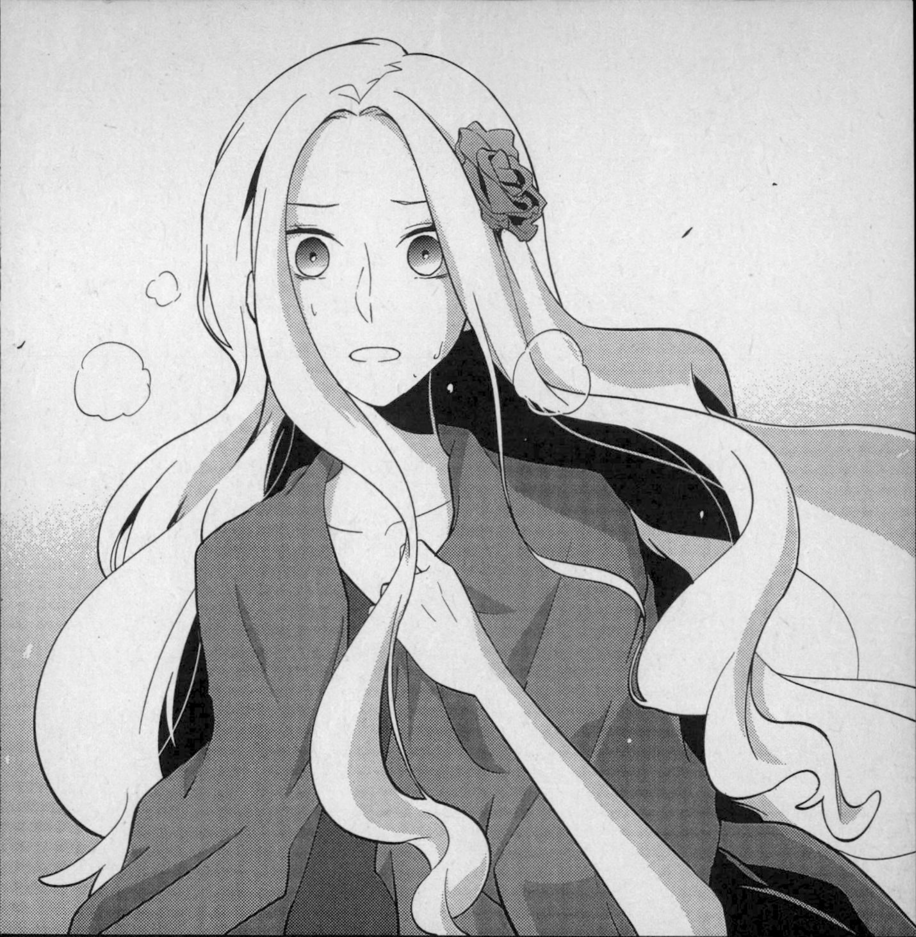

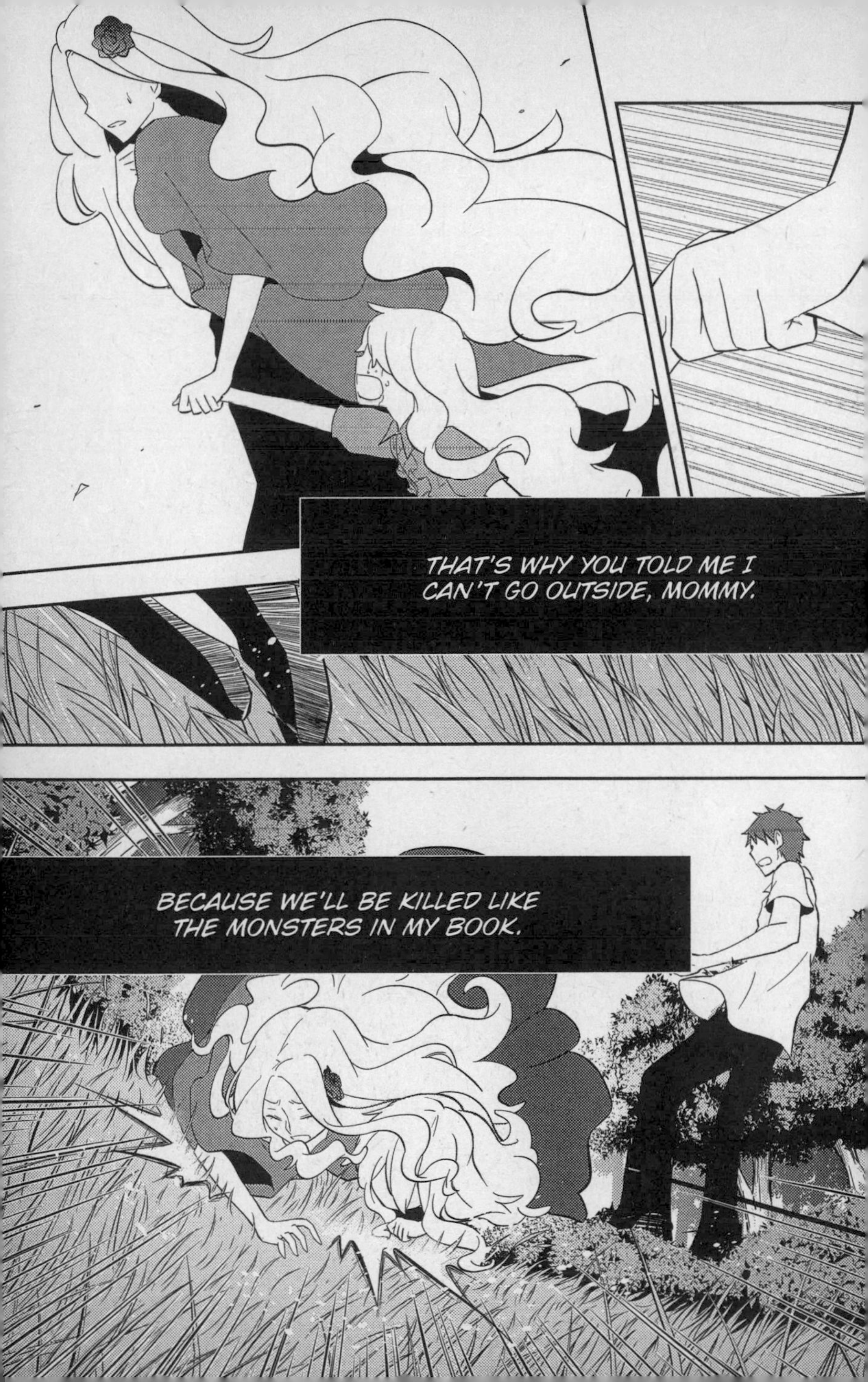
THAT'S WHY YOU TOLD ME I CAN'T GO OUTSIDE, MOMMY.
BECAUSE WE'LL BE KILLED LIKE THE MONSTERS IN MY BOOK.

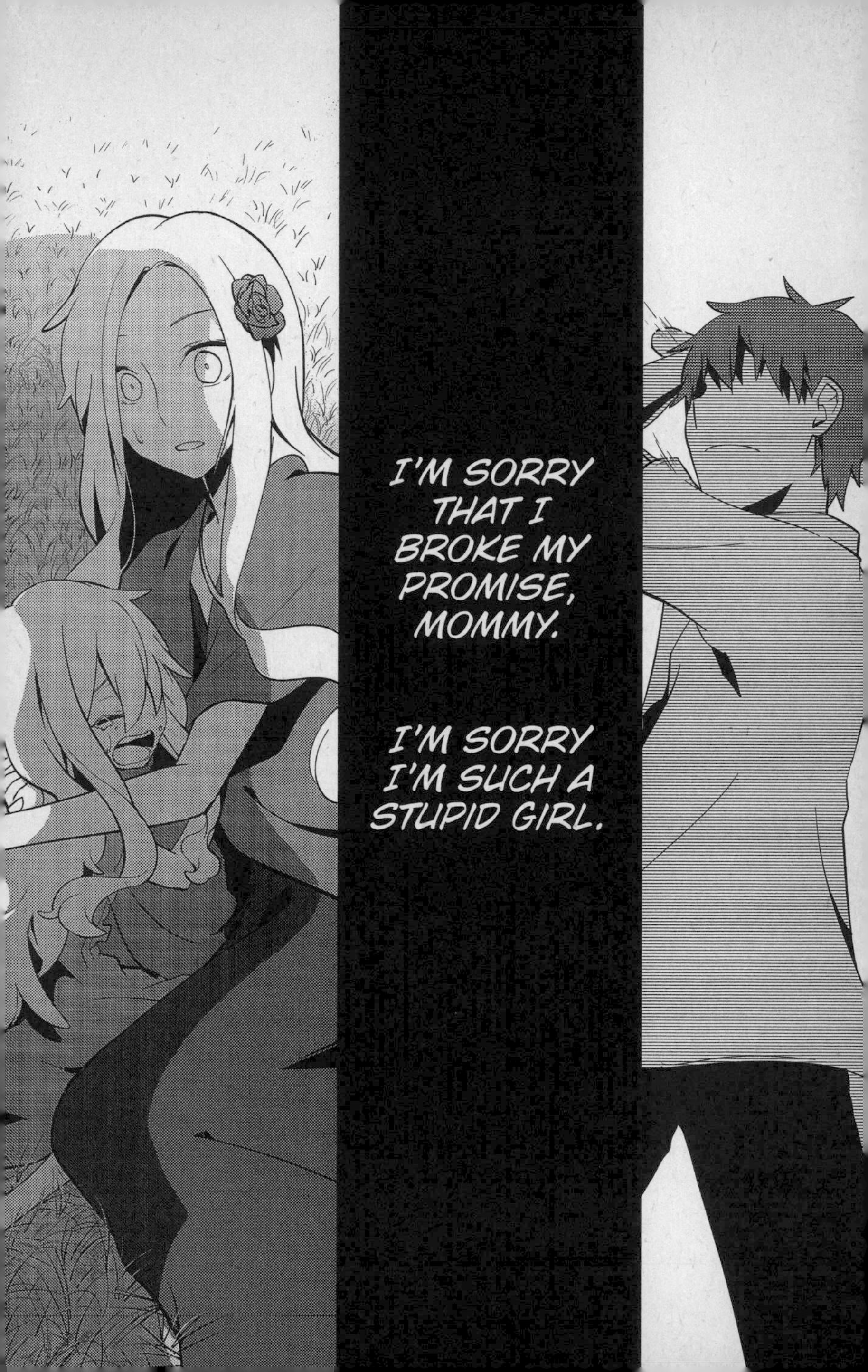
I'M SORRY THAT I BROKE MY PROMISE, MOMMY.
I'M SORRY I'M SUCH A STUPID GIRL.

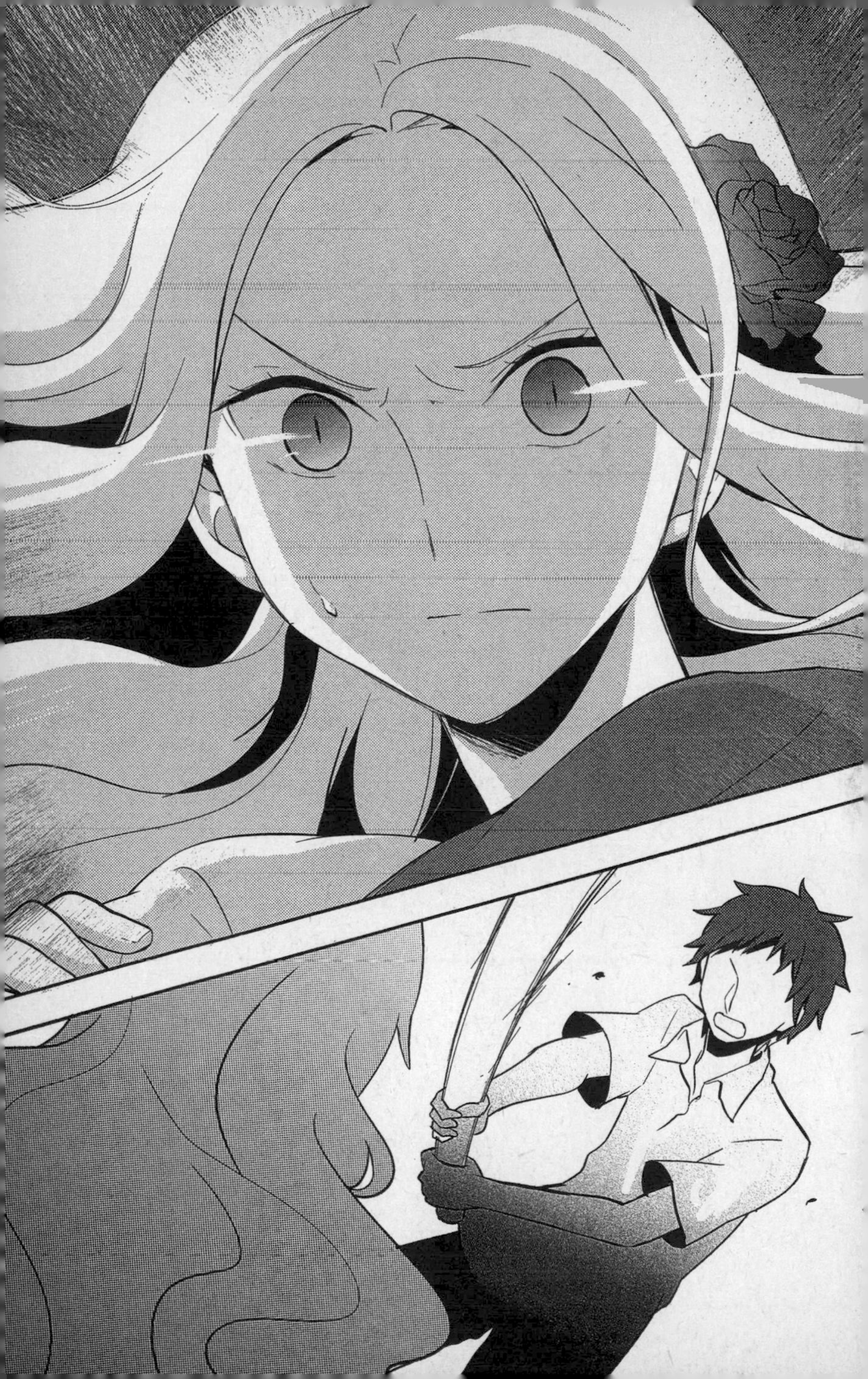

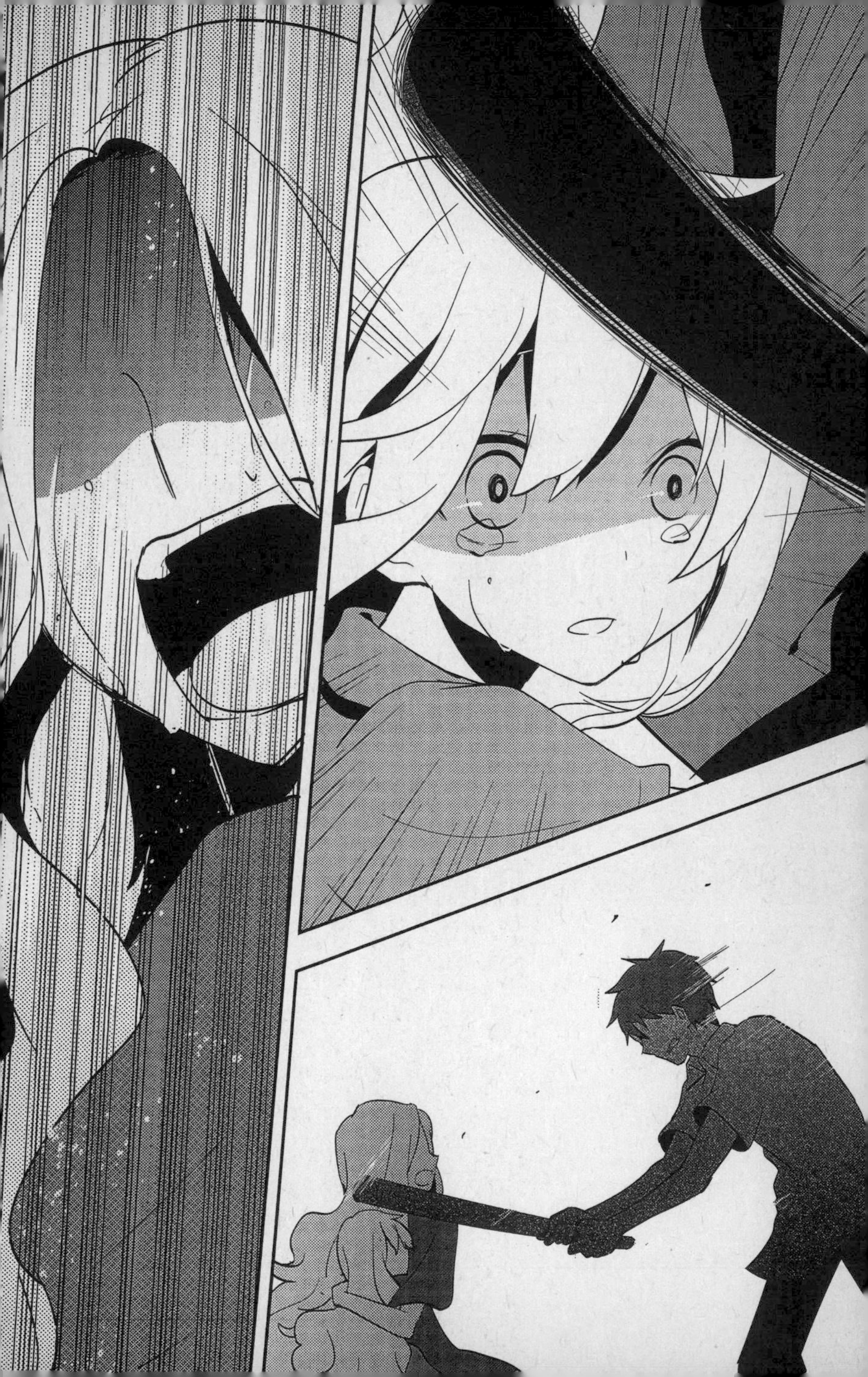

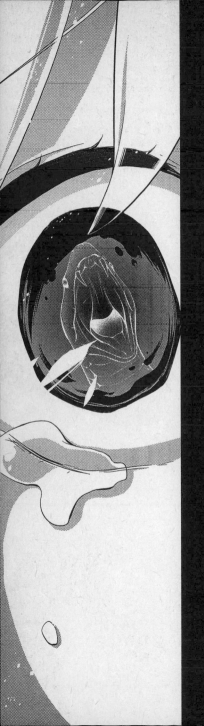

JUST BEING
TOGETHER WITH
YOU, MOMMY...

...MADE ME THE
HAPPIEST GIRL IN
THE WORLD...

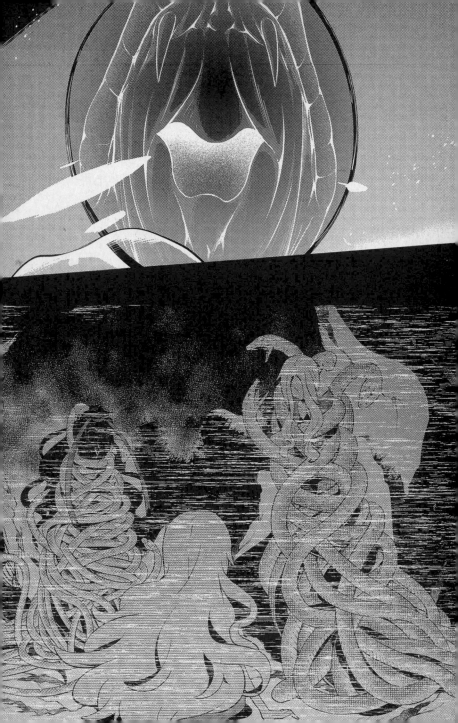

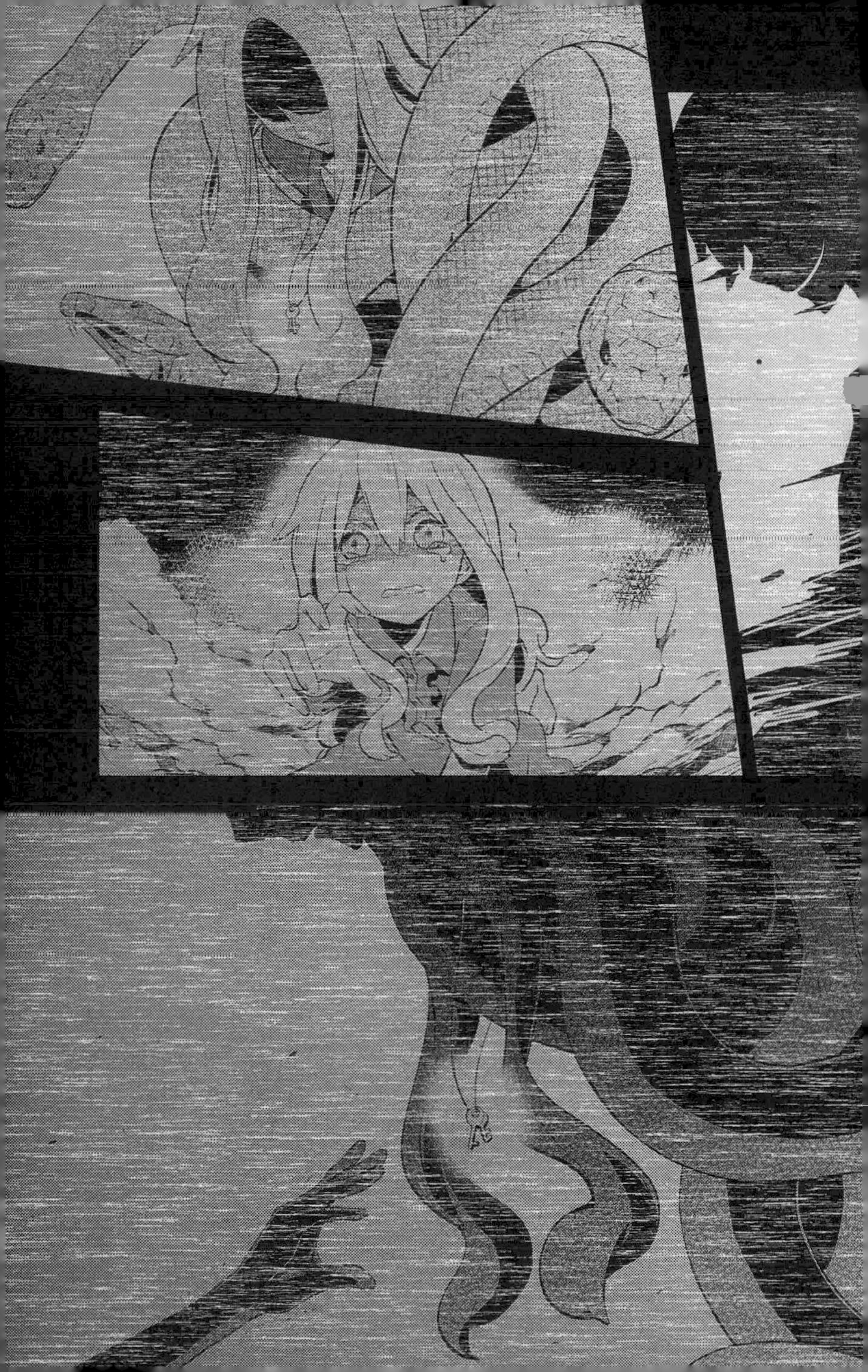

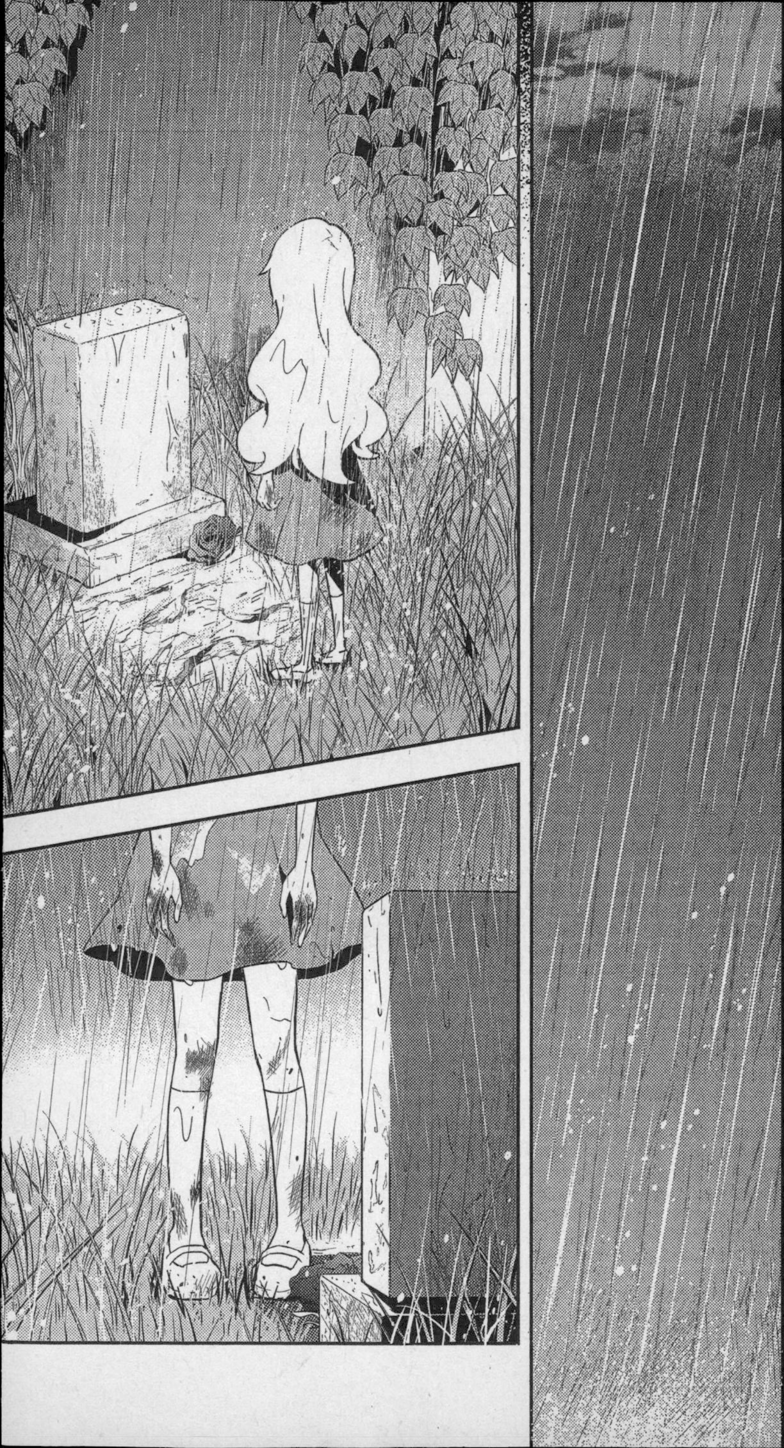

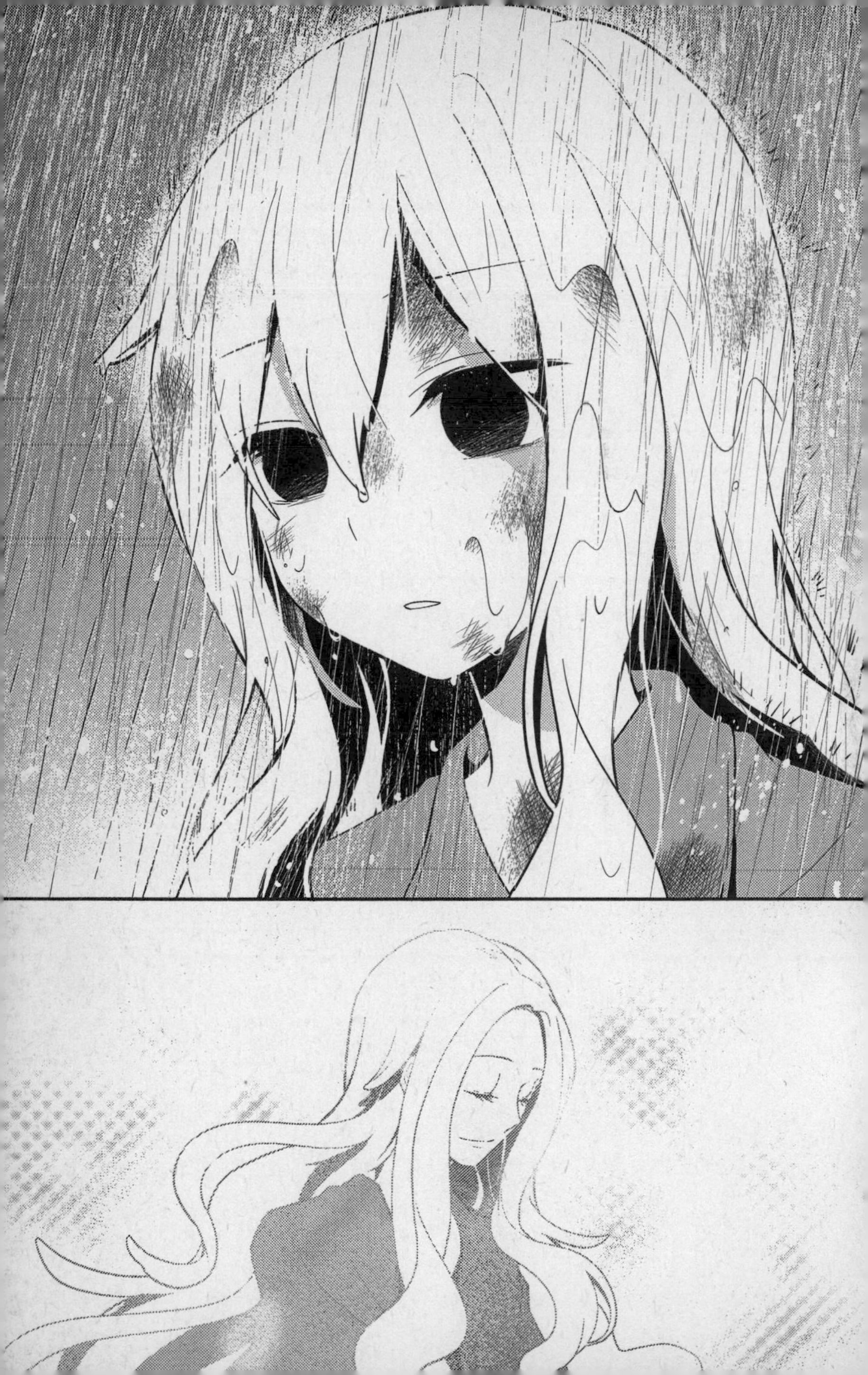

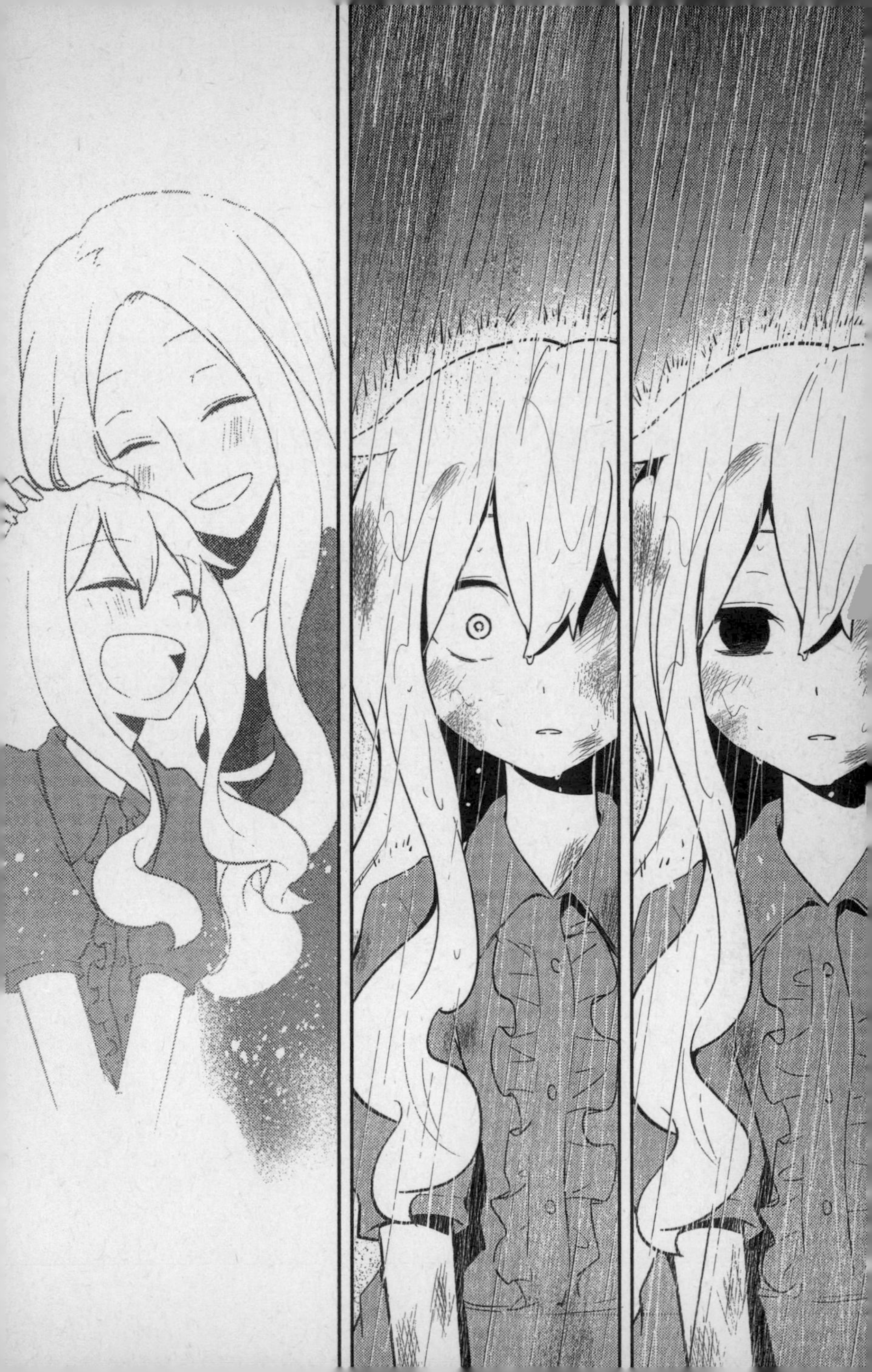

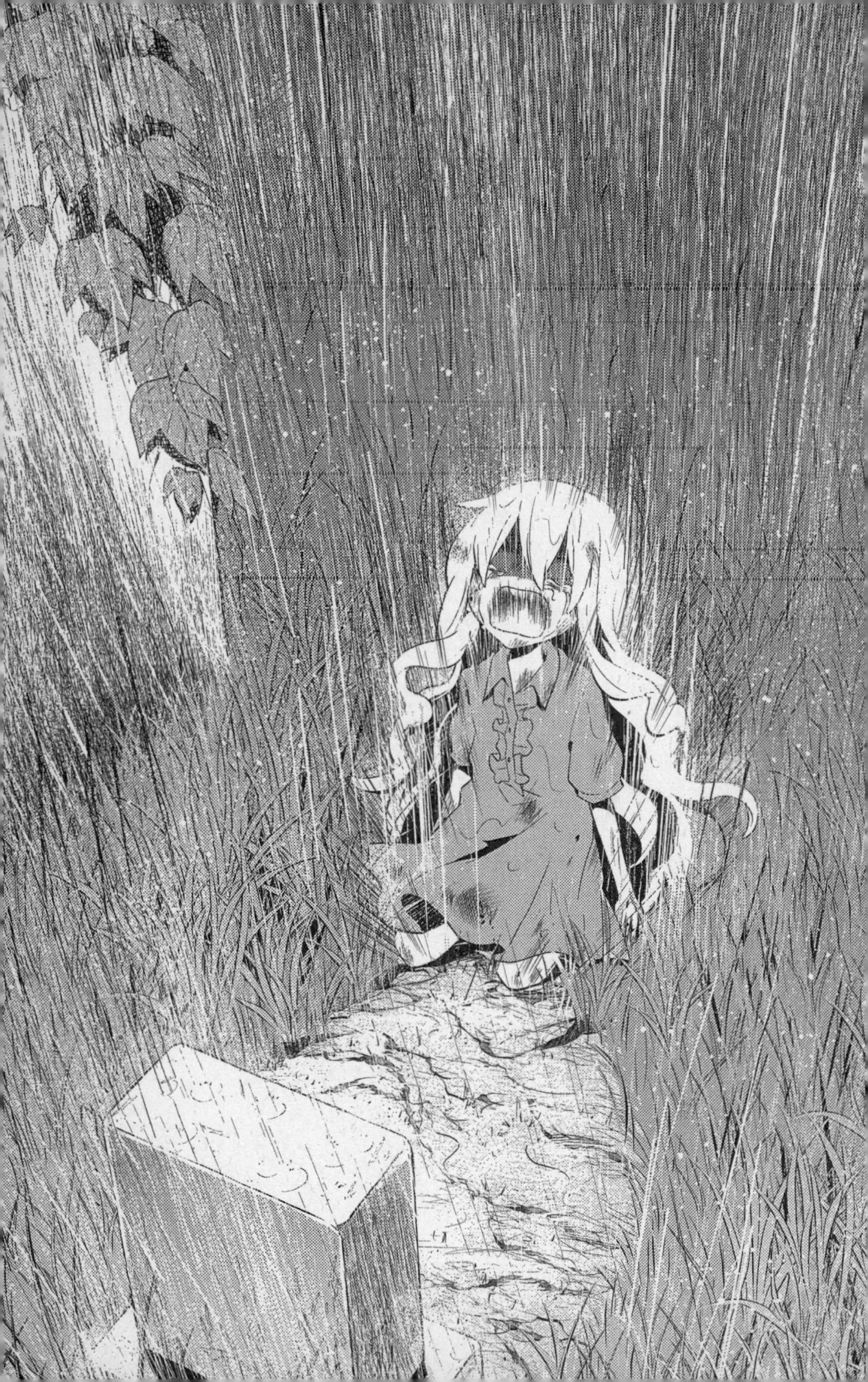

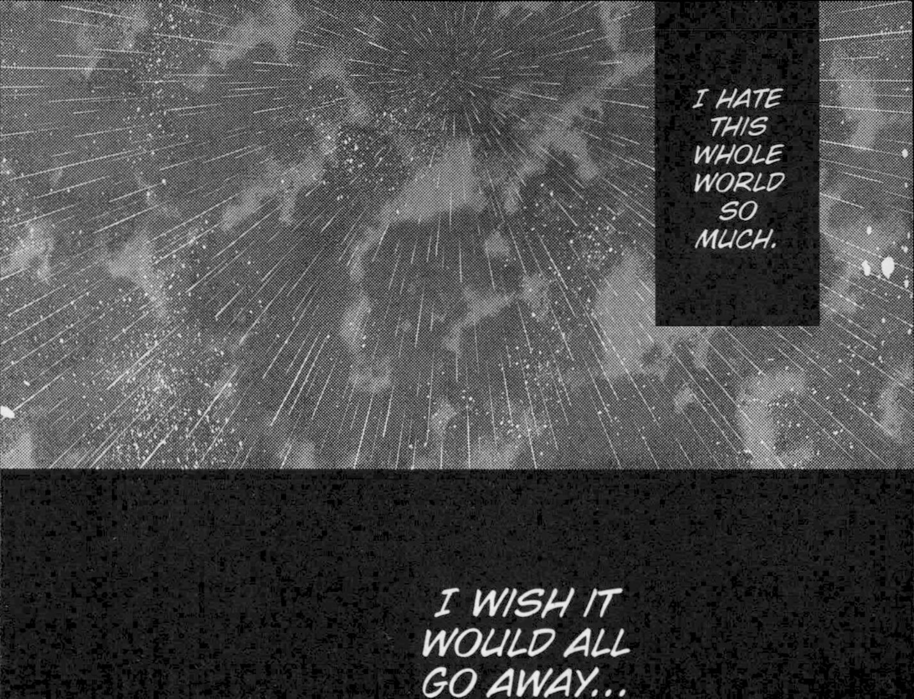
I HATE THIS WHOLE WORLD SO MUCH.
I WISH IT WOULD ALL GO AWAY...

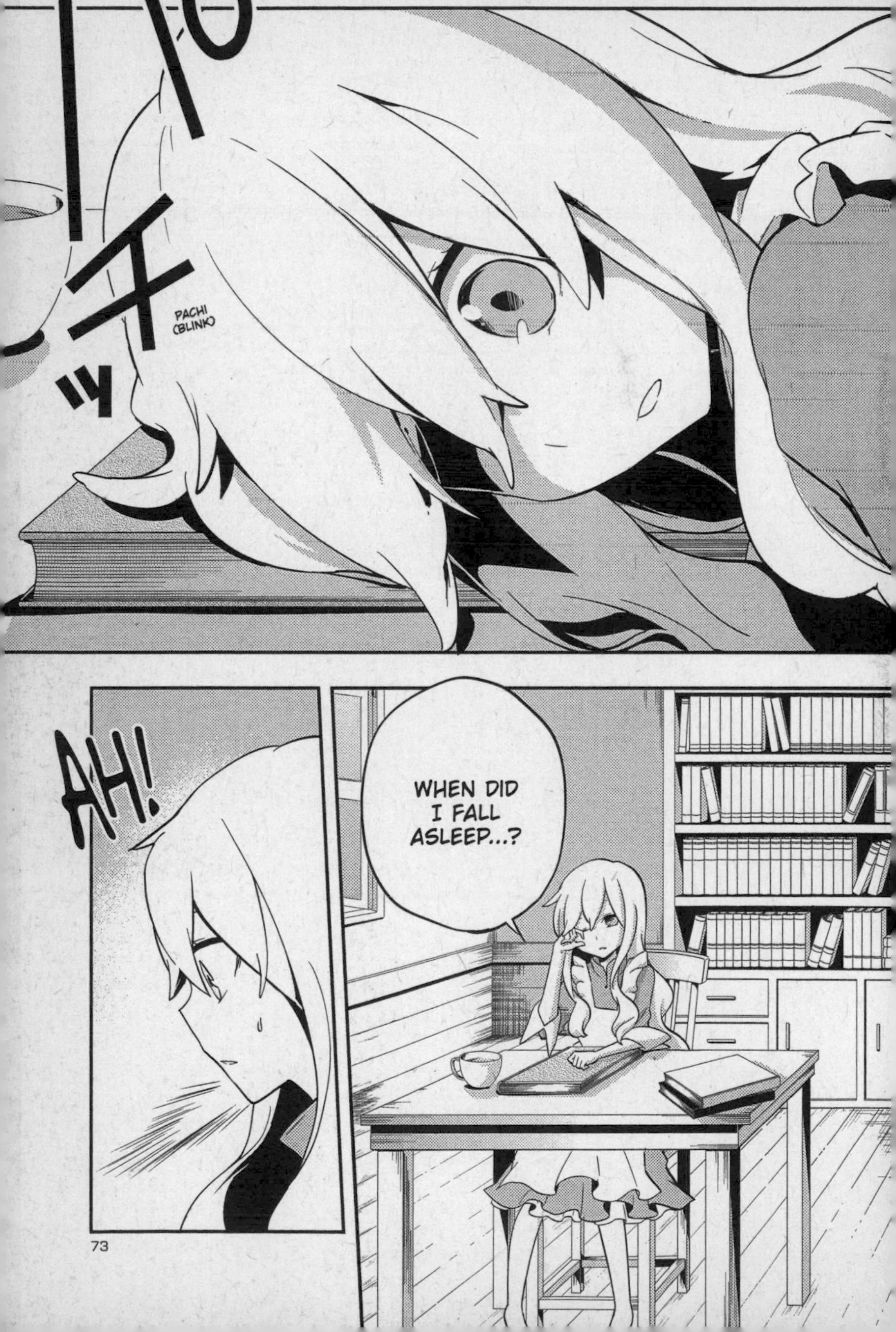
パチッ
PACHI (BLINK)
WHEN DID I FALL ASLEEP...?
AH!

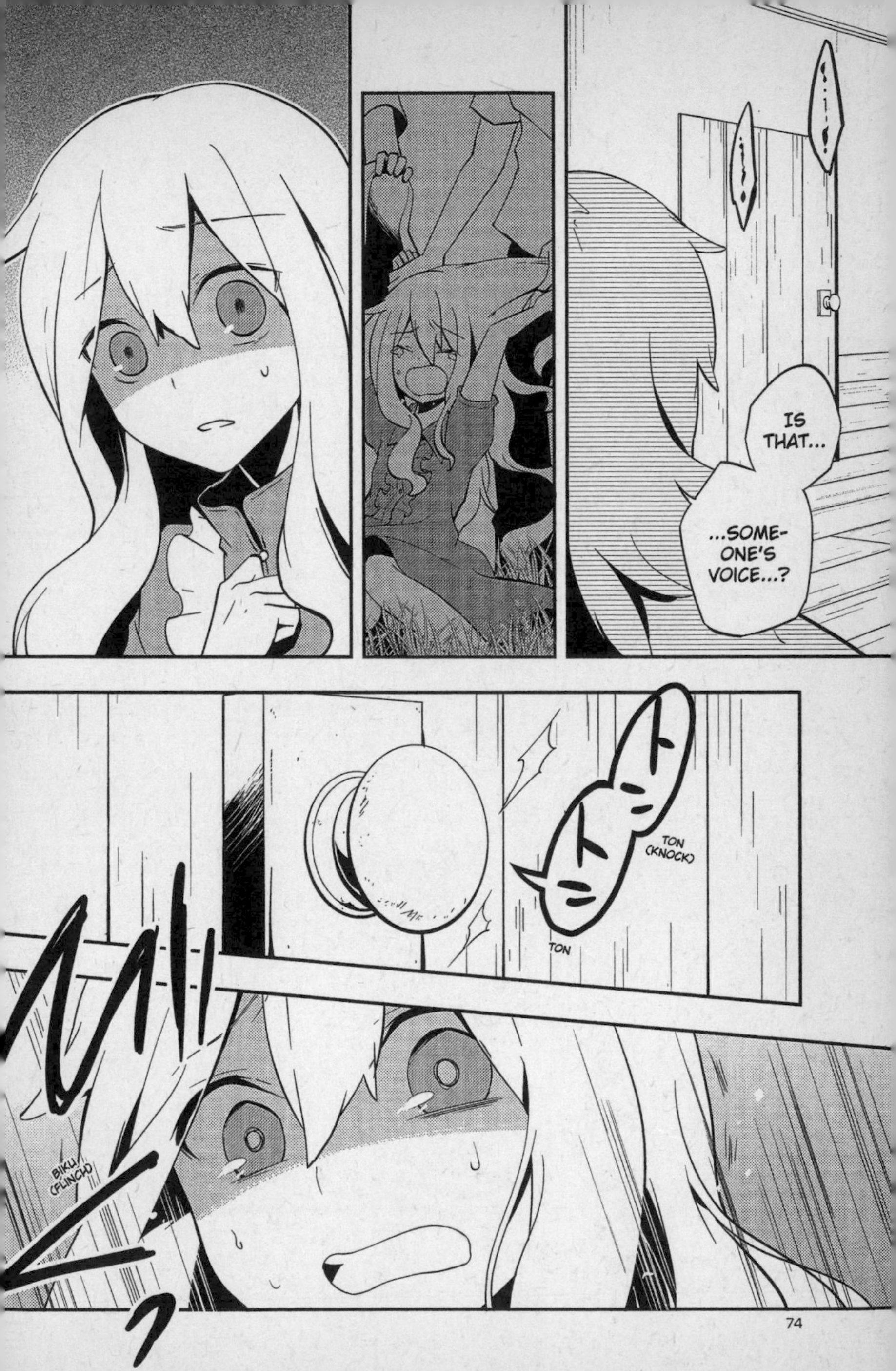
IS THAT...
...SOME-ONE'S VOICE...?
TON (KNOCK)
TON
BIKU (FLINCH)

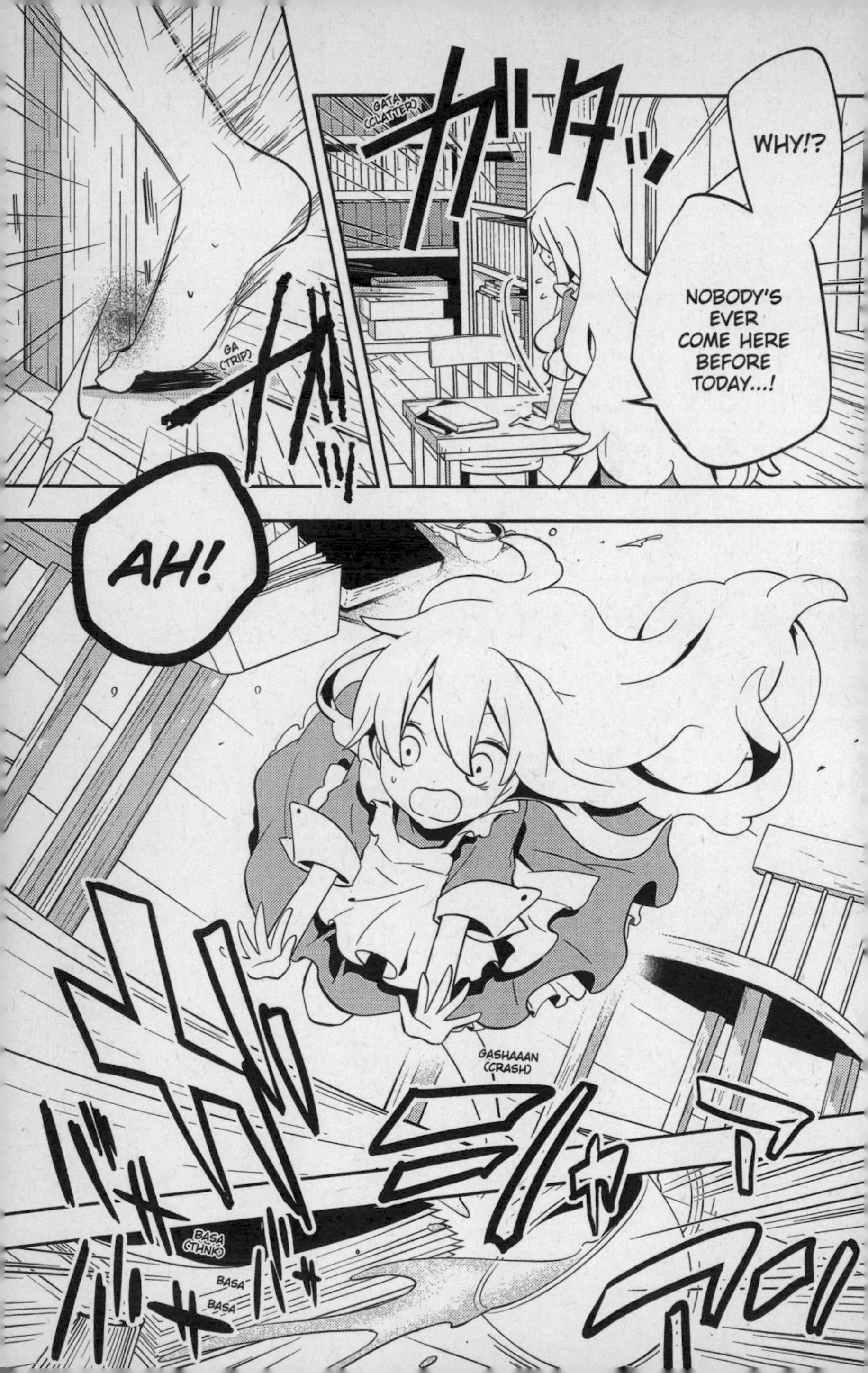
WHY!?
NOBODY'S EVER COME HERE BEFORE TODAY...!
GATA (CLATTER)
GA (TRIP)
AH!
GASHAAAN (CRASH)
BASA (THNK)
BASA
BASA

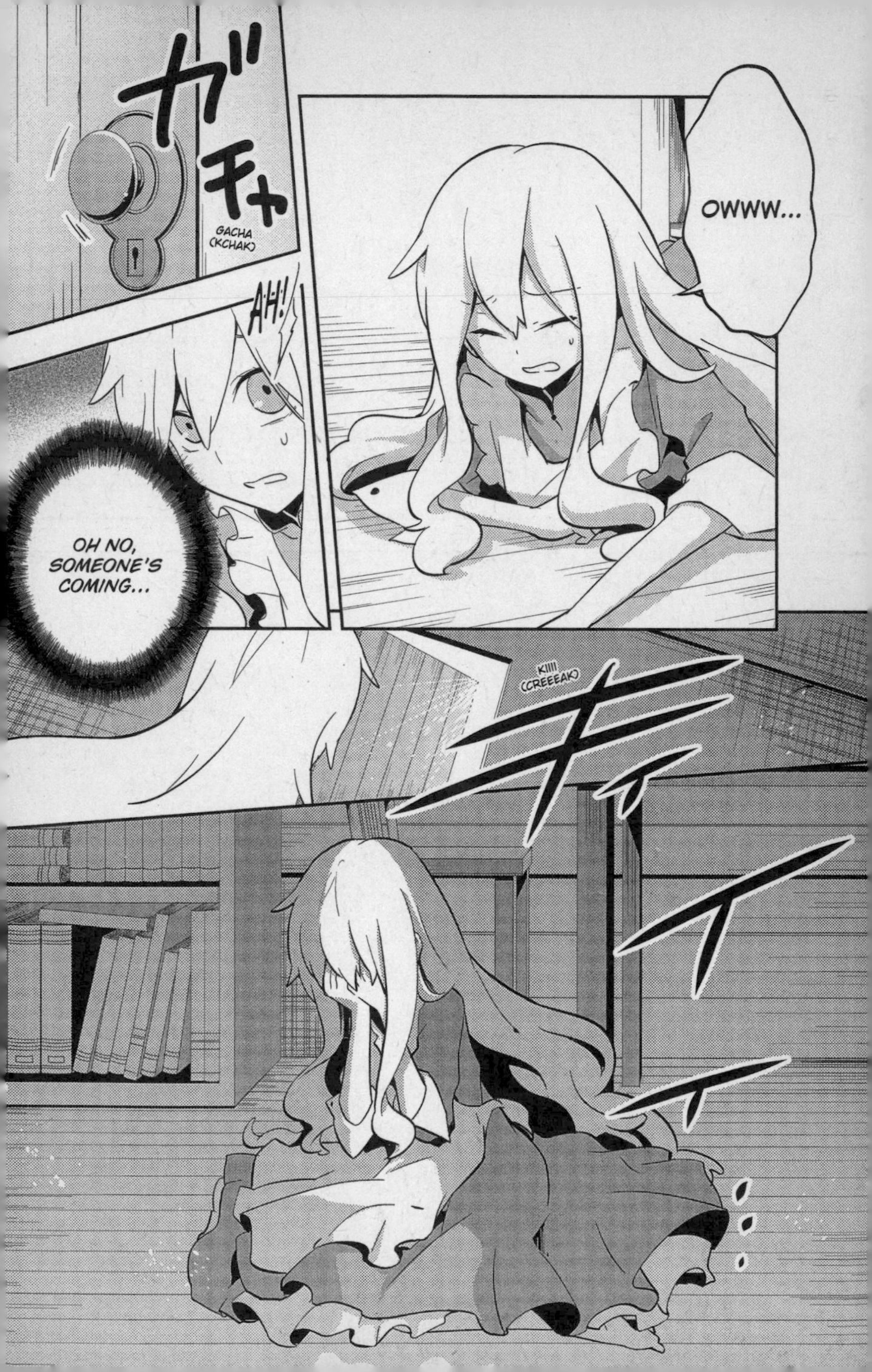
OWWW...
ガチャ
GACHA (KCHAK)
AH!
OH NO, SOMEONE'S COMING...
KIIII (CREEEAK)
キィィィ

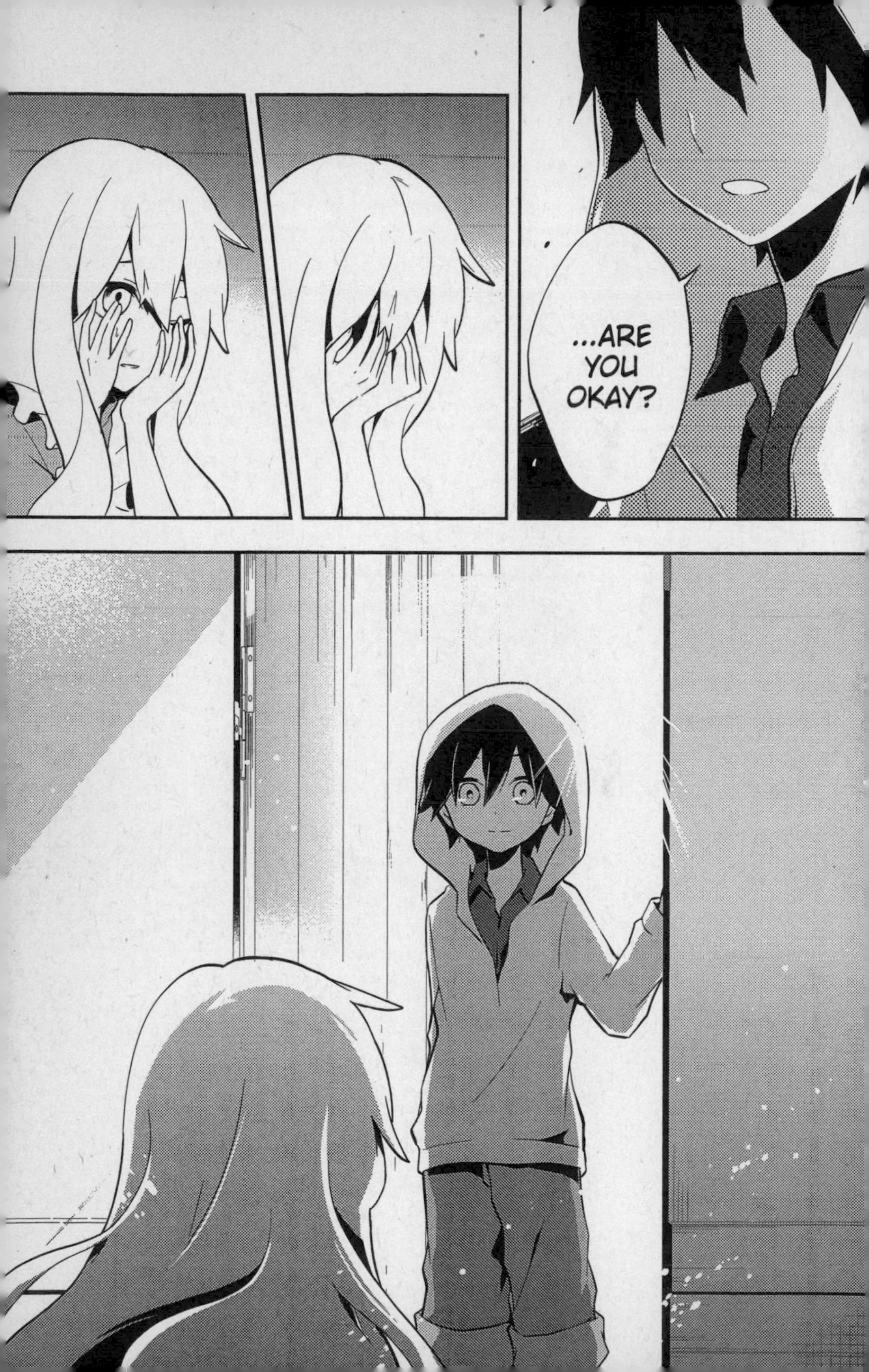
...ARE YOU OKAY?

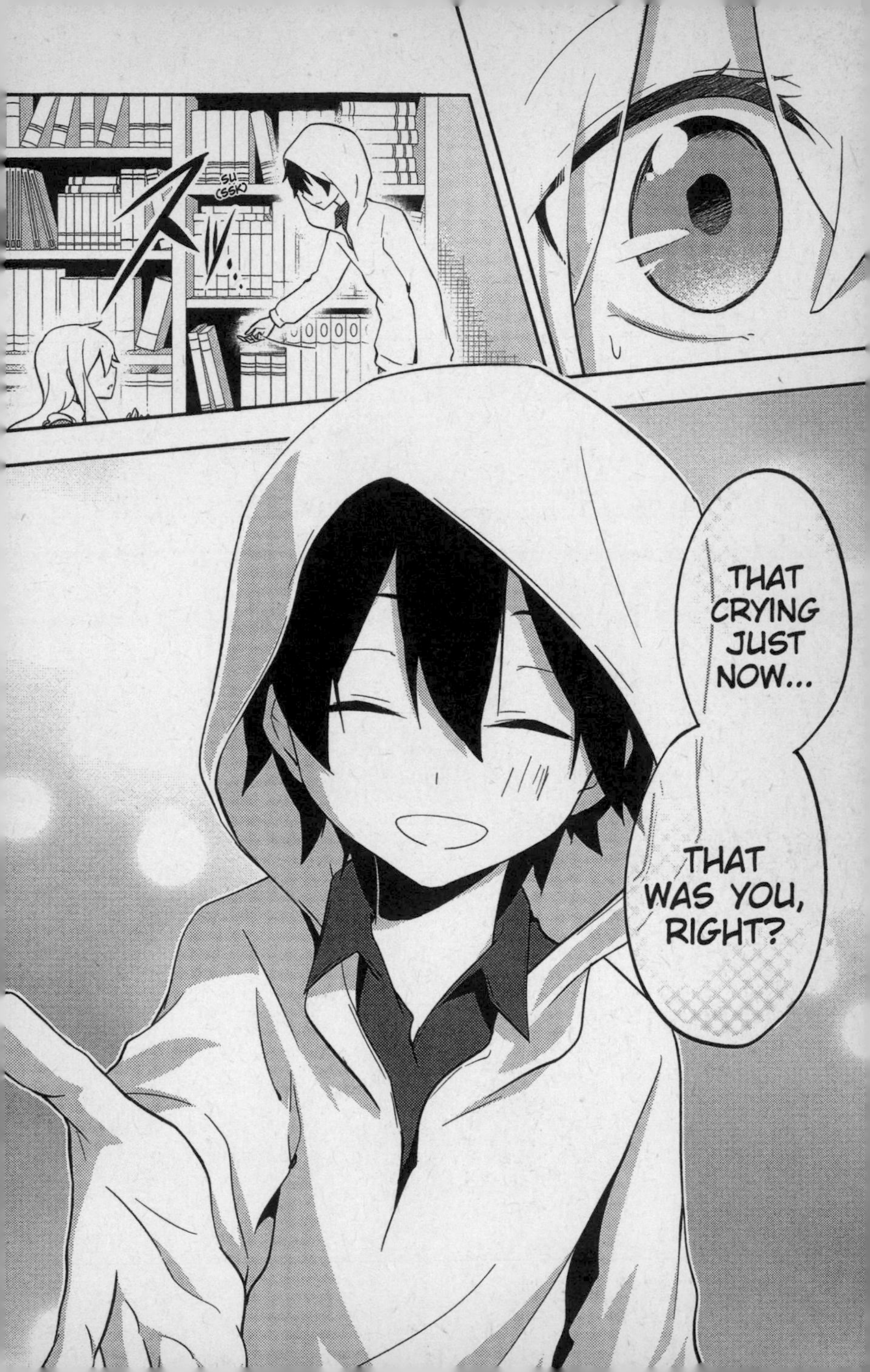
SU (SSK)
THAT CRYING JUST NOW...
THAT WAS YOU, RIGHT?

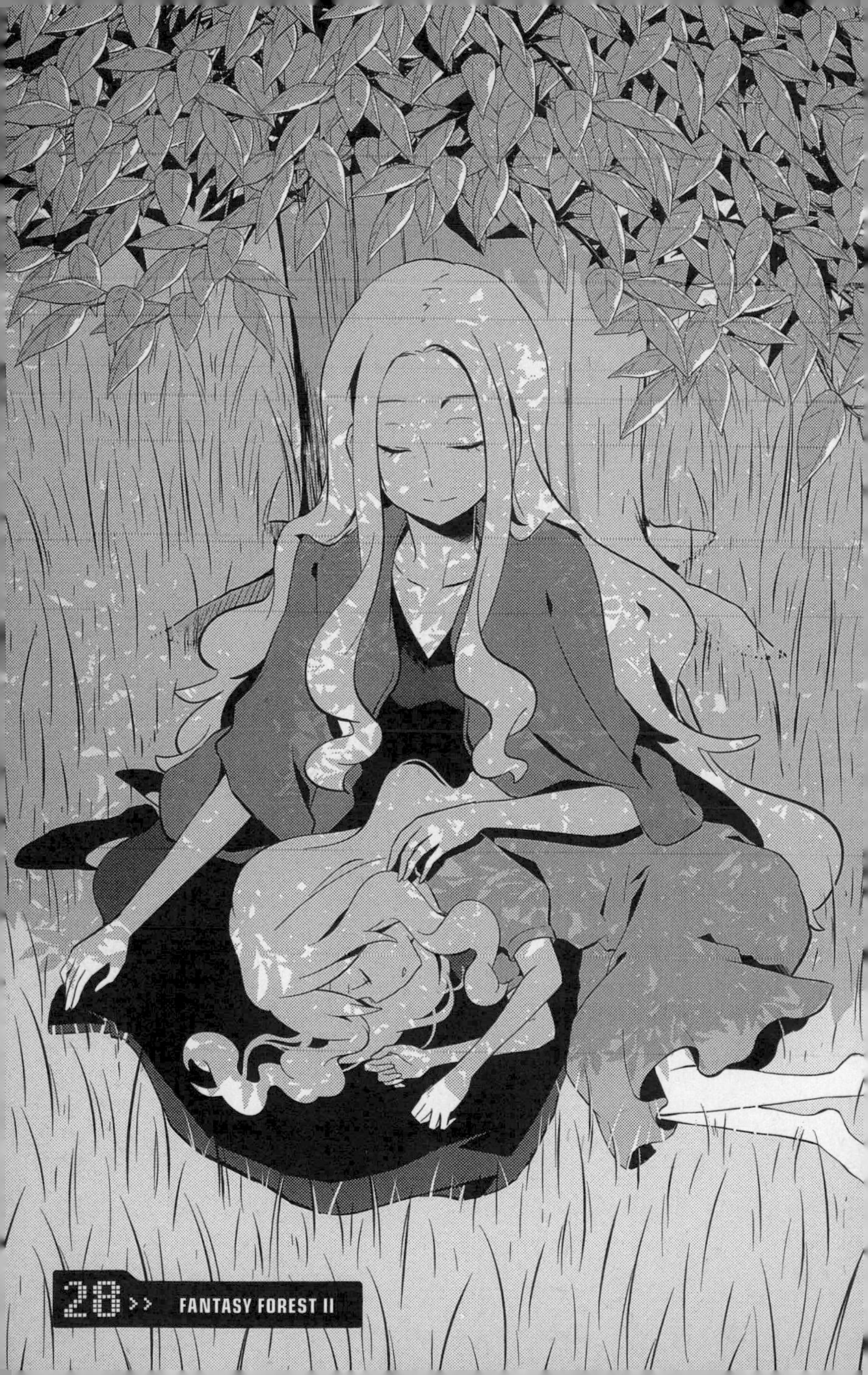

28 >> FANTASY FOREST II

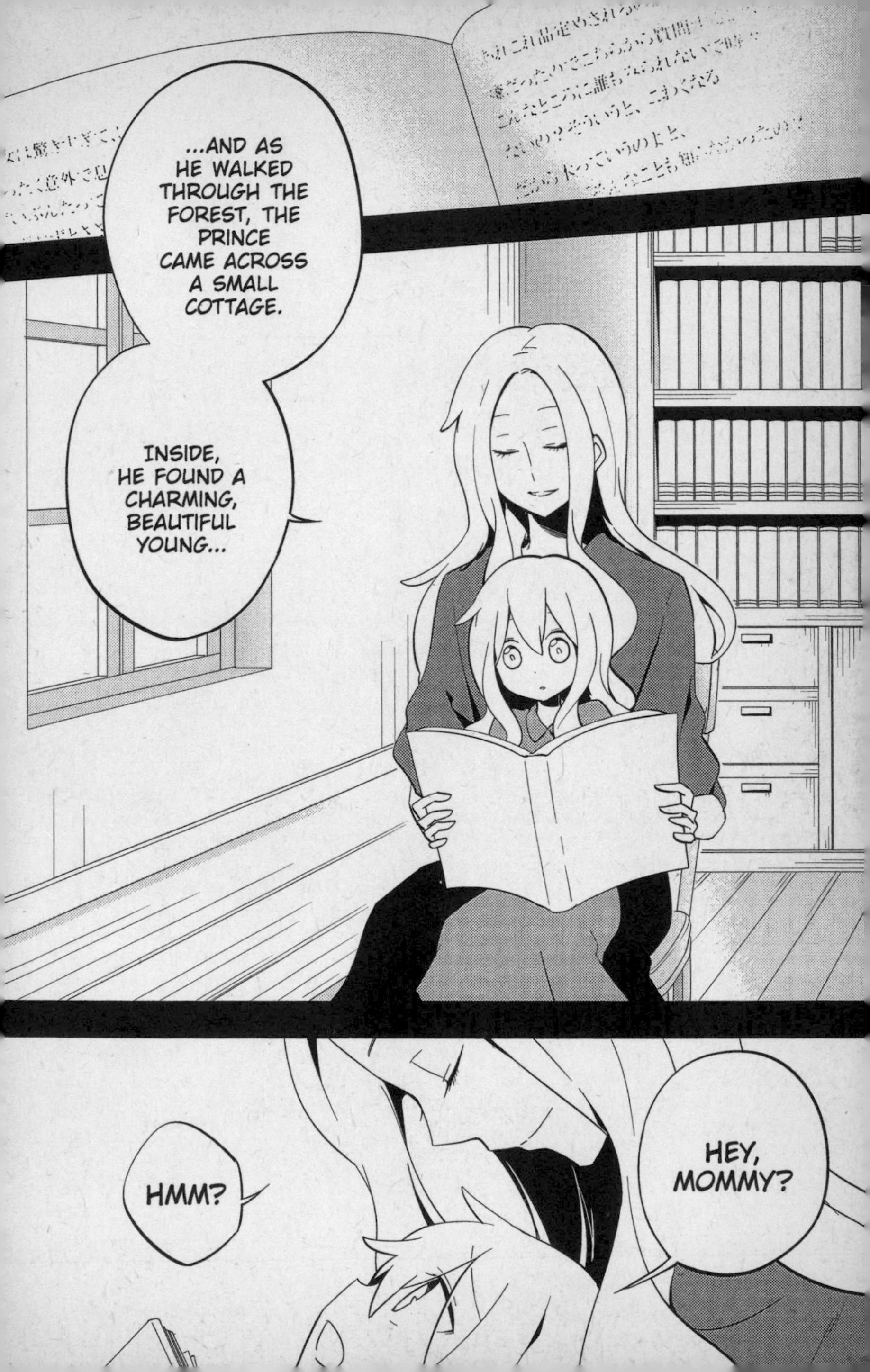
...AND AS HE WALKED THROUGH THE FOREST, THE PRINCE CAME ACROSS A SMALL COTTAGE.
INSIDE, HE FOUND A CHARMING, BEAUTIFUL YOUNG...
HEY, MOMMY?
HMM?

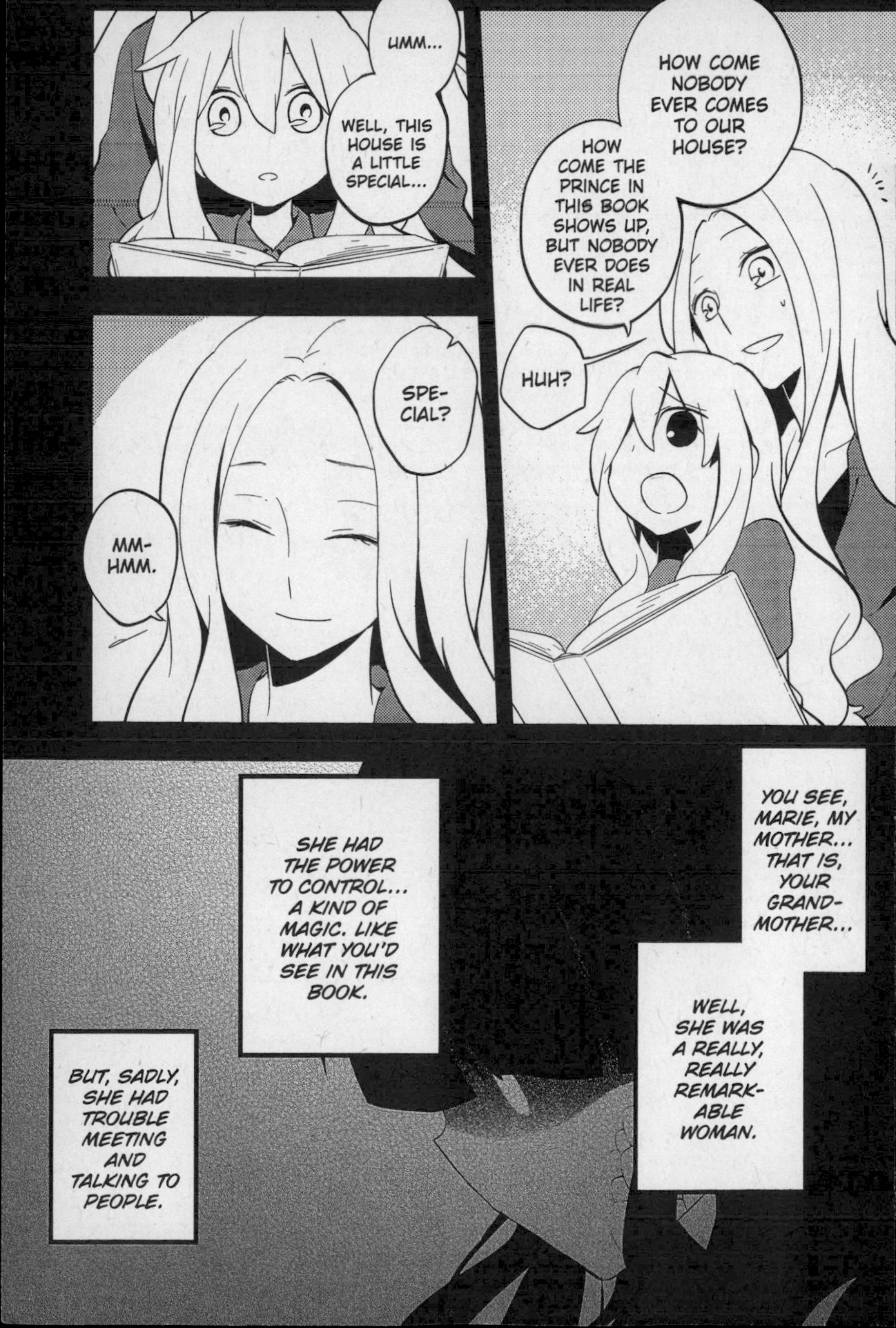

HOW COME NOBODY EVER COMES TO OUR HOUSE?
HOW COME THE PRINCE IN THIS BOOK SHOWS UP, BUT NOBODY EVER DOES IN REAL LIFE?
HUH?
UMM...
WELL, THIS HOUSE IS A LITTLE SPECIAL...
SPE-CIAL?
MM-HMM.
YOU SEE, MARIE, MY MOTHER... THAT IS, YOUR GRAND-MOTHER...
WELL, SHE WAS A REALLY, REALLY REMARK-ABLE WOMAN.
SHE HAD THE POWER TO CONTROL... A KIND OF MAGIC. LIKE WHAT YOU'D SEE IN THIS BOOK.
BUT, SADLY, SHE HAD TROUBLE MEETING AND TALKING TO PEOPLE.

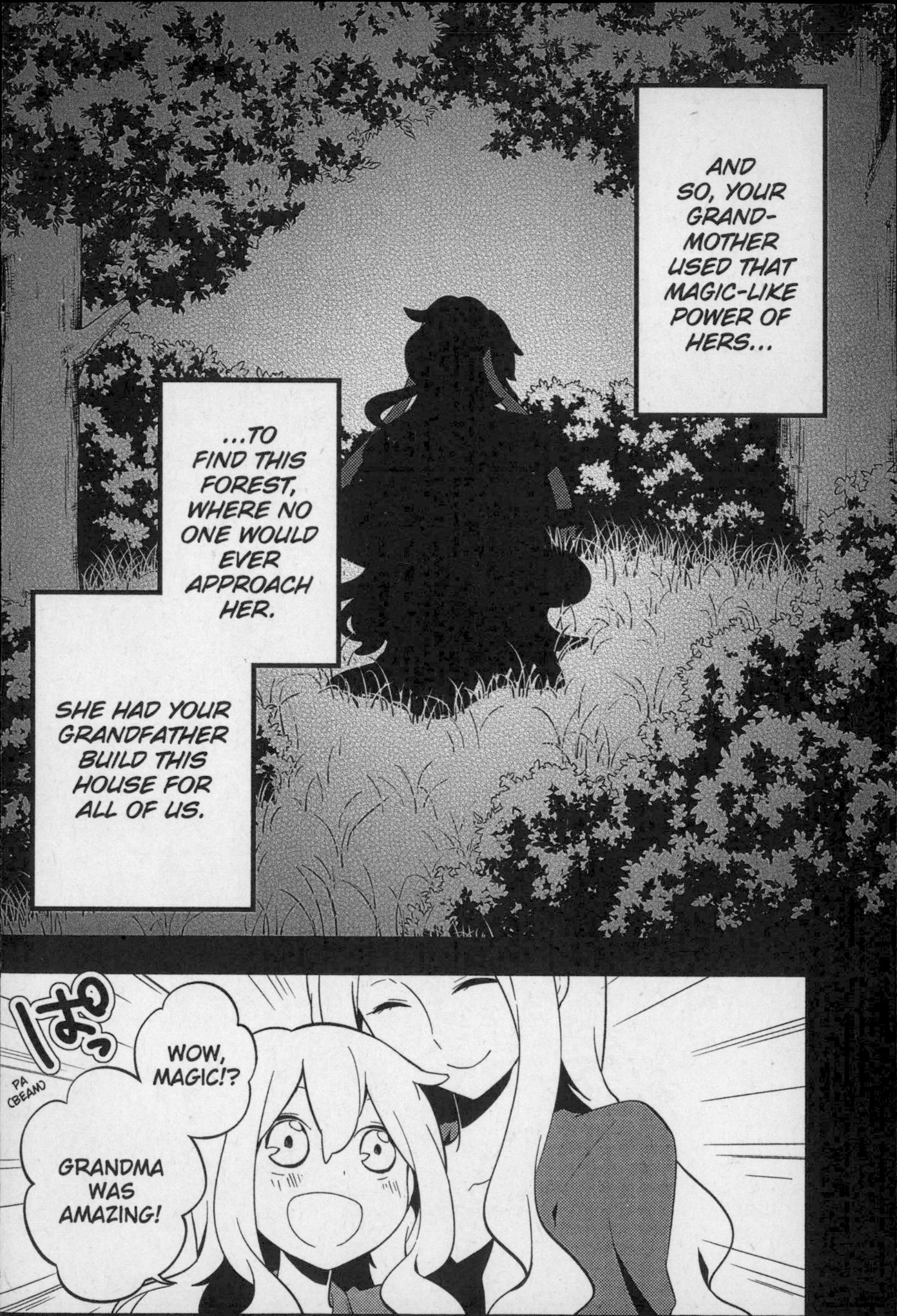
AND SO, YOUR GRAND-MOTHER USED THAT MAGIC-LIKE POWER OF HERS...
...TO FIND THIS FOREST, WHERE NO ONE WOULD EVER APPROACH HER.
SHE HAD YOUR GRANDFATHER BUILD THIS HOUSE FOR ALL OF US.
WOW, MAGIC!?
ぱっ
PA (BEAM)
GRANDMA WAS AMAZING!

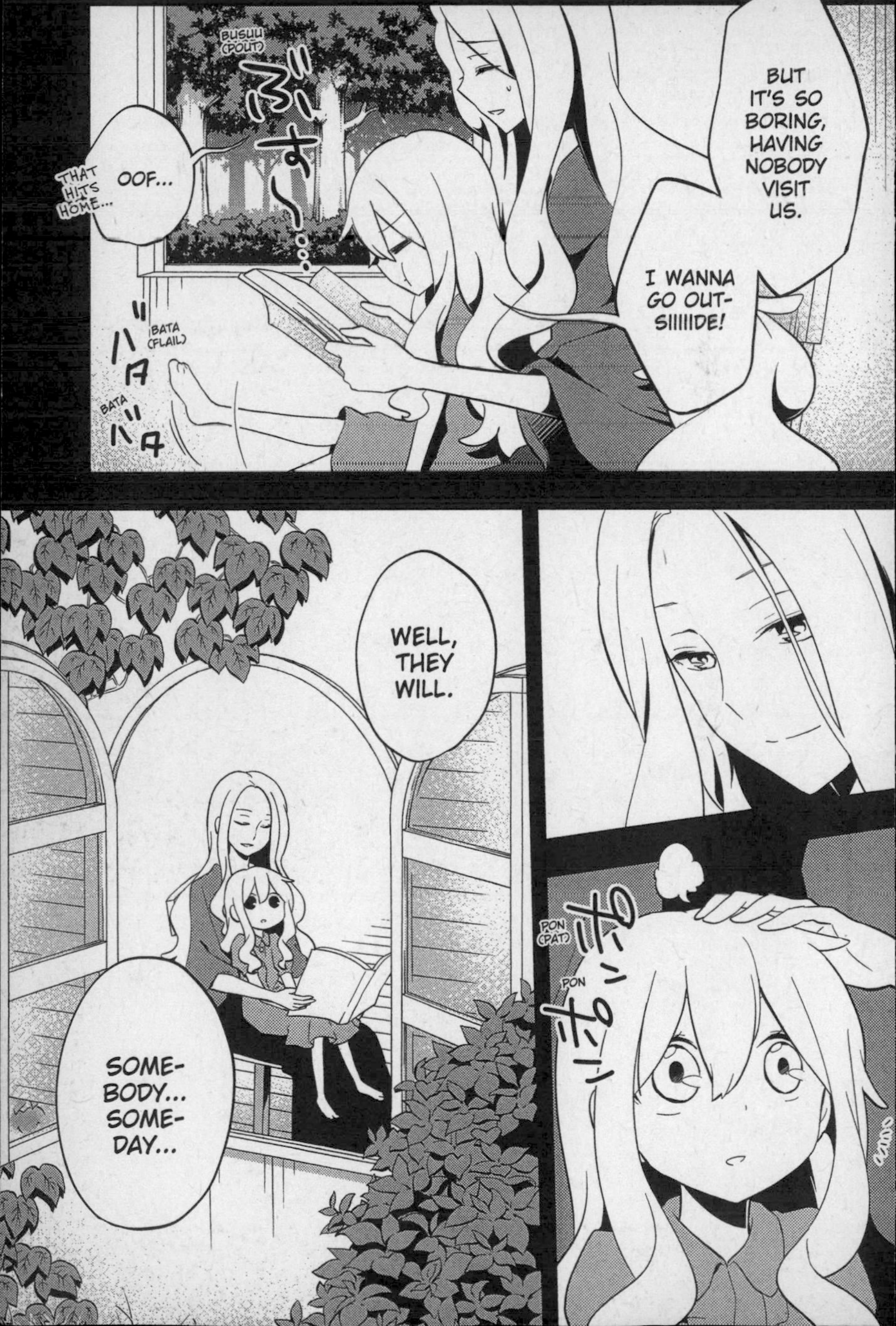
BUT IT'S SO BORING, HAVING NOBODY VISIT US.
I WANNA GO OUT-SIIIIIDE!
BUSUU (POUT)
ぶすー…
THAT HITS HOME...
OOF...
BATA (FLAIL)
バタ
BATA
バタ
PON (PAT)
ポン
PON
ポン
WELL, THEY WILL.
SOME-BODY... SOME-DAY...

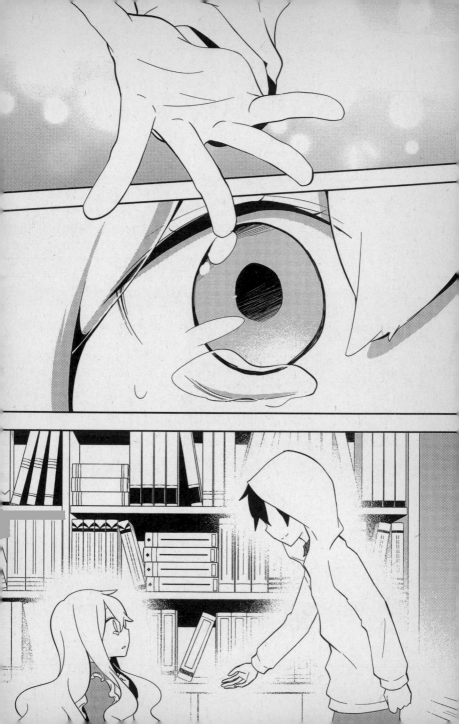

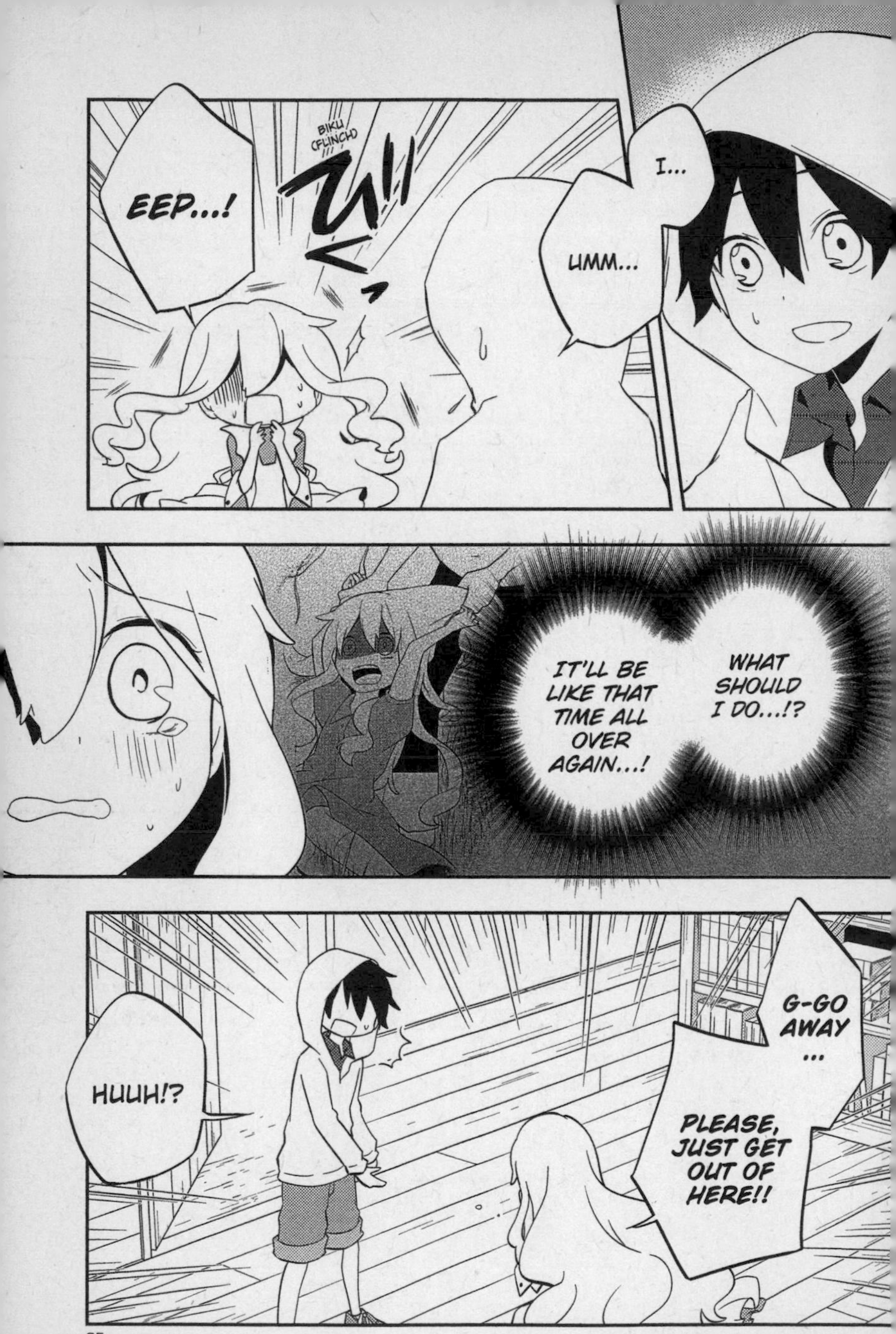
I...
UMM...
EEP...!
BIKU (FLINCH)
WHAT SHOULD I DO...!?
IT'LL BE LIKE THAT TIME ALL OVER AGAIN...!
G-GO AWAY ...
PLEASE, JUST GET OUT OF HERE!!
HUUH!?

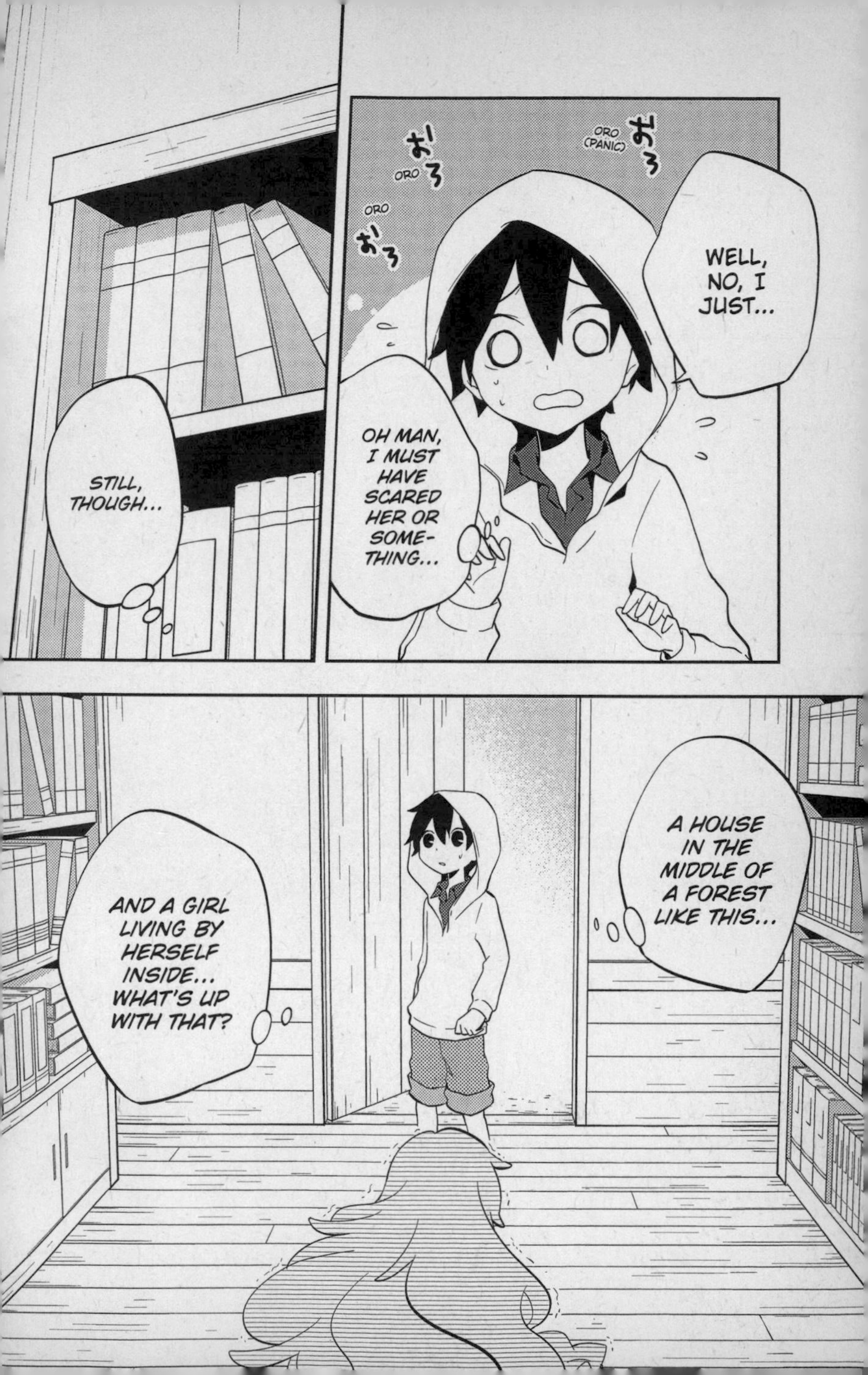
おろ
ORO (PANIC)
WELL, NO, I JUST...
おろ
ORO
おろ
ORO
OH MAN, I MUST HAVE SCARED HER OR SOME-THING...
STILL, THOUGH...
A HOUSE IN THE MIDDLE OF A FOREST LIKE THIS...
AND A GIRL LIVING BY HERSELF INSIDE... WHAT'S UP WITH THAT?

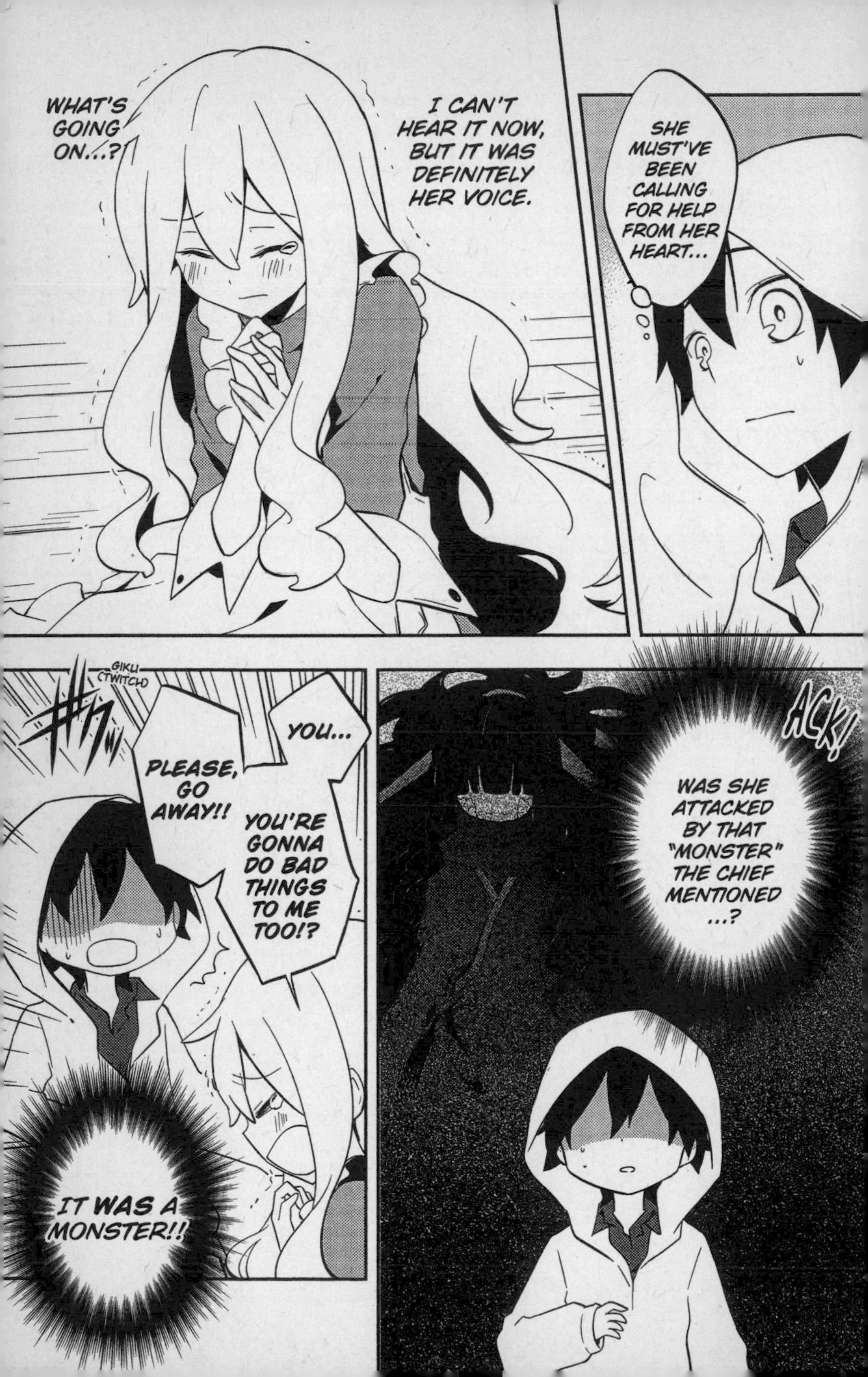
SHE MUST'VE BEEN CALLING FOR HELP FROM HER HEART...
I CAN'T HEAR IT NOW, BUT IT WAS DEFINITELY HER VOICE.
WHAT'S GOING ON...?
ACK!
WAS SHE ATTACKED BY THAT "MONSTER" THE CHIEF MENTIONED ...?
YOU...
PLEASE, GO AWAY!!
YOU'RE GONNA DO BAD THINGS TO ME TOO!?
GIKU (TWITCH)
IT WAS A MONSTER!!

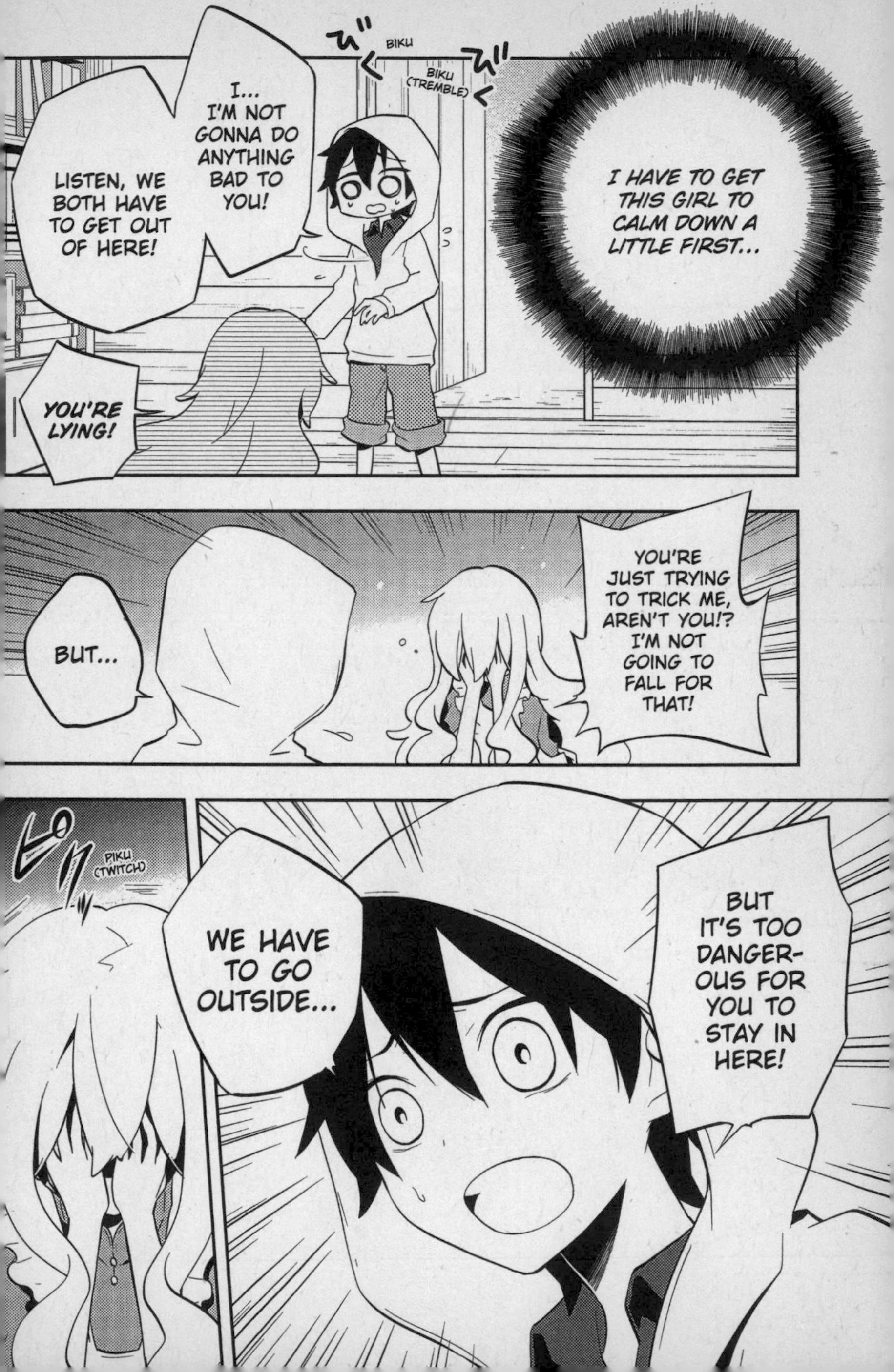
I HAVE TO GET THIS GIRL TO CALM DOWN A LITTLE FIRST...
BIKU
BIKU (TREMBLE)
I... I'M NOT GONNA DO ANYTHING BAD TO YOU!
LISTEN, WE BOTH HAVE TO GET OUT OF HERE!
YOU'RE LYING!
YOU'RE JUST TRYING TO TRICK ME, AREN'T YOU!? I'M NOT GOING TO FALL FOR THAT!
BUT...
BUT IT'S TOO DANGER-OUS FOR YOU TO STAY IN HERE!
WE HAVE TO GO OUTSIDE...
PIKU (TWITCH)

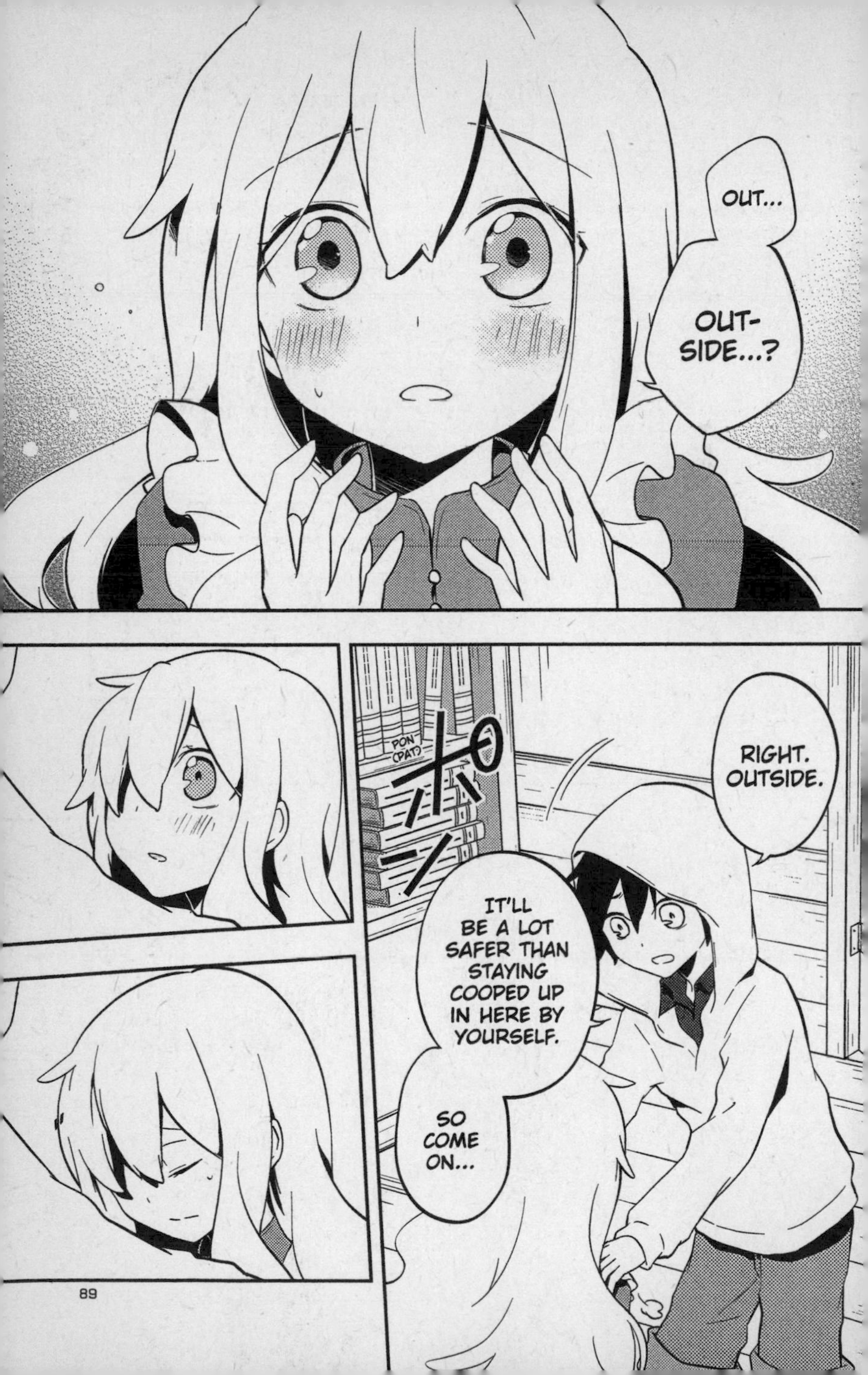
OUT...
OUT-SIDE...?
RIGHT. OUTSIDE.
PON (PAT)
IT'LL BE A LOT SAFER THAN STAYING COOPED UP IN HERE BY YOURSELF.
SO COME ON...

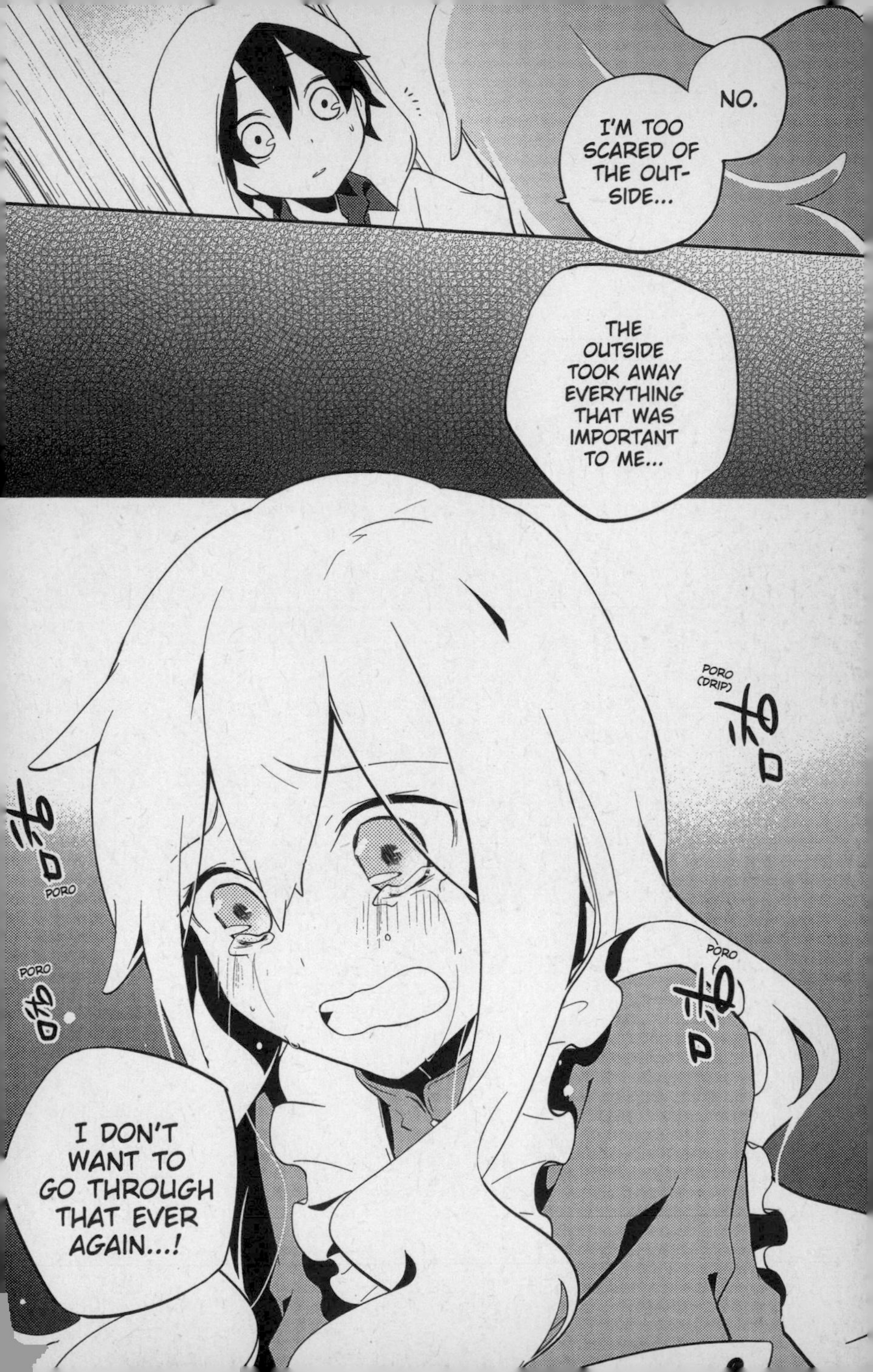
NO.
I'M TOO SCARED OF THE OUT-SIDE...
THE OUTSIDE TOOK AWAY EVERYTHING THAT WAS IMPORTANT TO ME...
PORO (DRIP)
PORO
PORO
PORO
I DON'T WANT TO GO THROUGH THAT EVER AGAIN...!

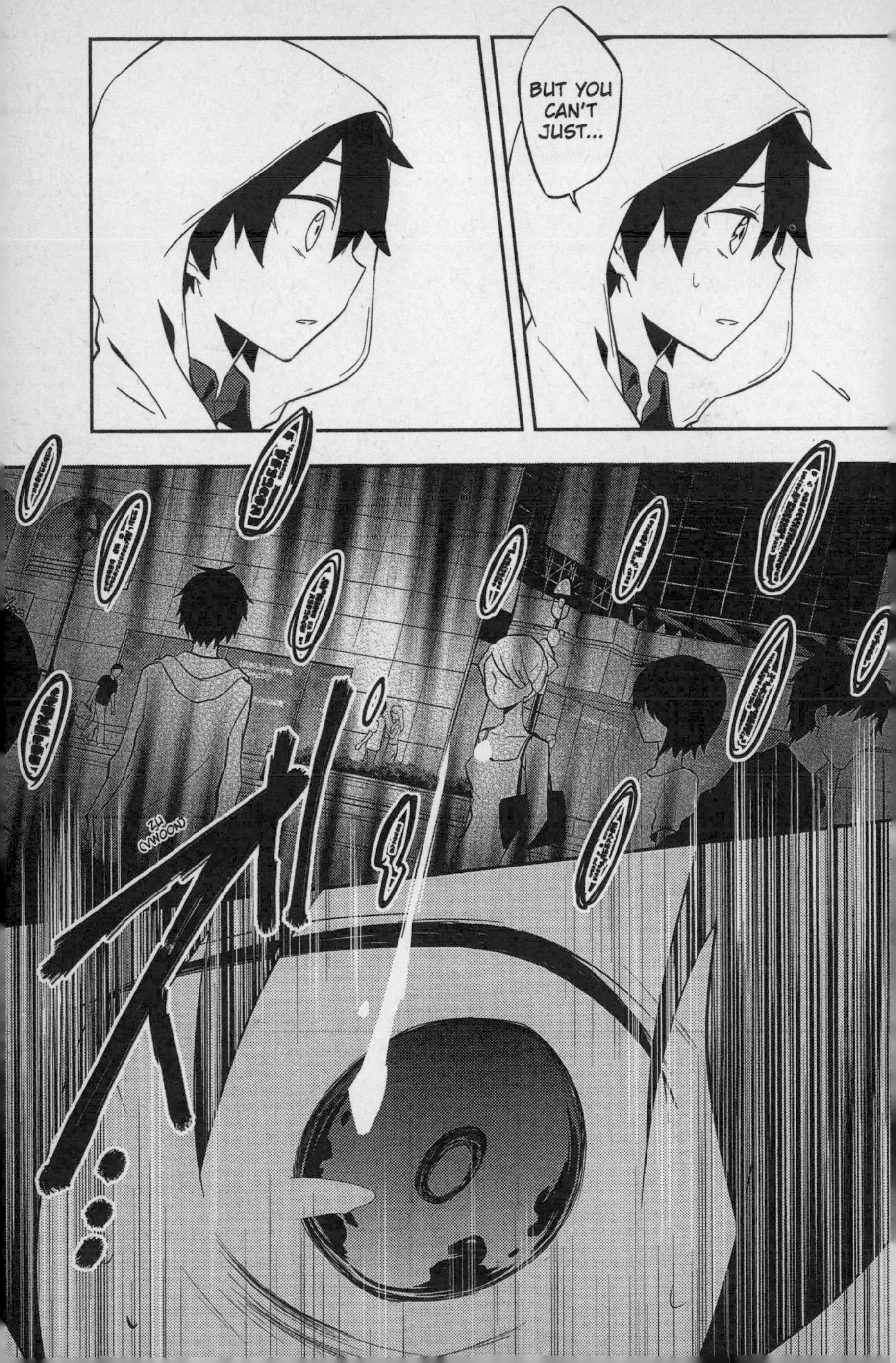
BUT YOU CAN'T JUST...
ZU (VWOON)

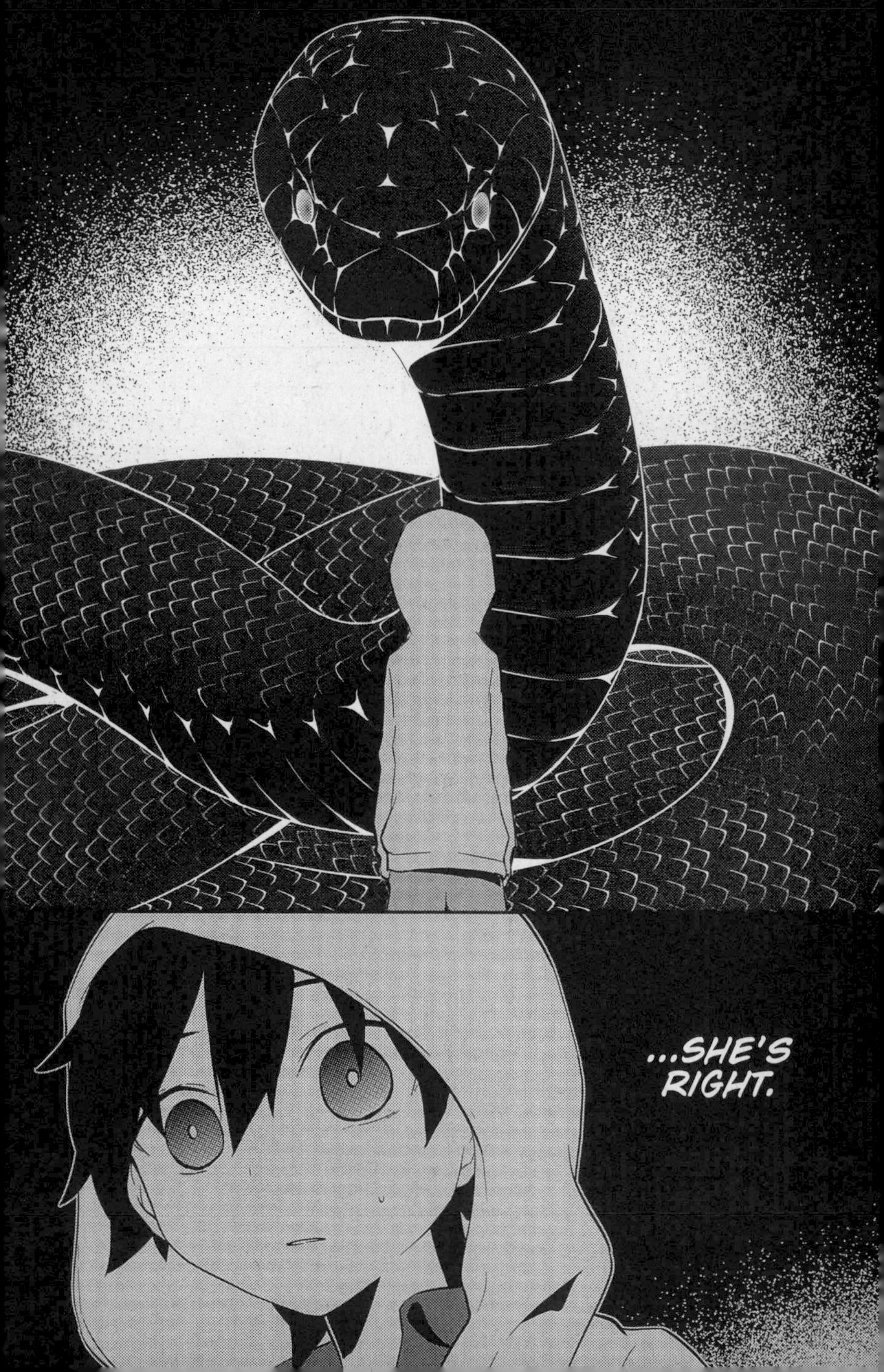
...SHE'S
RIGHT.

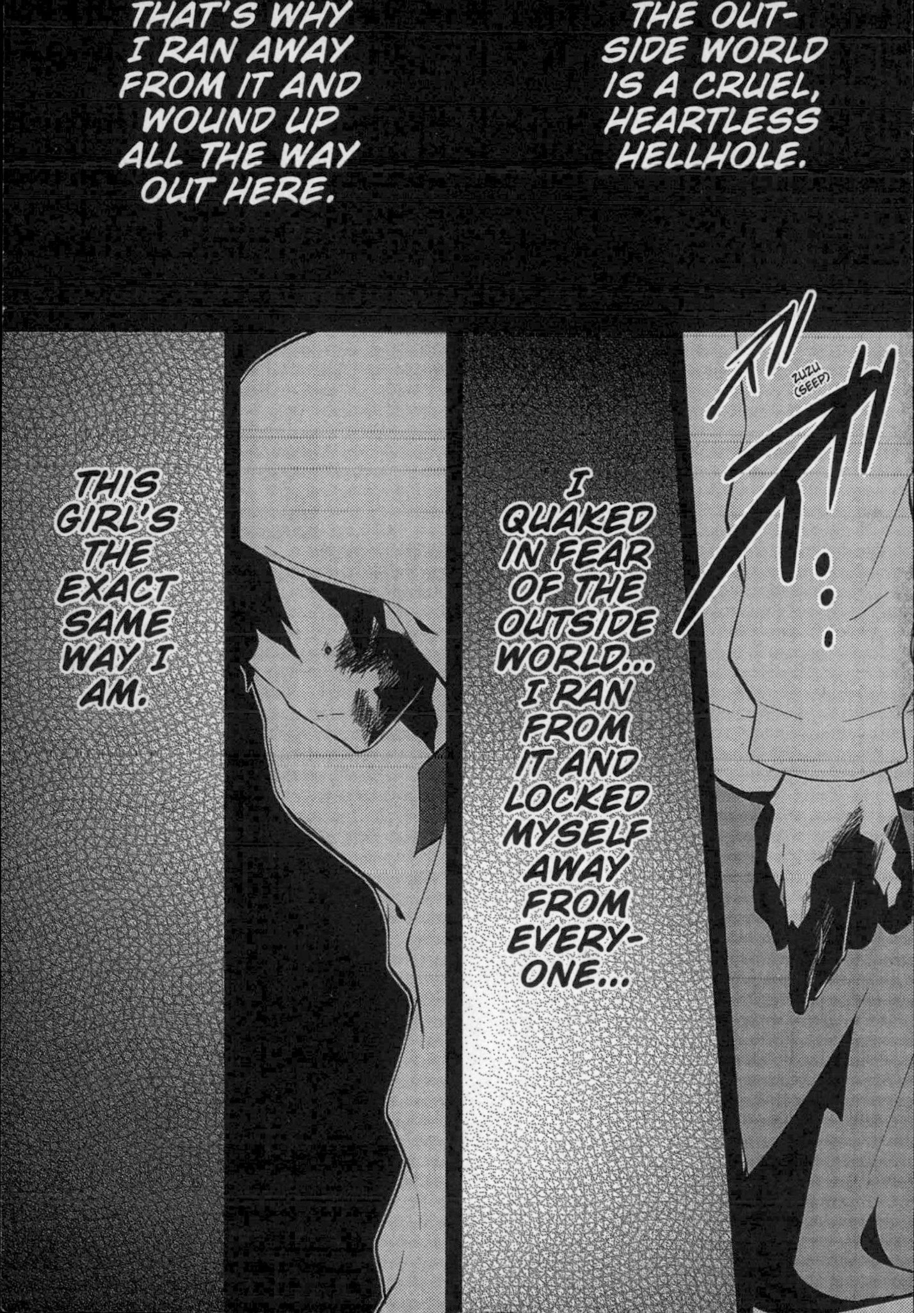
THE OUT-SIDE WORLD IS A CRUEL, HEARTLESS HELLHOLE.
THAT'S WHY I RAN AWAY FROM IT AND WOUND UP ALL THE WAY OUT HERE.
ZUZU (SEEP)
I QUAKED IN FEAR OF THE OUTSIDE WORLD... I RAN FROM IT AND LOCKED MYSELF AWAY FROM EVERY-ONE...
THIS GIRL'S THE EXACT SAME WAY I AM.

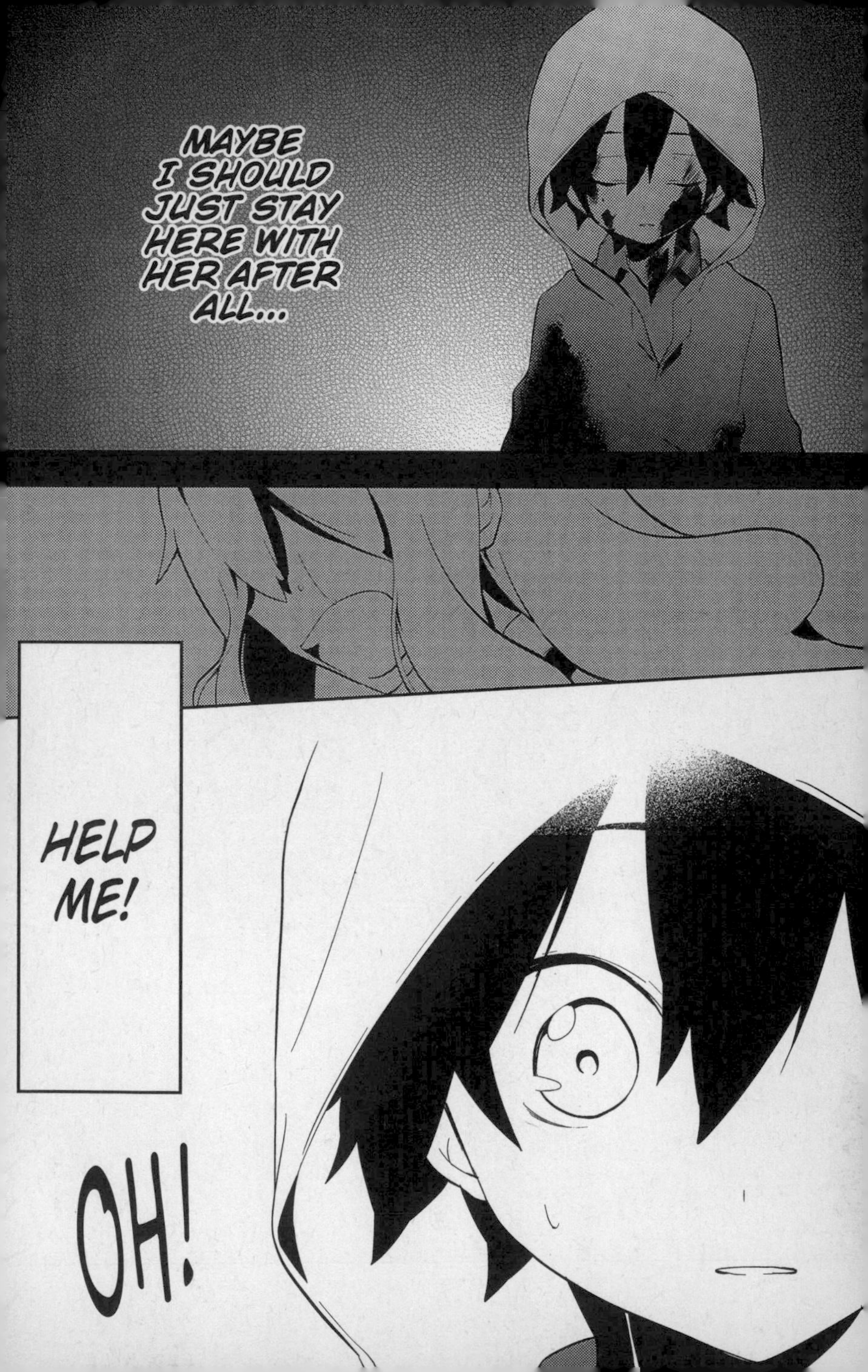
MAYBE I SHOULD JUST STAY HERE WITH HER AFTER ALL...
HELP ME!
OH!

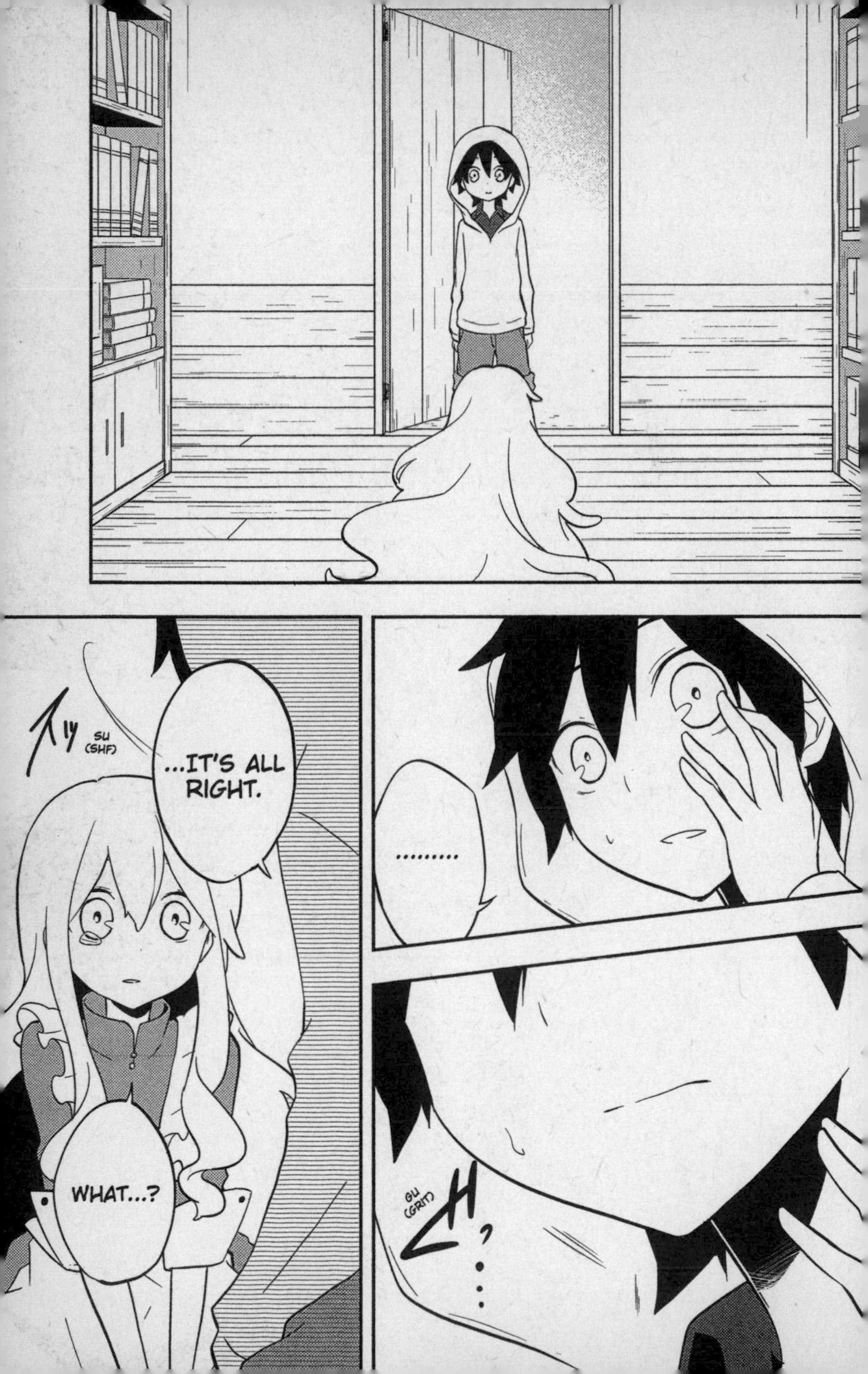
....
GU (GRIT)
SU (SHF)
...IT'S ALL RIGHT.
WHAT...?

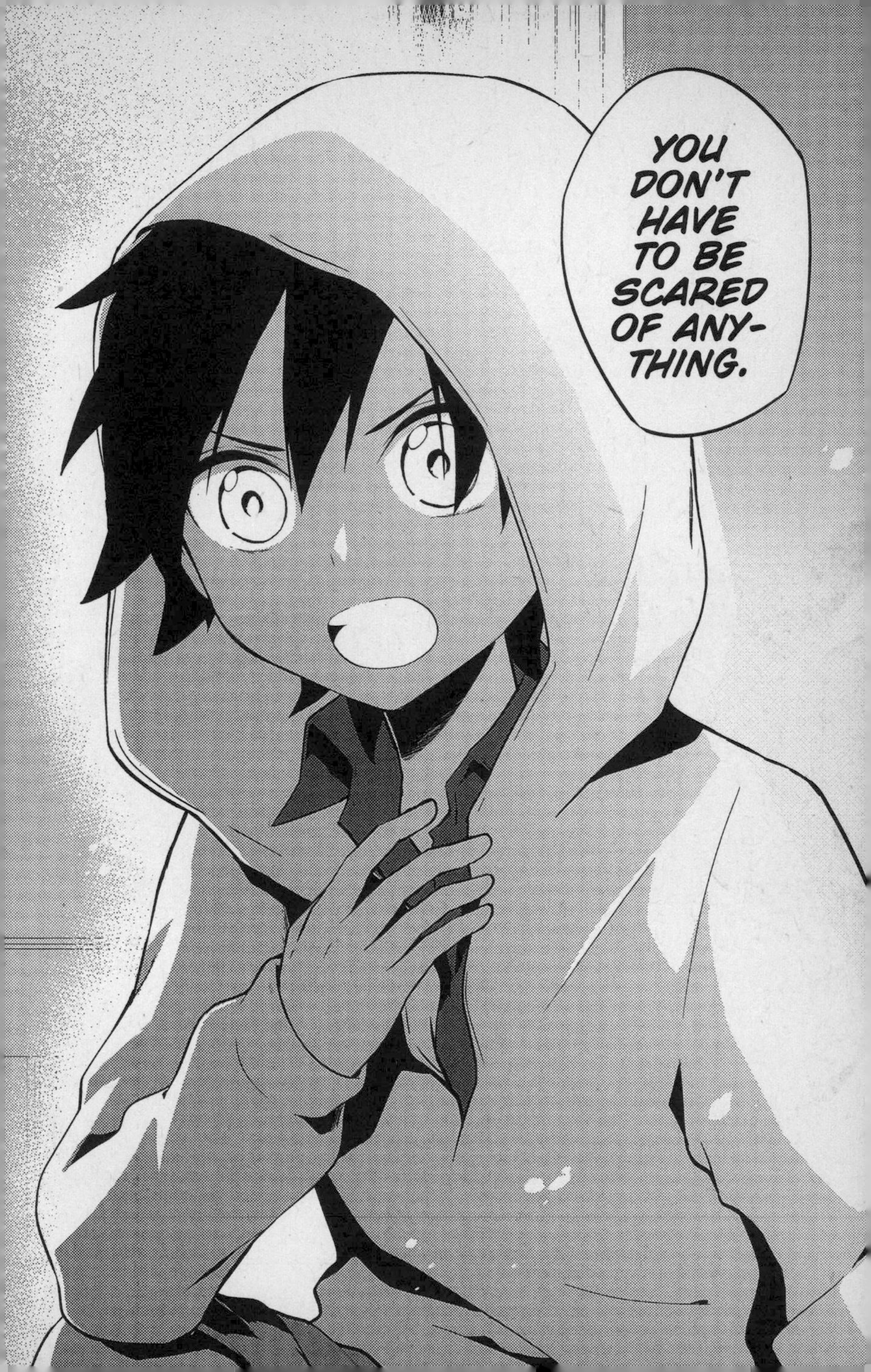
YOU DON'T HAVE TO BE SCARED OF ANY-THING.

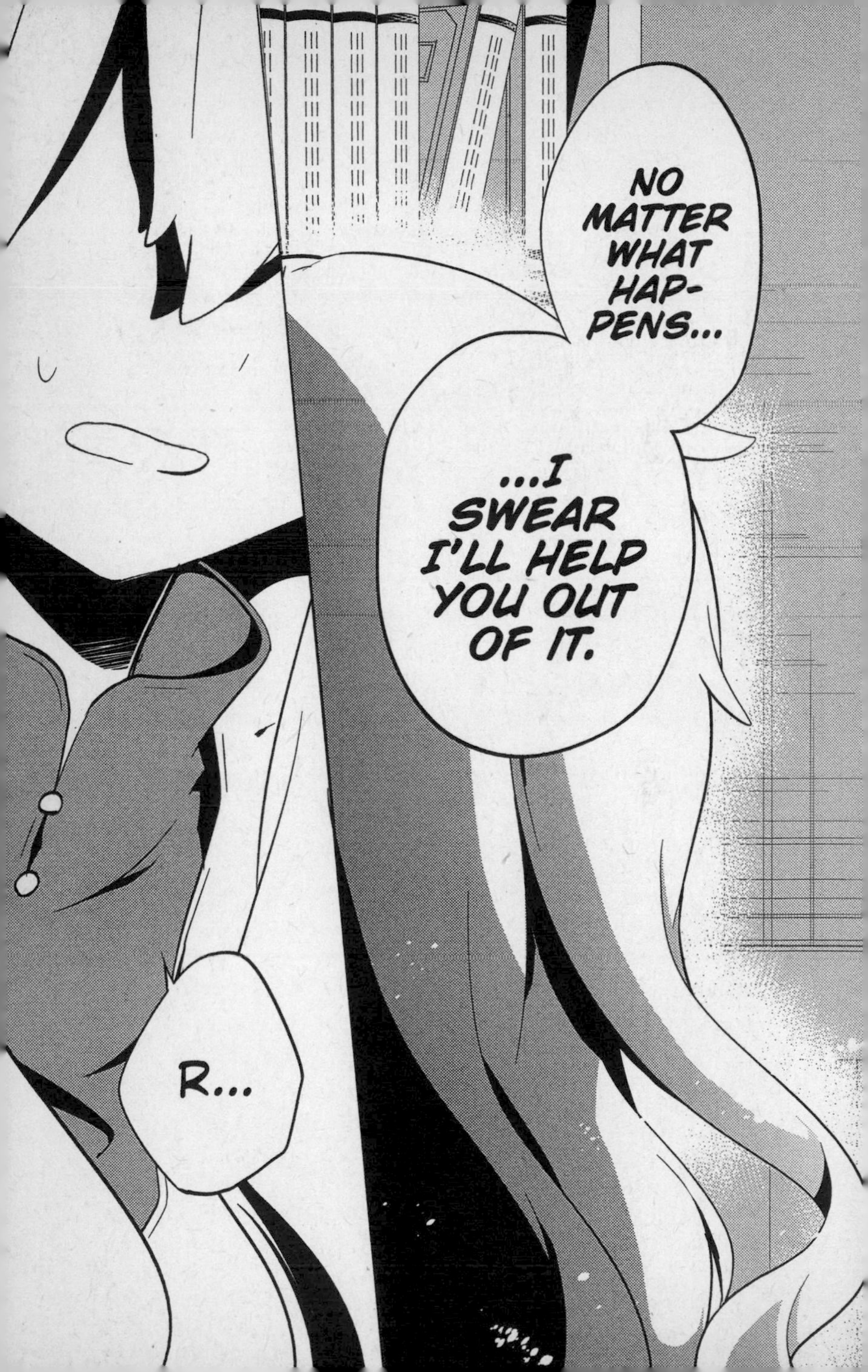
NO MATTER WHAT HAP-PENS...
...I SWEAR I'LL HELP YOU OUT OF IT.
R...

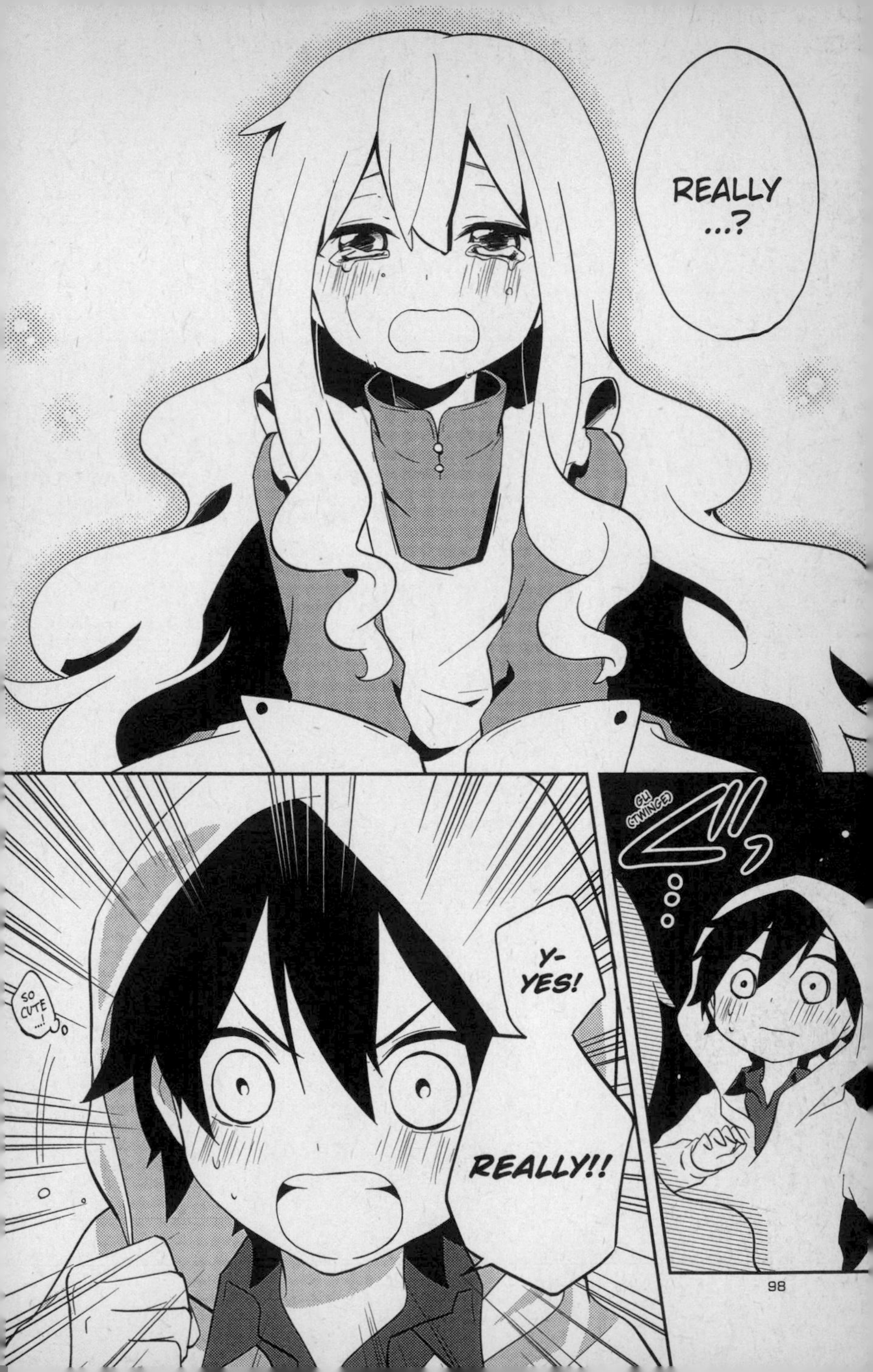
REALLY ...?
GU (TWINGE)
Y- YES!
REALLY!!
SO CUTE ...!

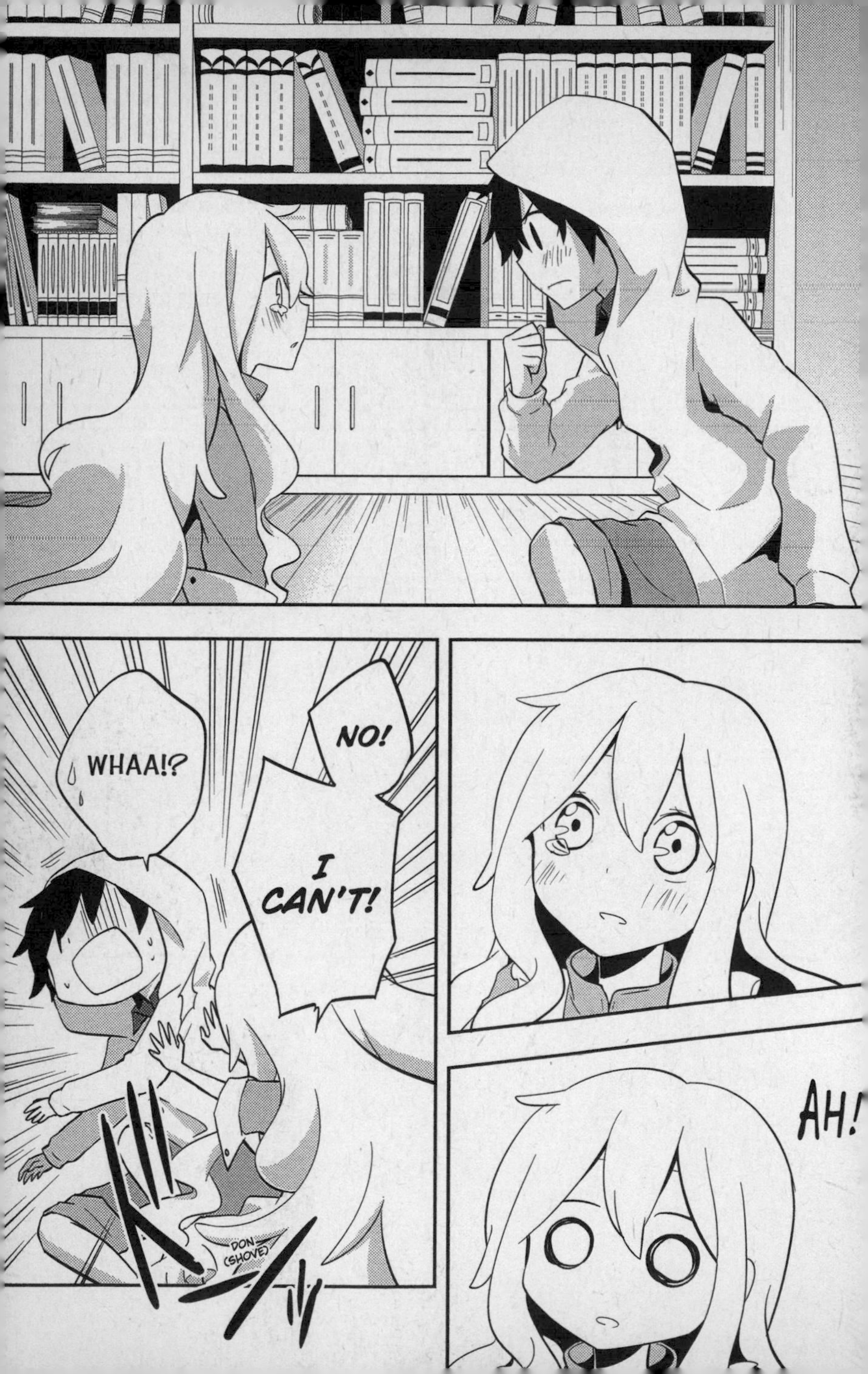
AH!
NO!
I CAN'T!
WHAA!?
DON (SHOVE)

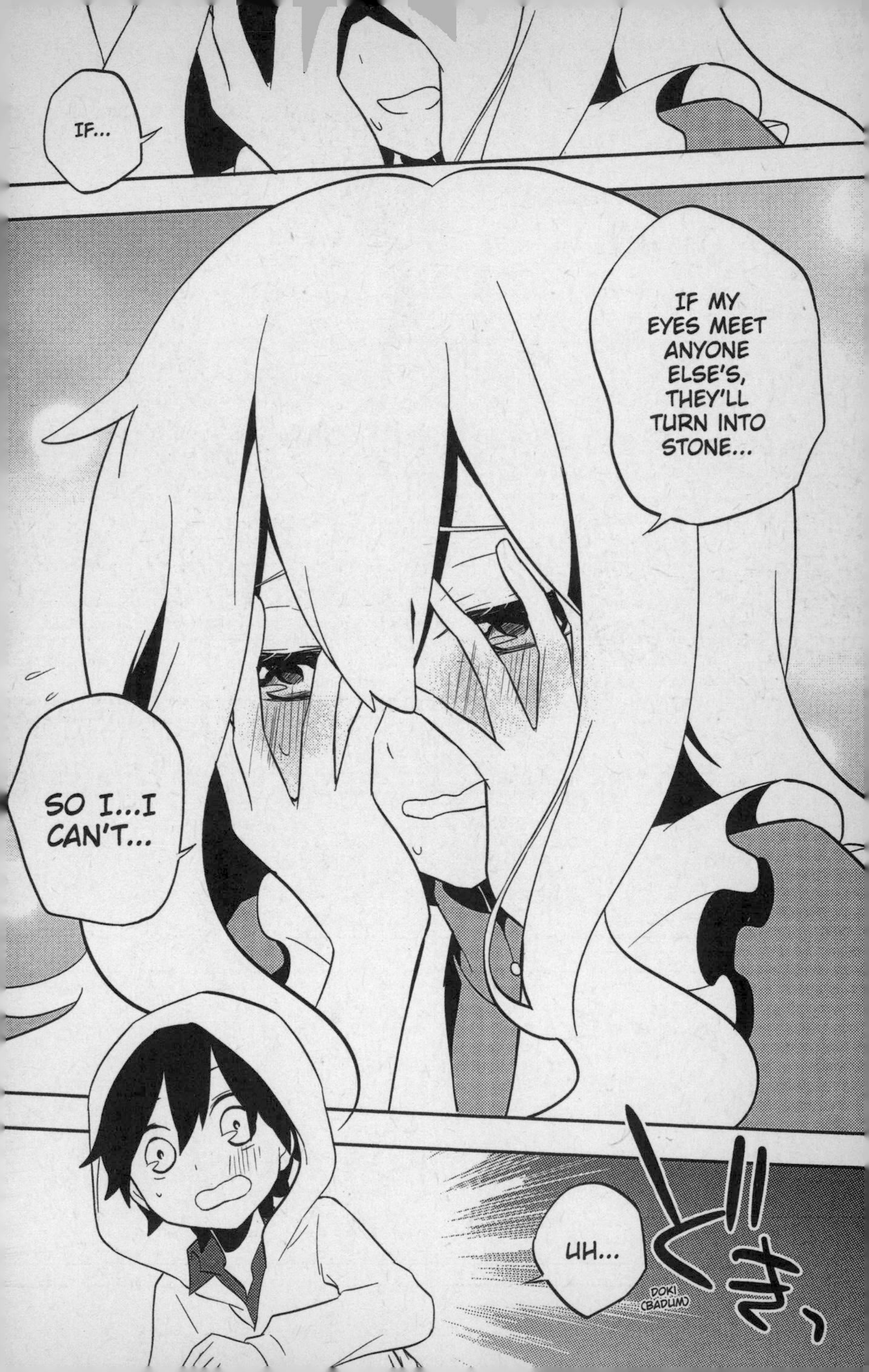
IF...
IF MY EYES MEET ANYONE ELSE'S, THEY'LL TURN INTO STONE...
SO I...I CAN'T...
DOKI (BADUM)
UH...

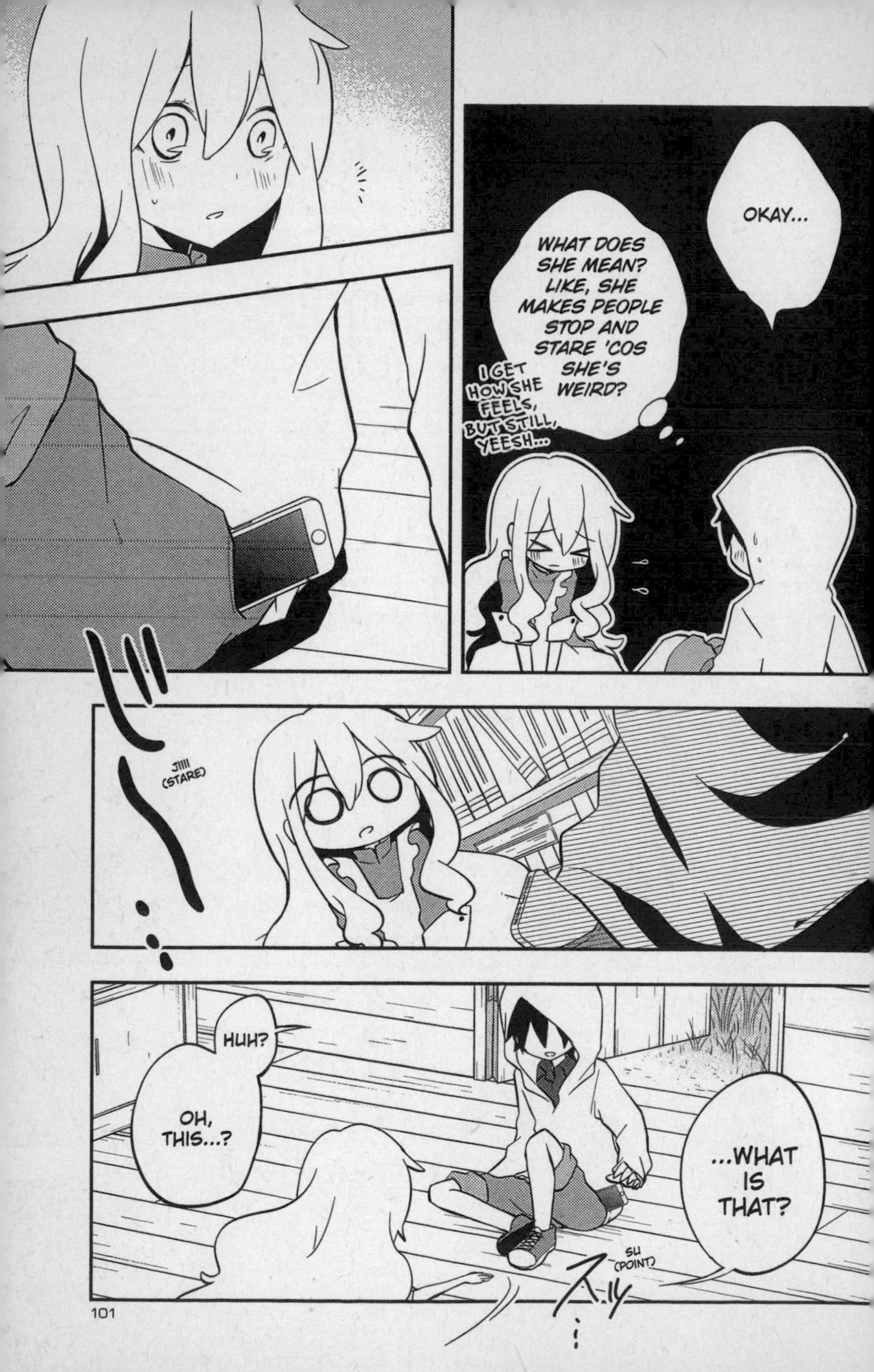
OKAY...
WHAT DOES SHE MEAN? LIKE, SHE MAKES PEOPLE STOP AND STARE 'COS SHE'S WEIRD?
I GET HOW SHE FEELS, BUT STILL, YEESH...
JIIII (STARE)
...WHAT IS THAT?
SU (POINT)
HUH?
OH, THIS...?

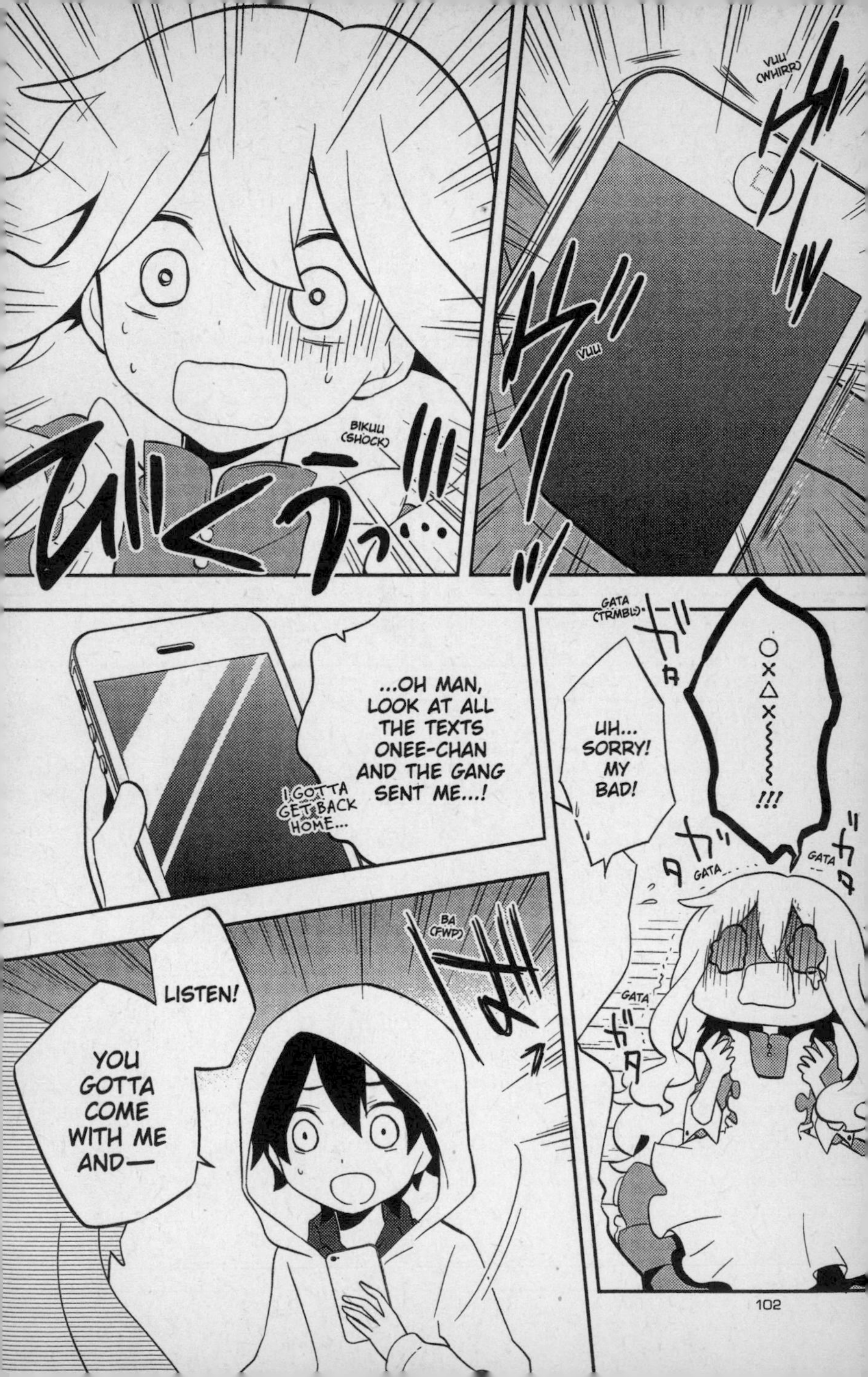
VUU (WHIRR)
VUU
BIKUU (SHOCK)
GATA (TRMBL)
○×△×~~~!!!
UH... SORRY! MY BAD!
GATA
GATA
GATA
...OH MAN, LOOK AT ALL THE TEXTS ONEE-CHAN AND THE GANG SENT ME...!
I GOTTA GET BACK HOME...
BA (FWP)
LISTEN!
YOU GOTTA COME WITH ME AND—

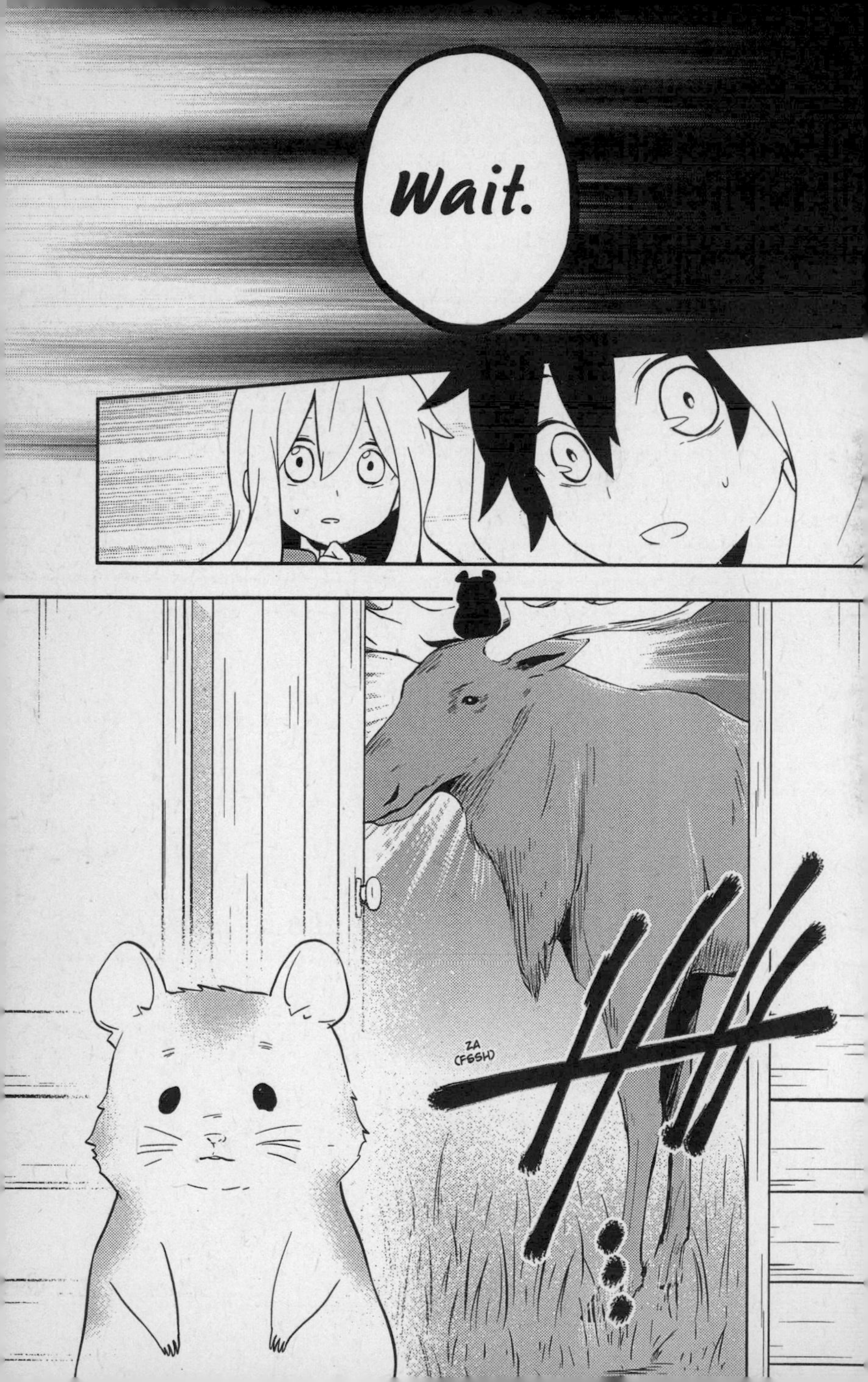
Wait.
ZA
(FSSH)

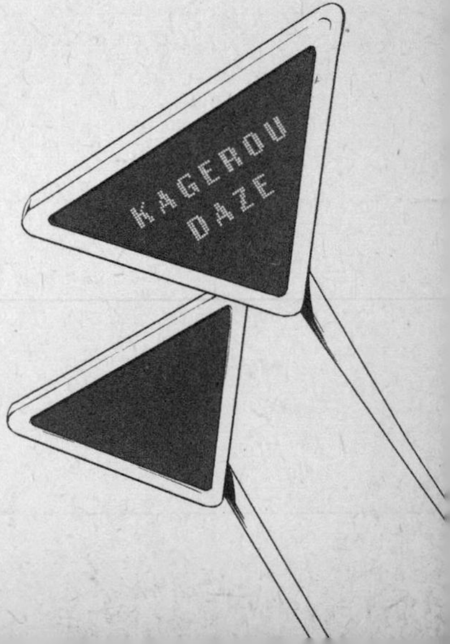
KAGEROU
DAZE

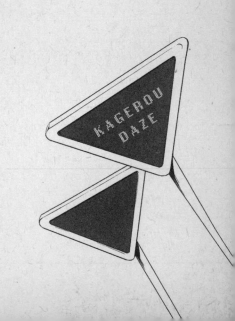

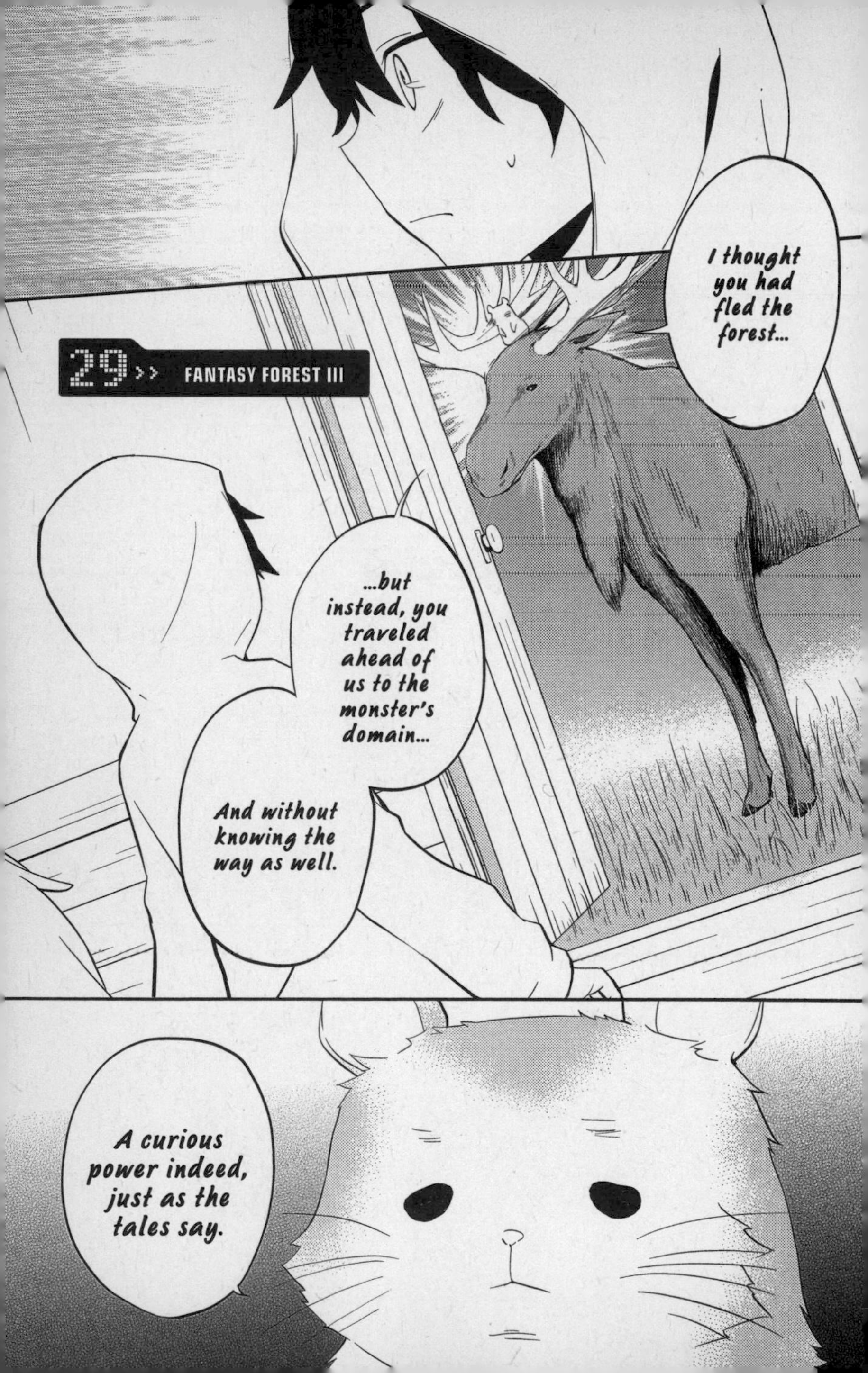
29 >> FANTASY FOREST III
I thought you had fled the forest...
...but instead, you traveled ahead of us to the monster's domain...
And without knowing the way as well.
A curious power indeed, just as the tales say.

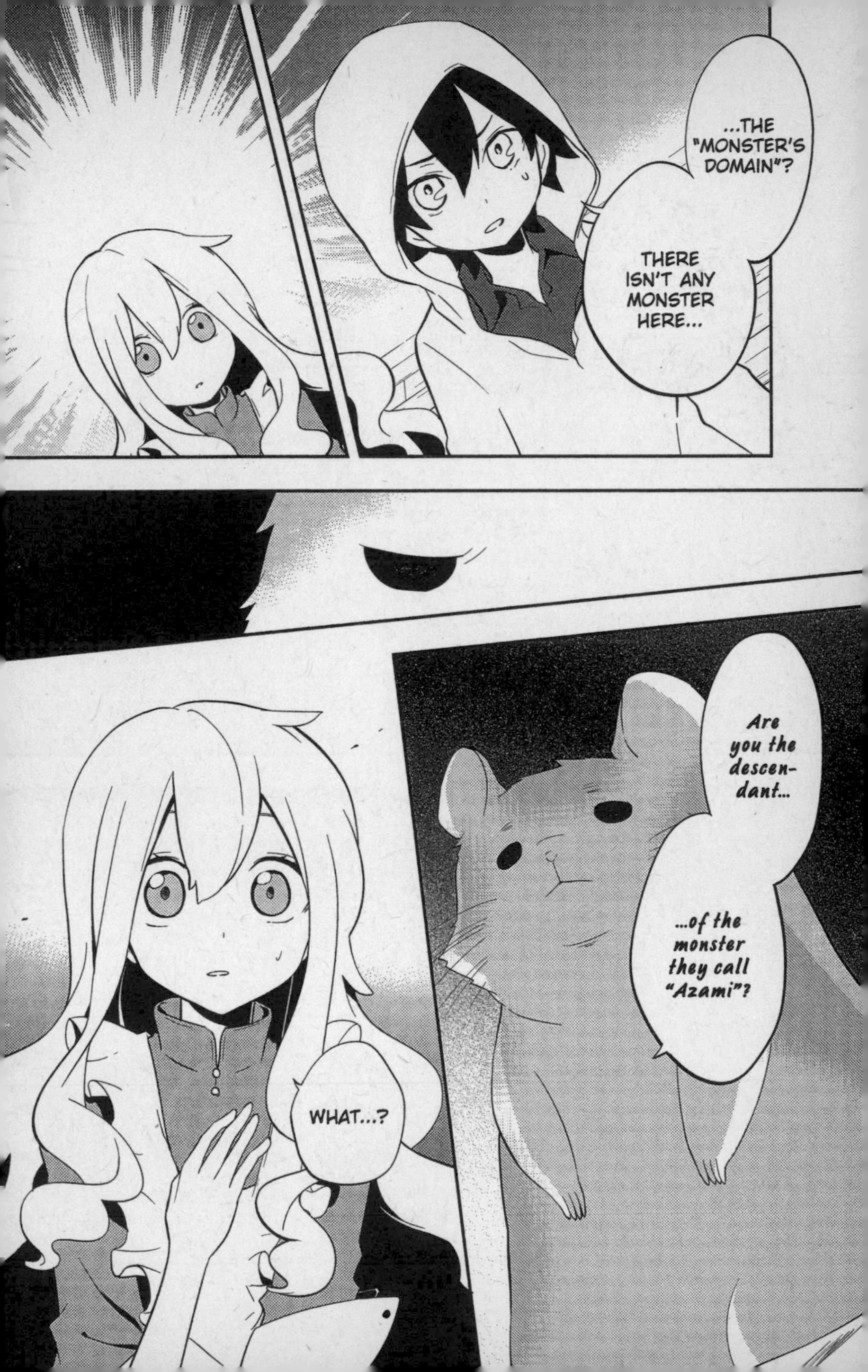
...THE "MONSTER'S DOMAIN"?
THERE ISN'T ANY MONSTER HERE...
Are you the descen-dant...
...of the monster they call "Azami"?
WHAT...?

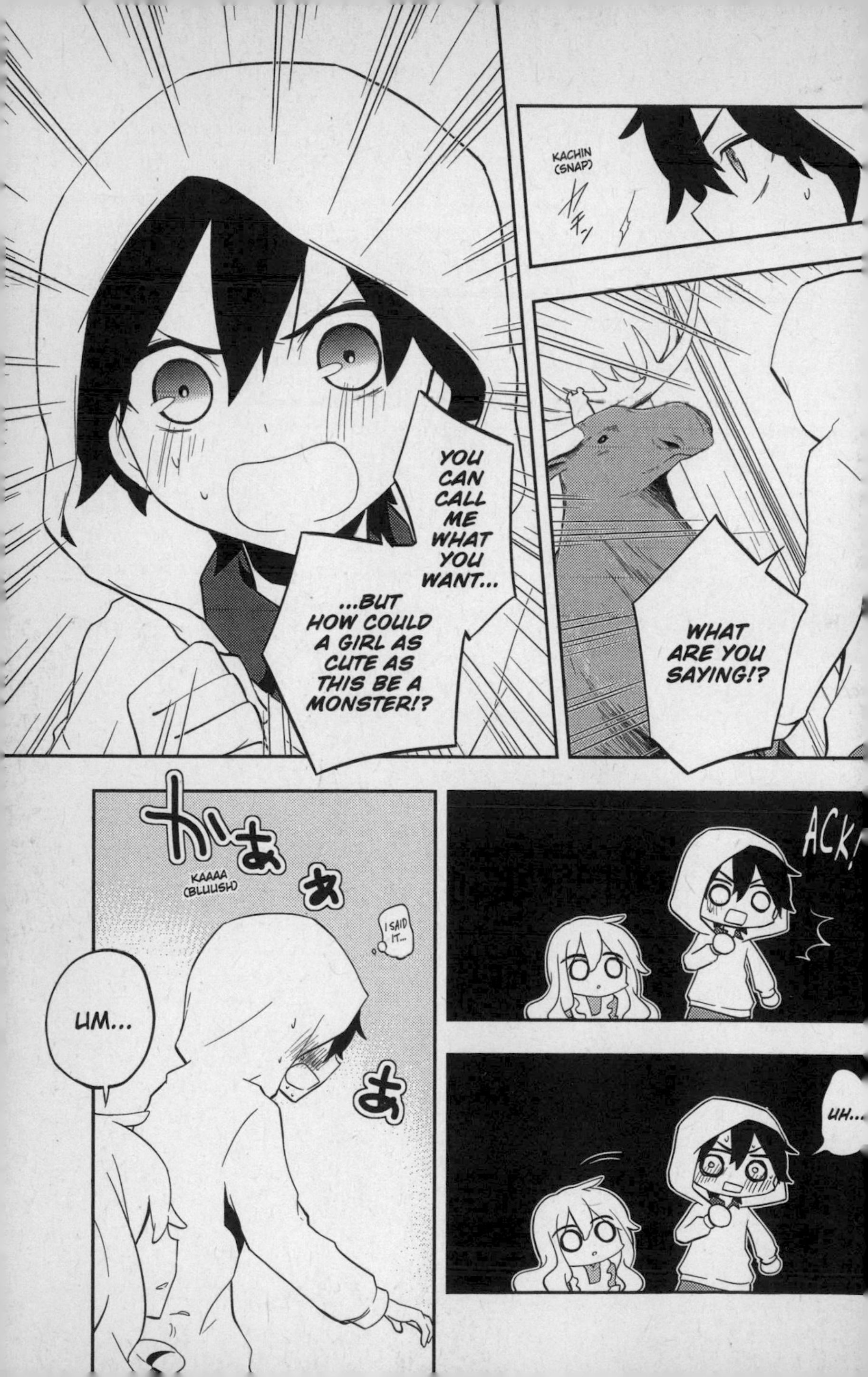
KACHIN (SNAP)
カチン
WHAT ARE YOU SAYING!?
YOU CAN CALL ME WHAT YOU WANT...
...BUT HOW COULD A GIRL AS CUTE AS THIS BE A MONSTER!?
ACK!
UH...
KAAAA (BLUUSH)
I SAID IT...
UM...

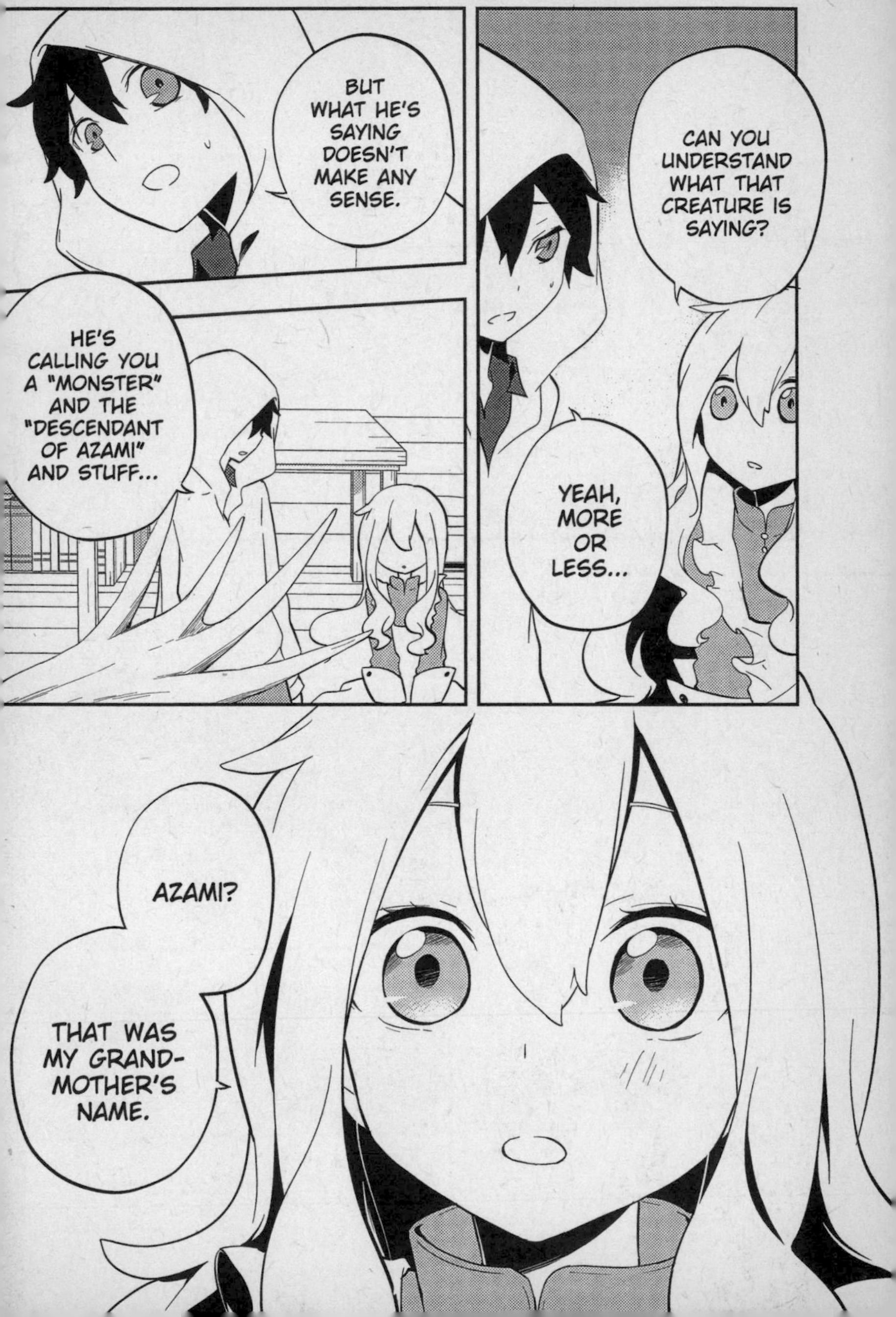
CAN YOU UNDERSTAND WHAT THAT CREATURE IS SAYING?
YEAH, MORE OR LESS...
BUT WHAT HE'S SAYING DOESN'T MAKE ANY SENSE.
HE'S CALLING YOU A "MONSTER" AND THE "DESCENDANT OF AZAMI" AND STUFF...
AZAMI?
THAT WAS MY GRAND-MOTHER'S NAME.

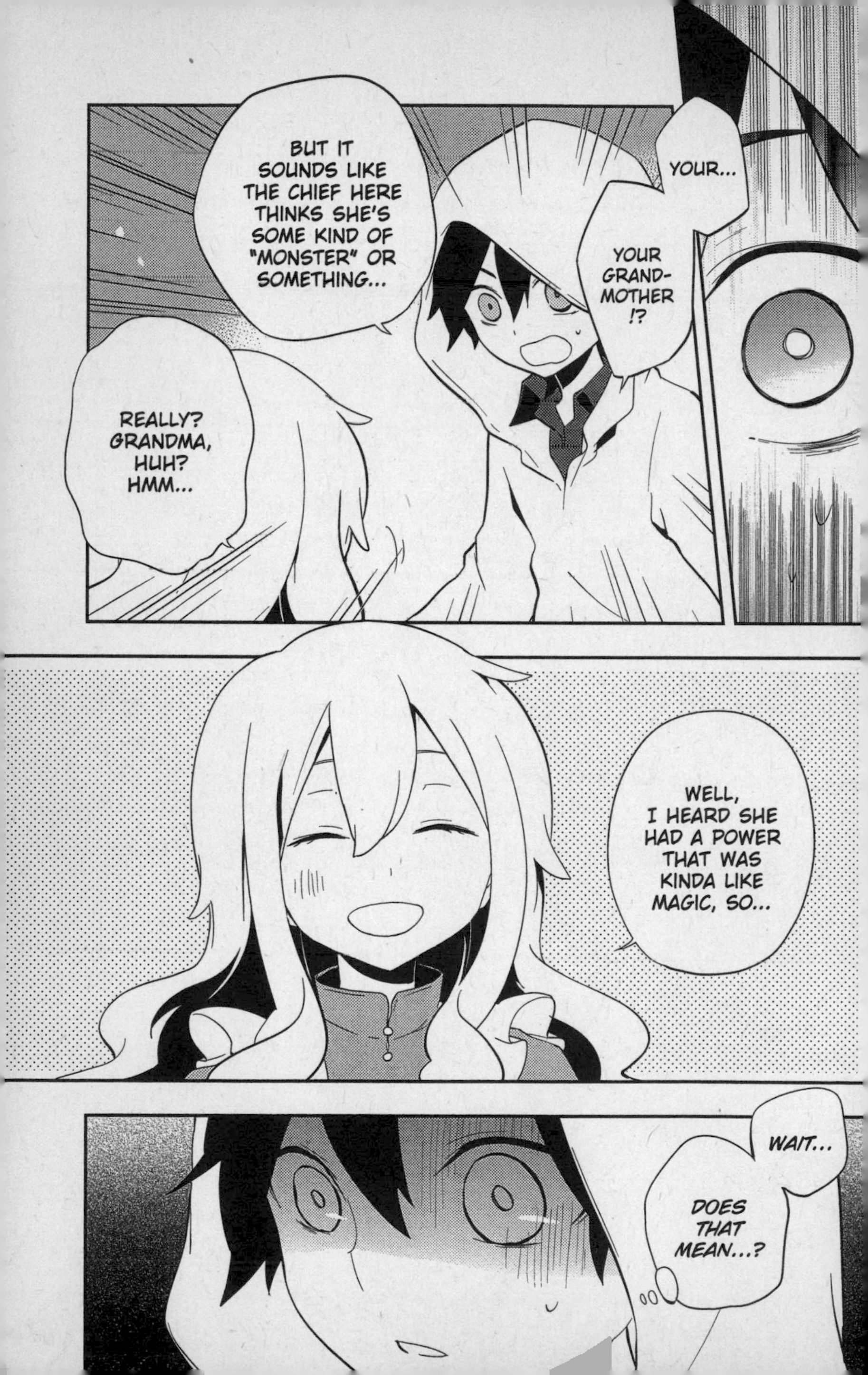
YOUR...
YOUR GRAND-MOTHER !?
BUT IT SOUNDS LIKE THE CHIEF HERE THINKS SHE'S SOME KIND OF "MONSTER" OR SOMETHING...
REALLY? GRANDMA, HUH? HMM...
WELL, I HEARD SHE HAD A POWER THAT WAS KINDA LIKE MAGIC, SO...
WAIT...
DOES THAT MEAN...?

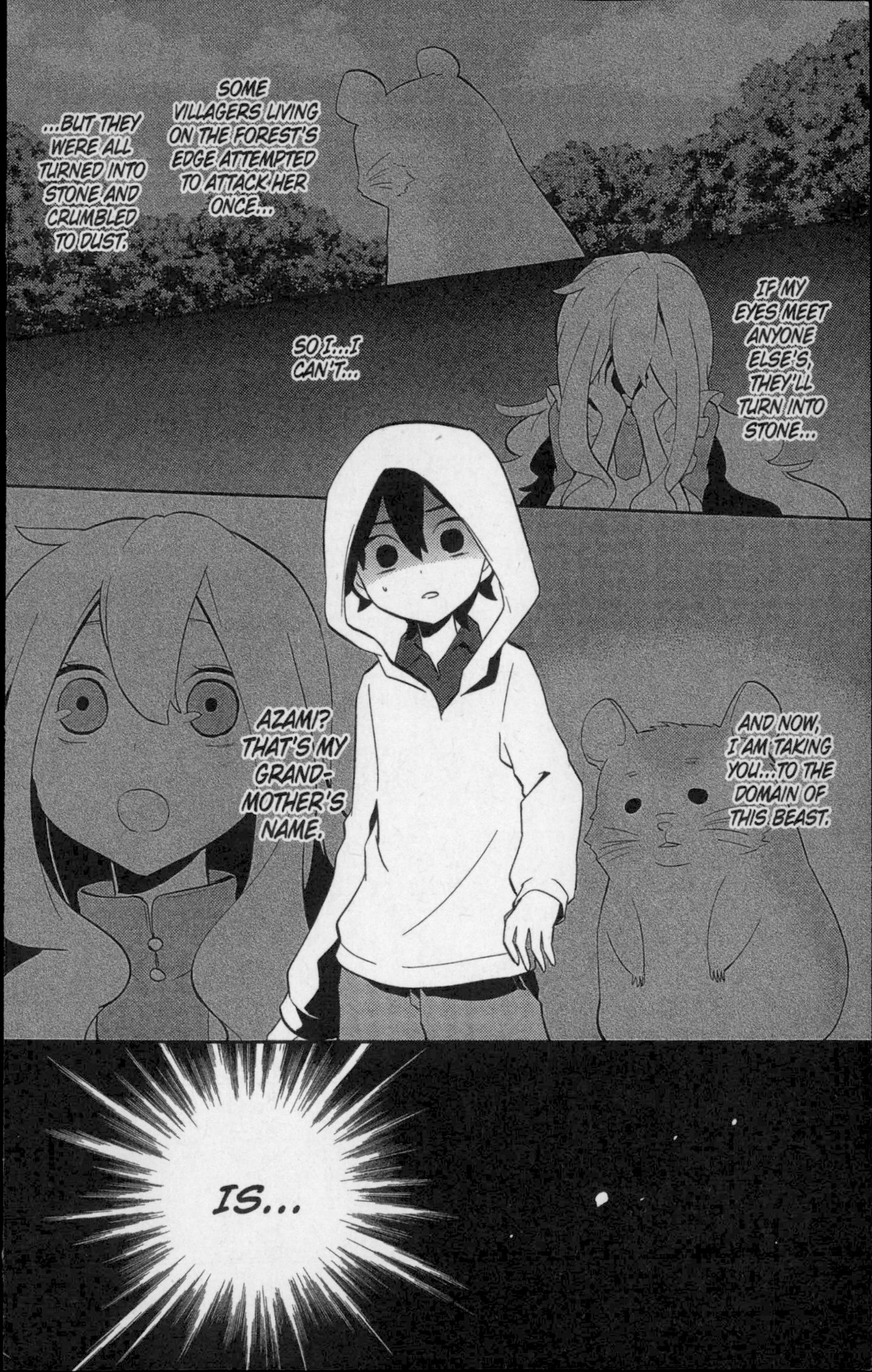
SOME VILLAGERS LIVING ON THE FOREST'S EDGE ATTEMPTED TO ATTACK HER ONCE...
...BUT THEY WERE ALL TURNED INTO STONE AND CRUMBLED TO DUST.
IF MY EYES MEET ANYONE ELSE'S, THEY'LL TURN INTO STONE...
SO I...I CAN'T...
AND NOW, I AM TAKING YOU...TO THE DOMAIN OF THIS BEAST.
AZAMI? THAT'S MY GRAND-MOTHER'S NAME.
IS...

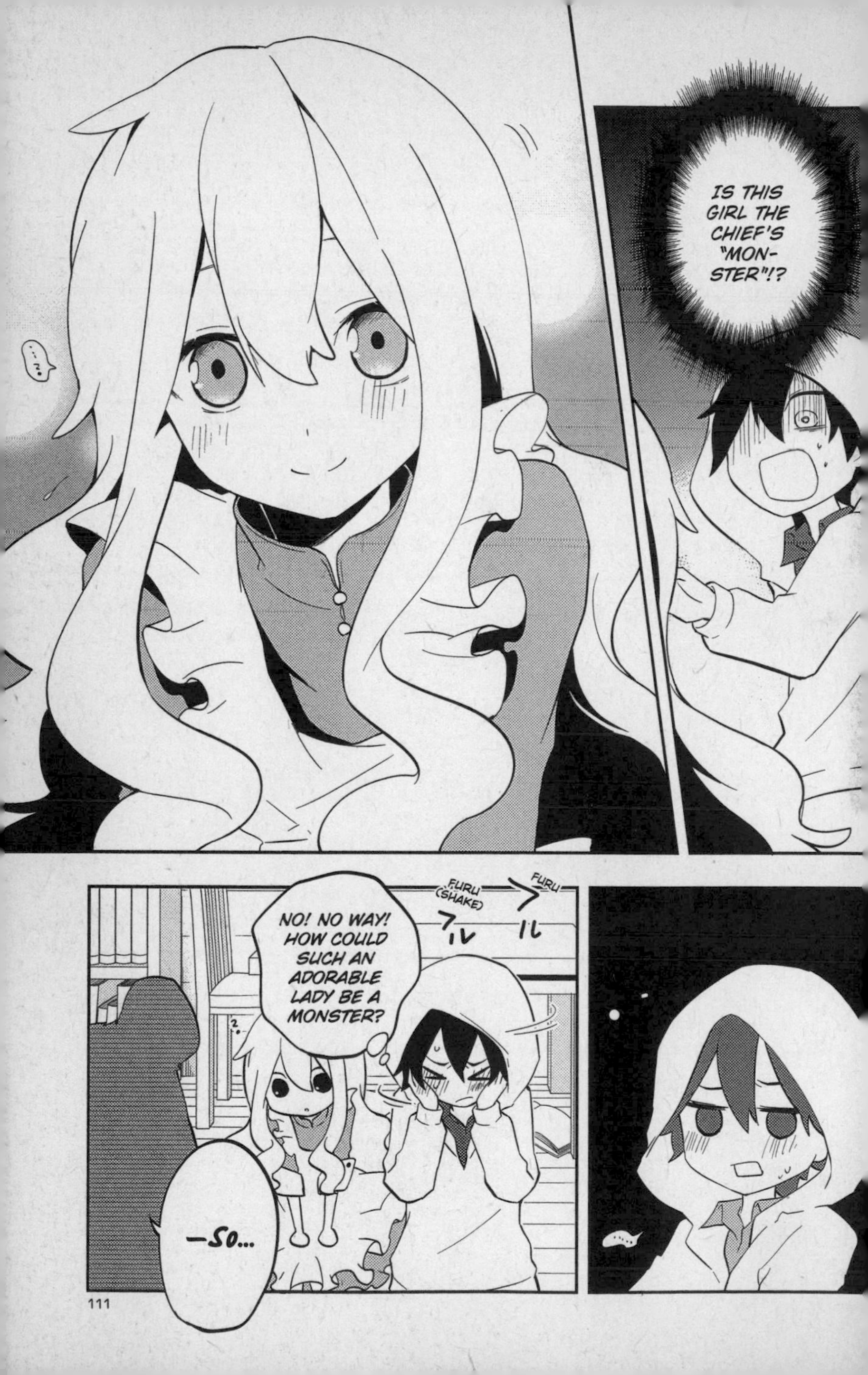
IS THIS GIRL THE CHIEF'S "MON-STER"!?
...?
...
FURU (SHAKE)
FURU
NO! NO WAY! HOW COULD SUCH AN ADORABLE LADY BE A MONSTER?
?
—SO...

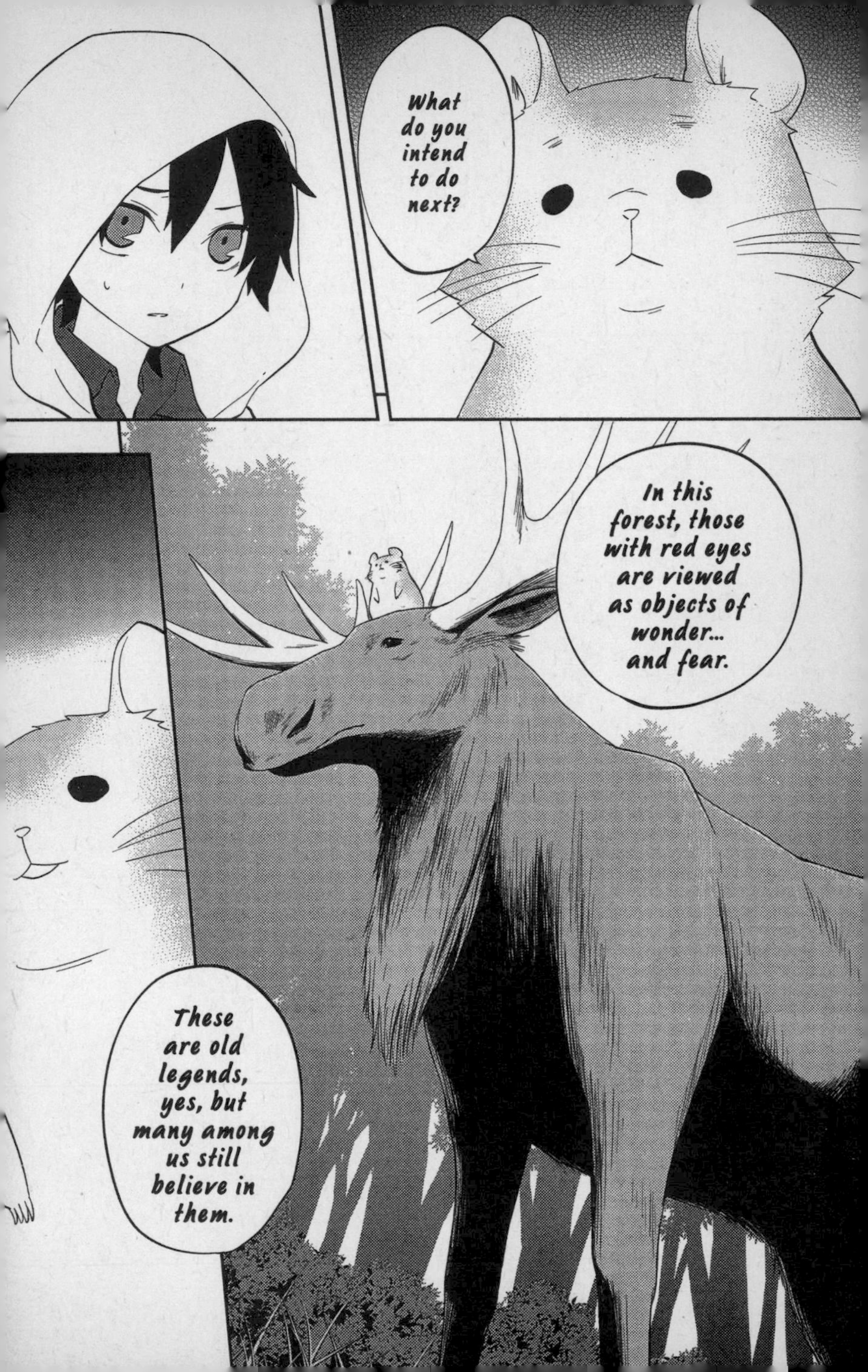
What do you intend to do next?
In this forest, those with red eyes are viewed as objects of wonder... and fear.
These are old legends, yes, but many among us still believe in them.

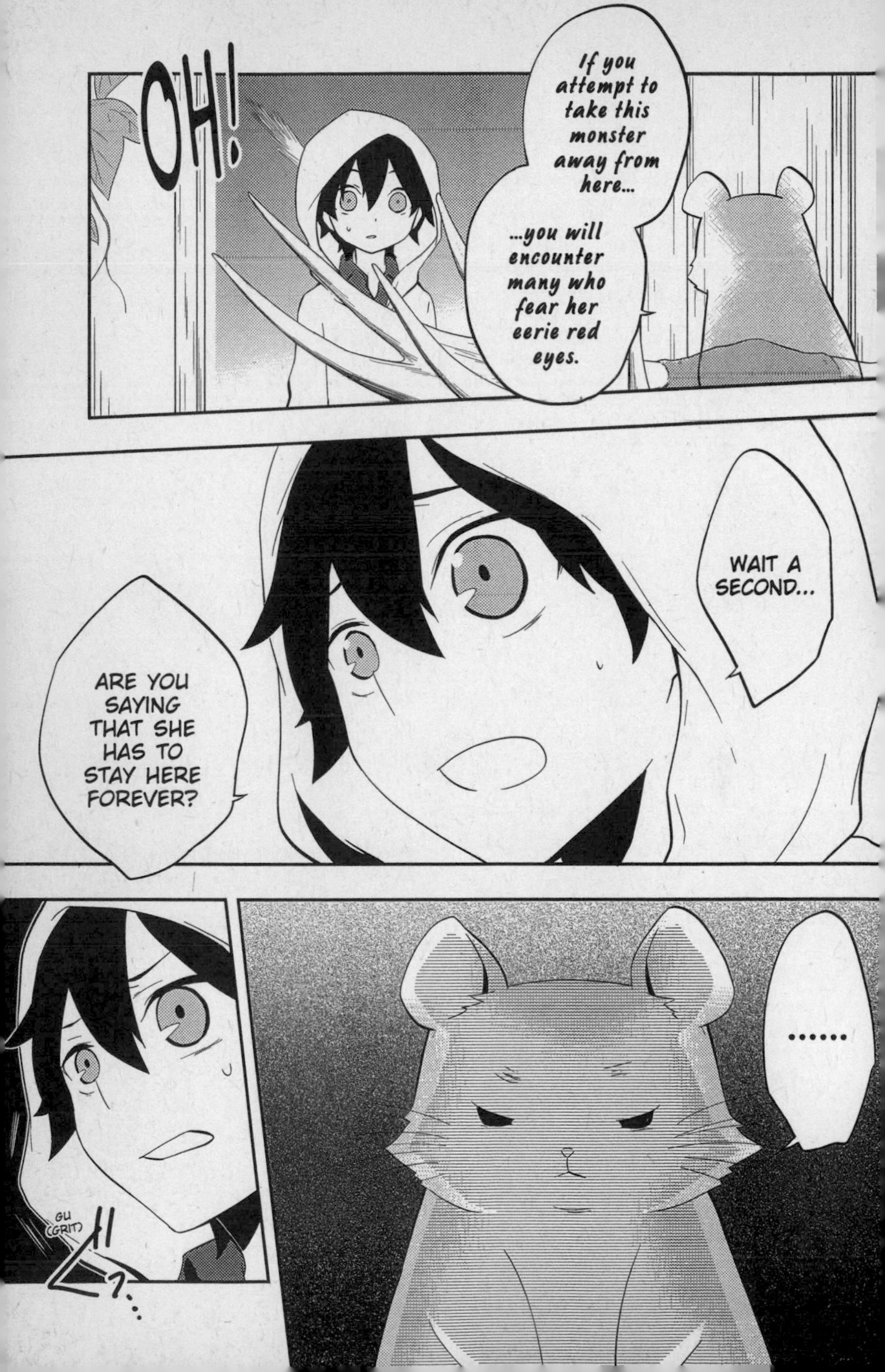
If you attempt to take this monster away from here...
...you will encounter many who fear her eerie red eyes.
OH!
WAIT A SECOND...
ARE YOU SAYING THAT SHE HAS TO STAY HERE FOREVER?
......
GU (GRIT)

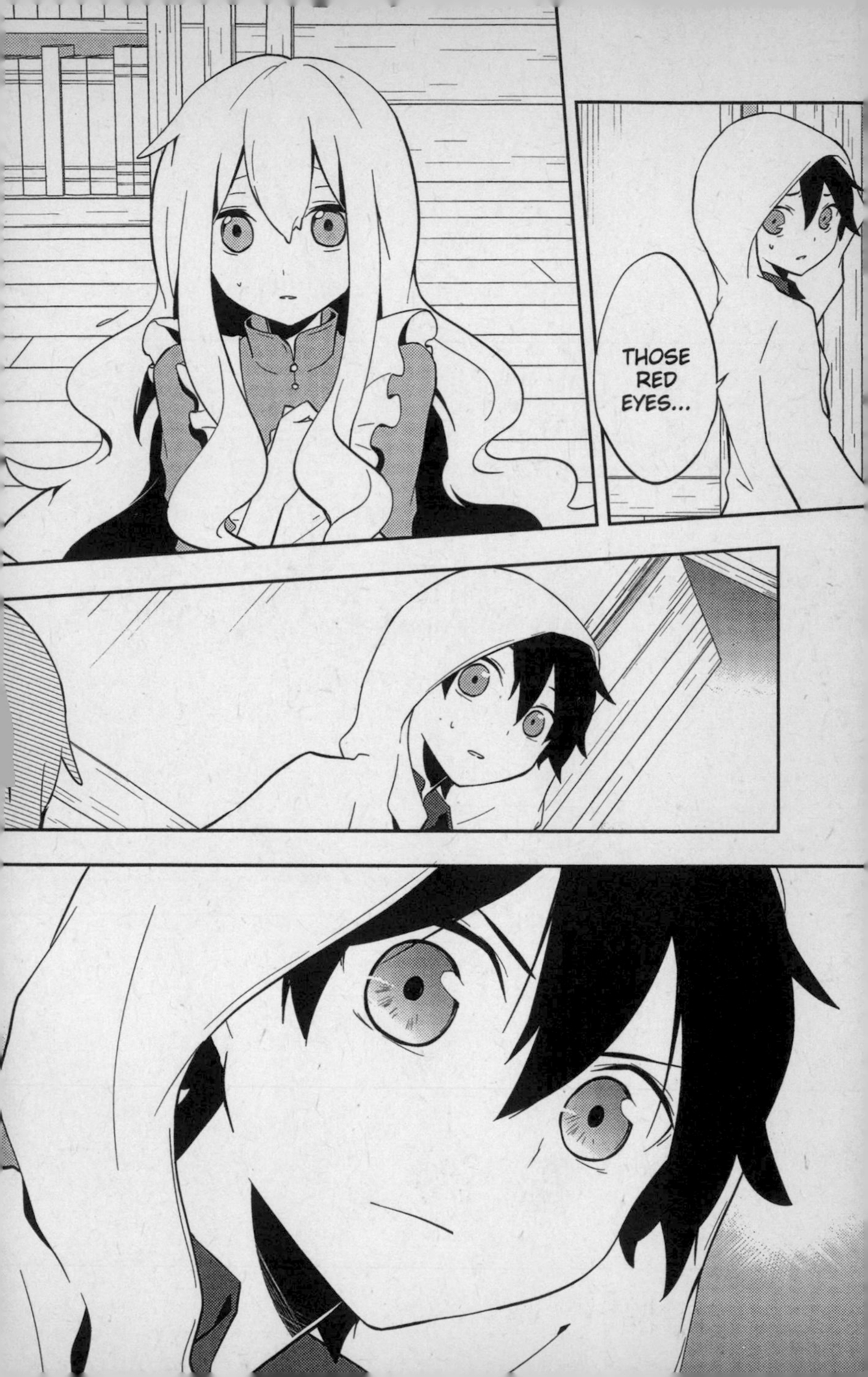
THOSE RED EYES...

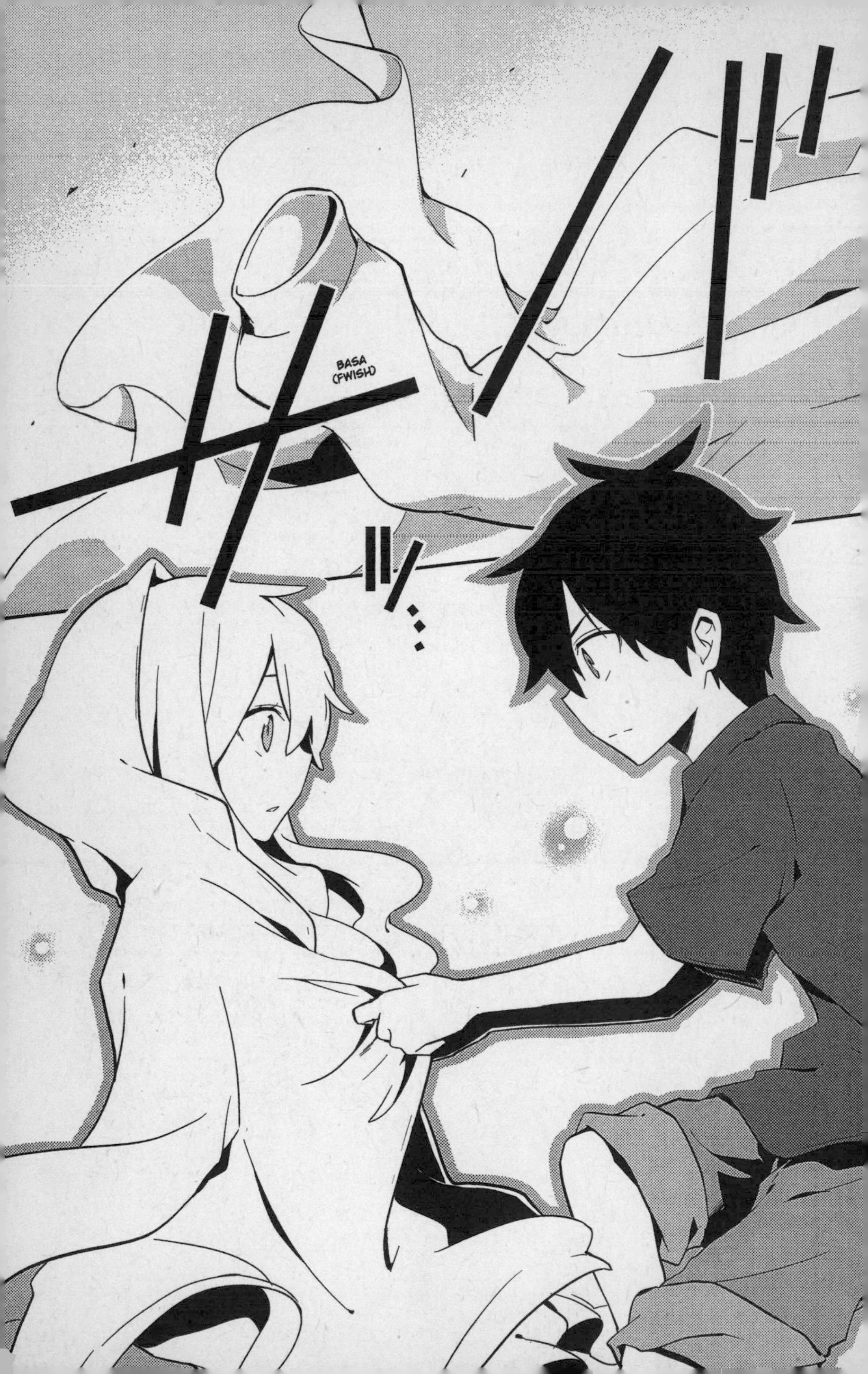
BASA
(FWISH)

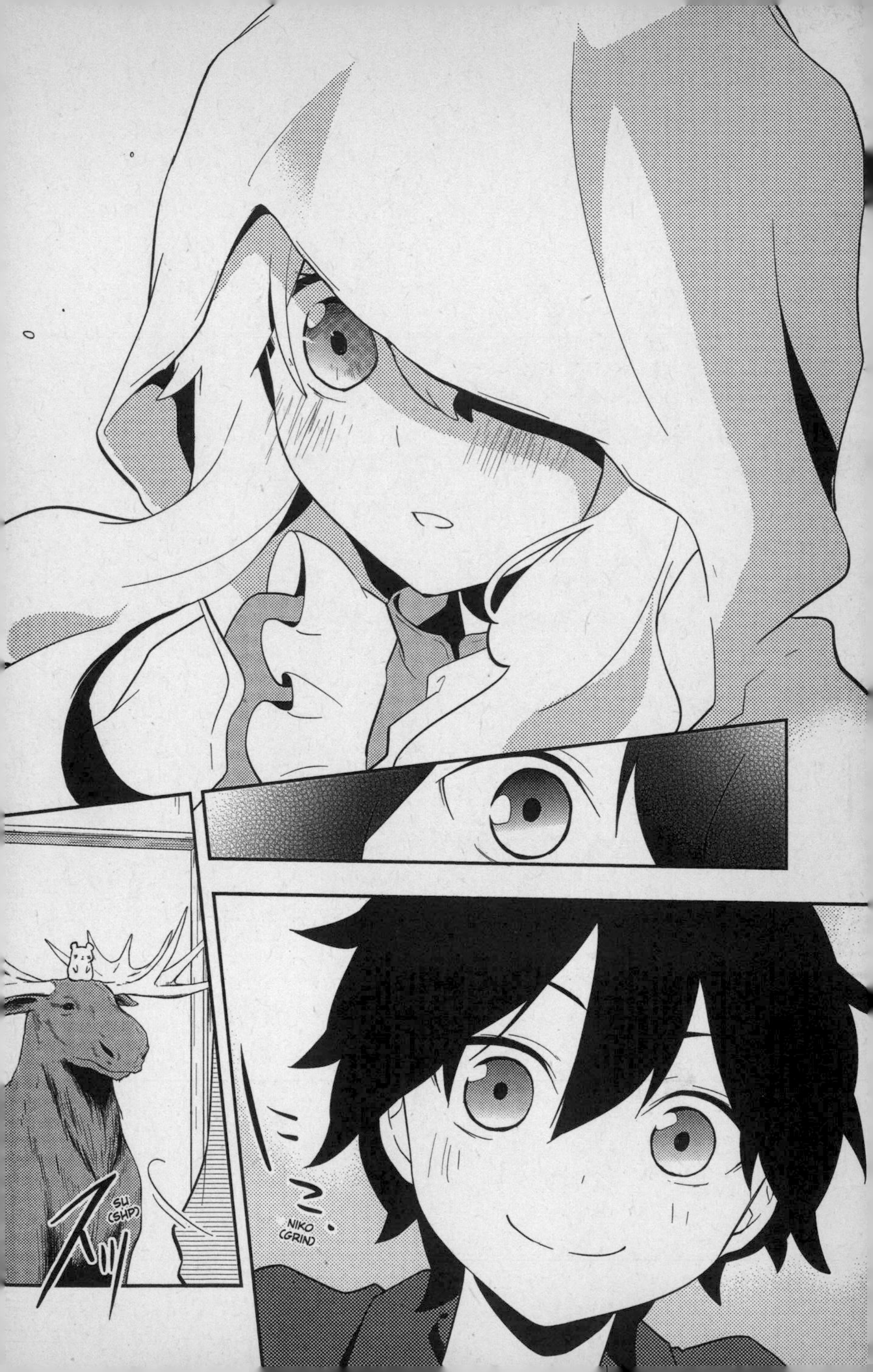
NIKO (GRIN)
SU (SHP)

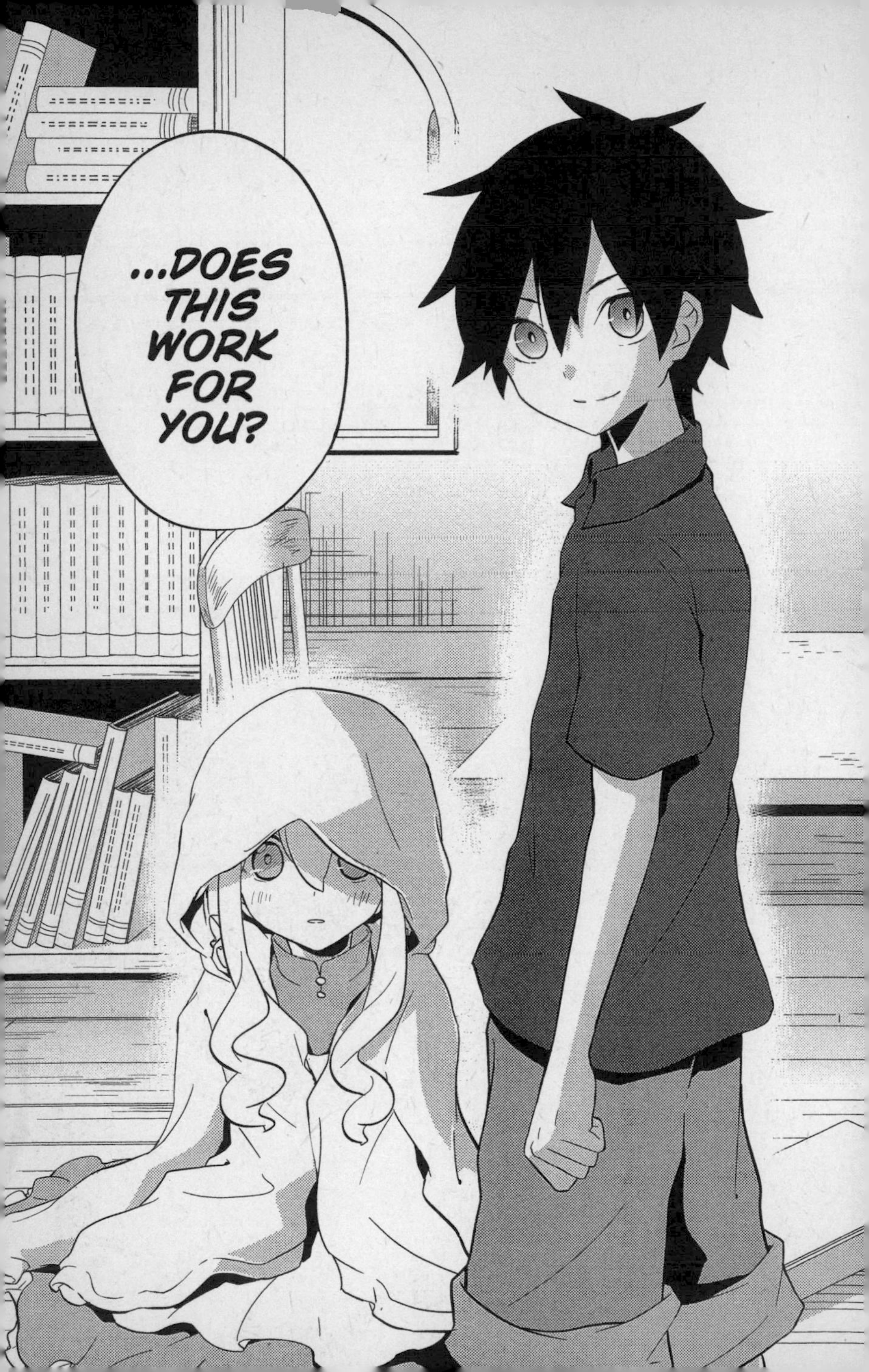
...DOES THIS WORK FOR YOU?

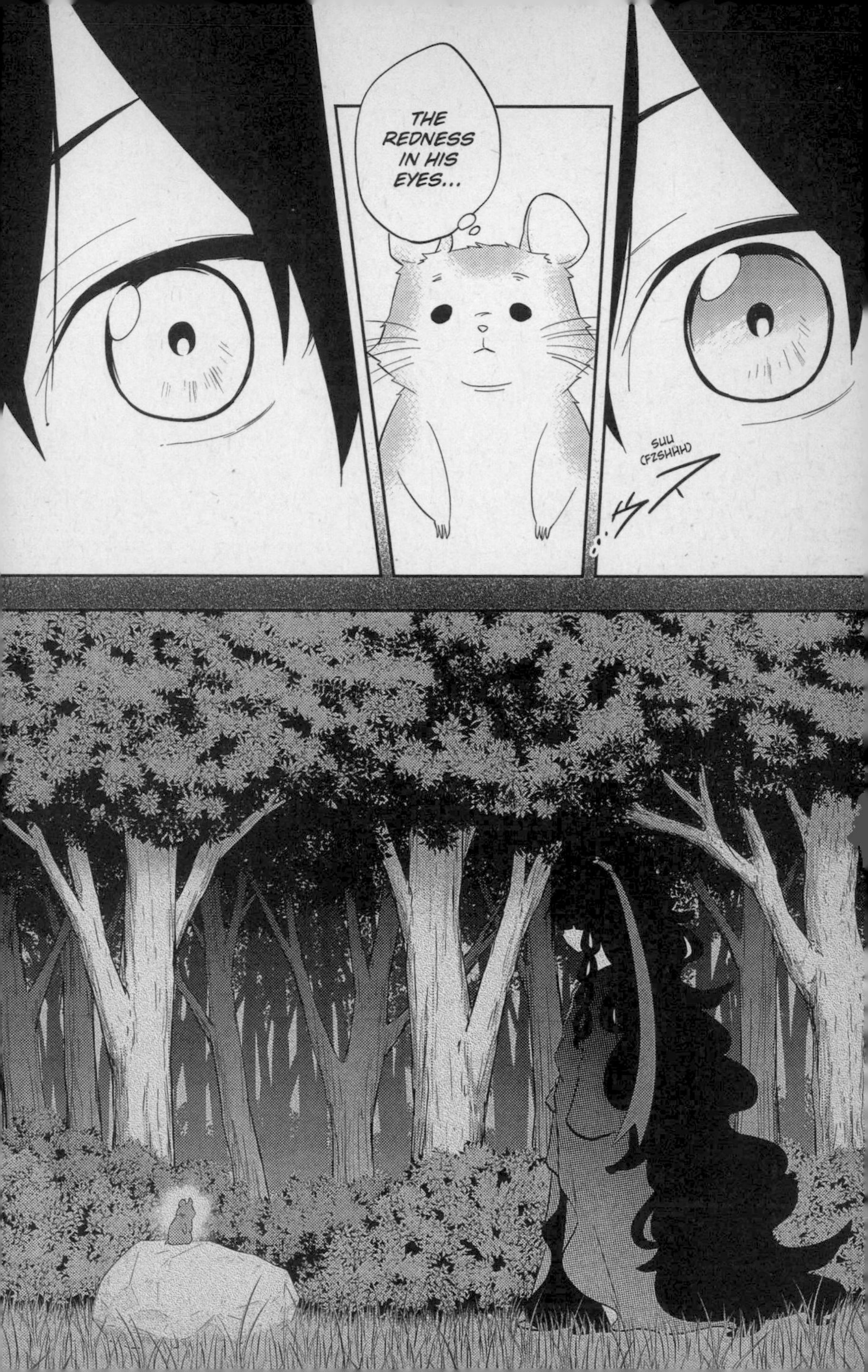
SUU (FZSHHH)
THE REDNESS IN HIS EYES...

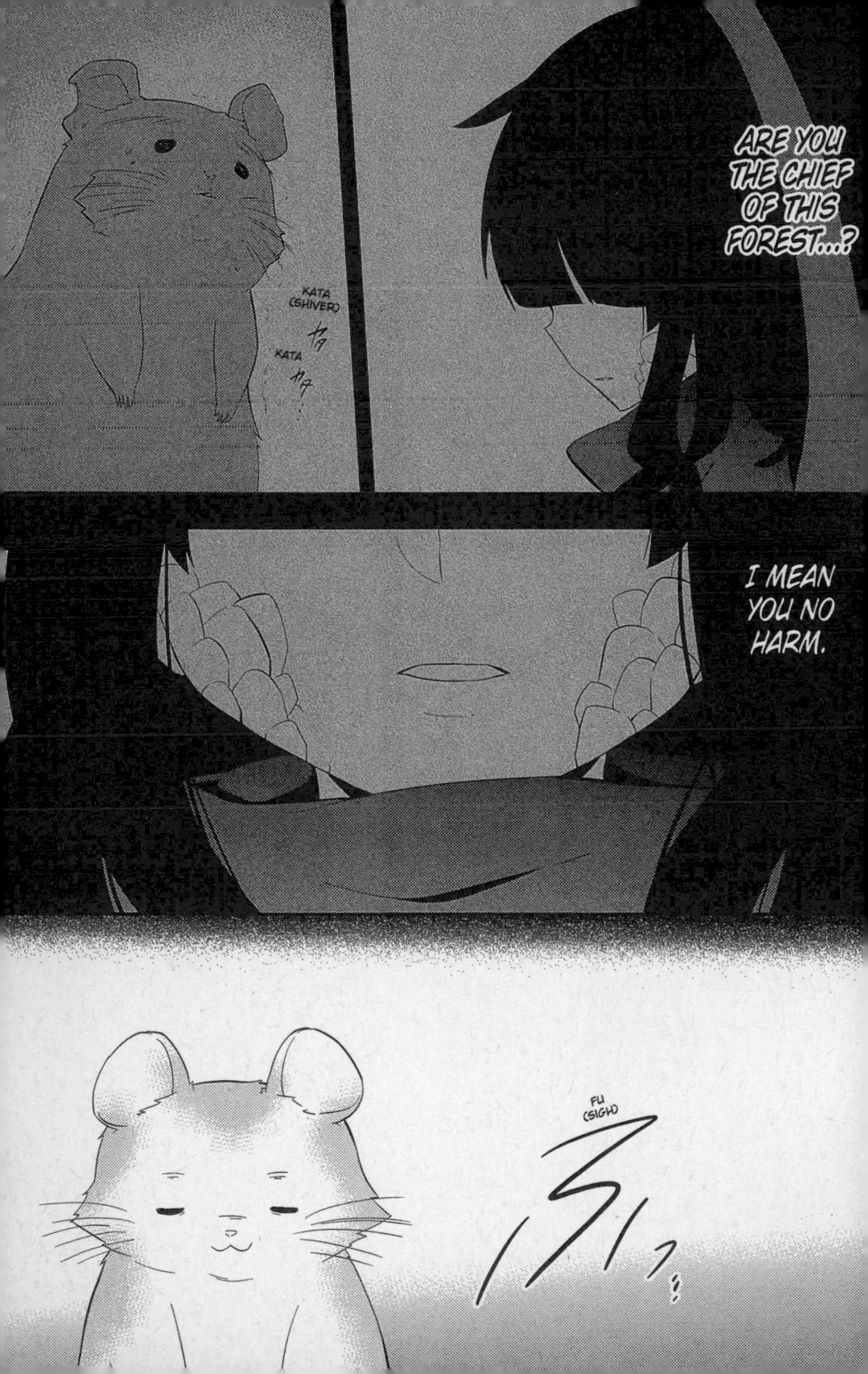
ARE YOU THE CHIEF OF THIS FOREST...?
KATA (SHIVER)
KATA
I MEAN YOU NO HARM.
FU (SIGH)

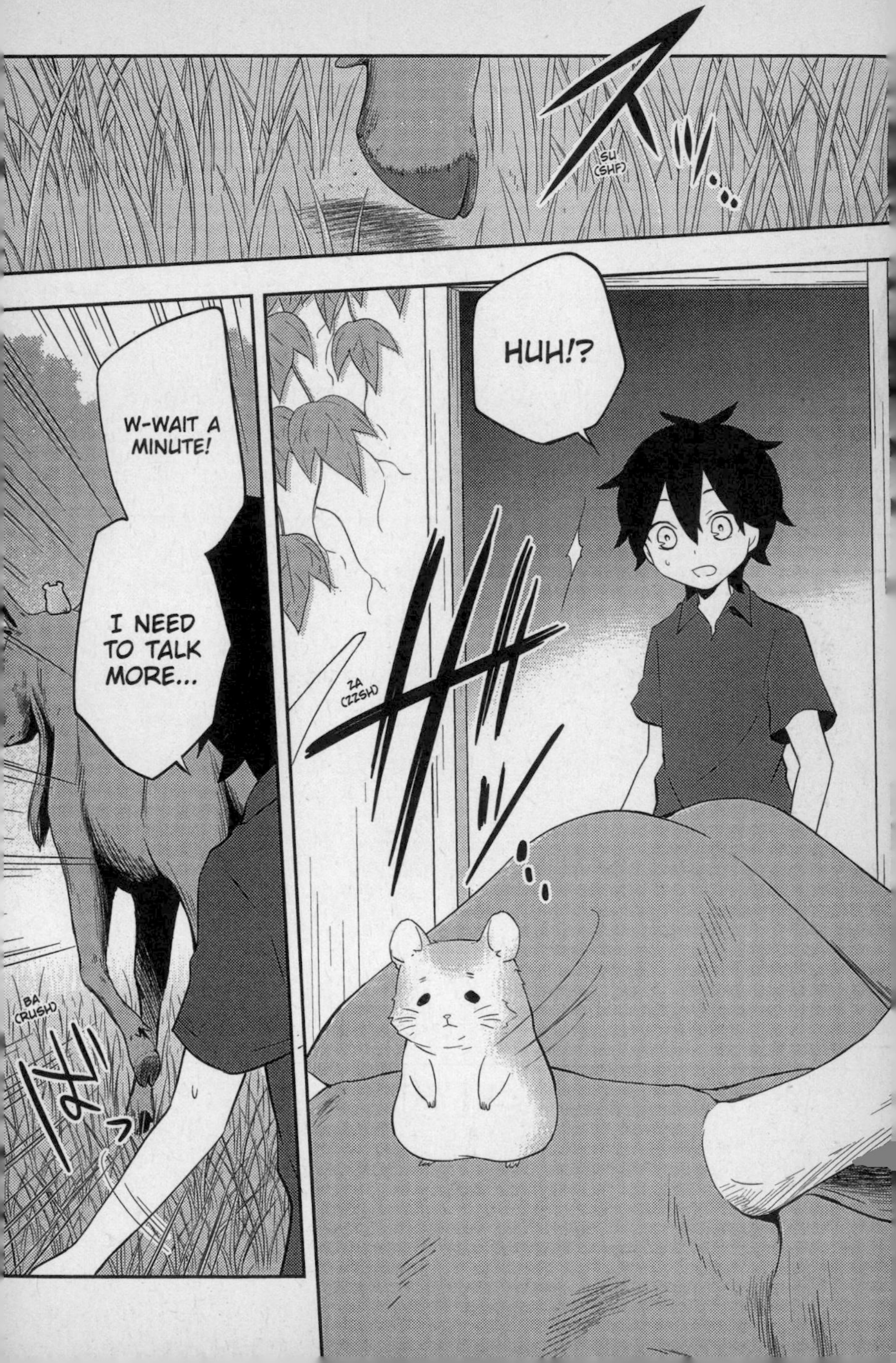
SU (SHF)
HUH!?
ZA (ZZSH)
W-WAIT A MINUTE!
I NEED TO TALK MORE...
BA (RUSH)

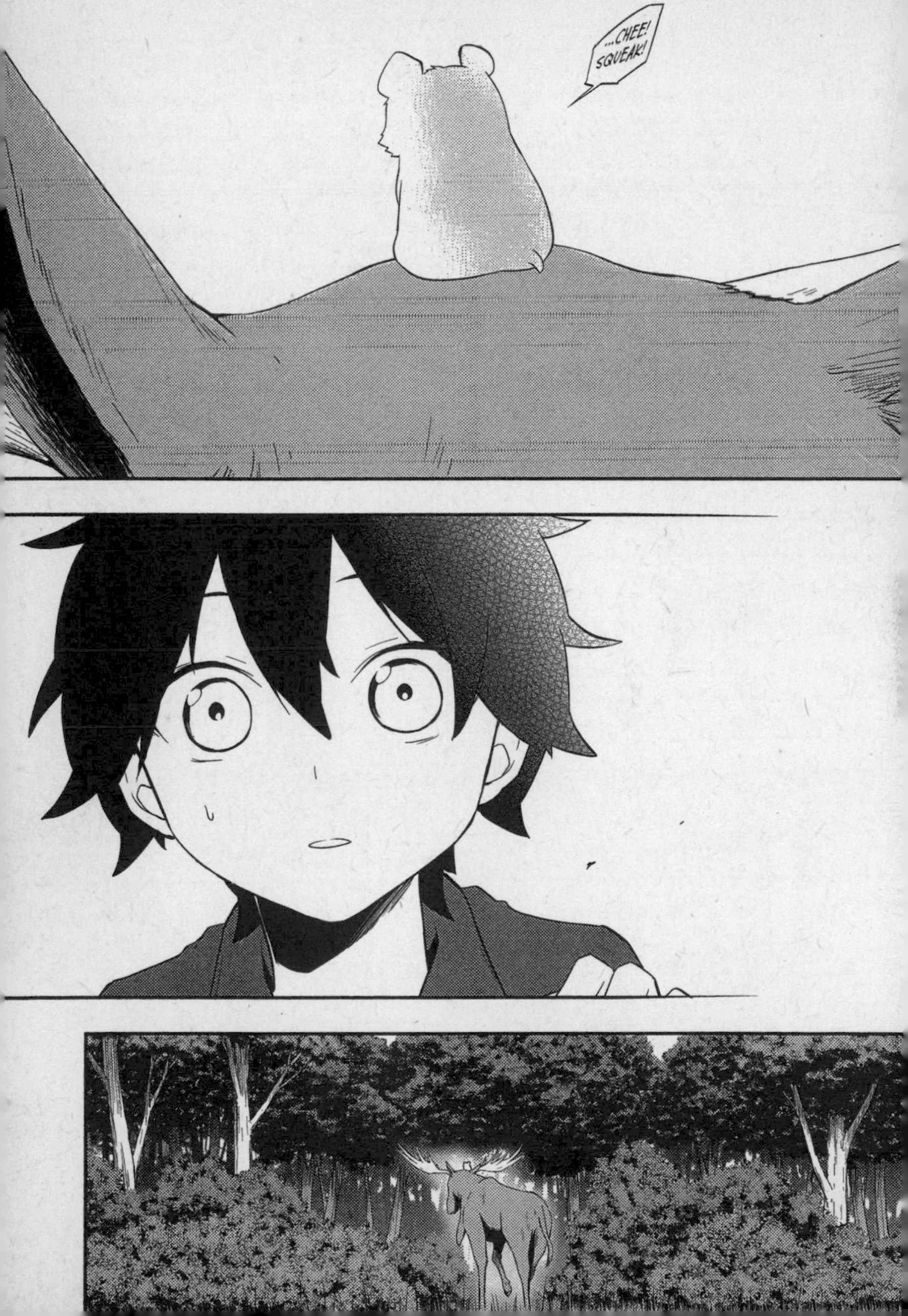
...CHEE! SQUEAK!

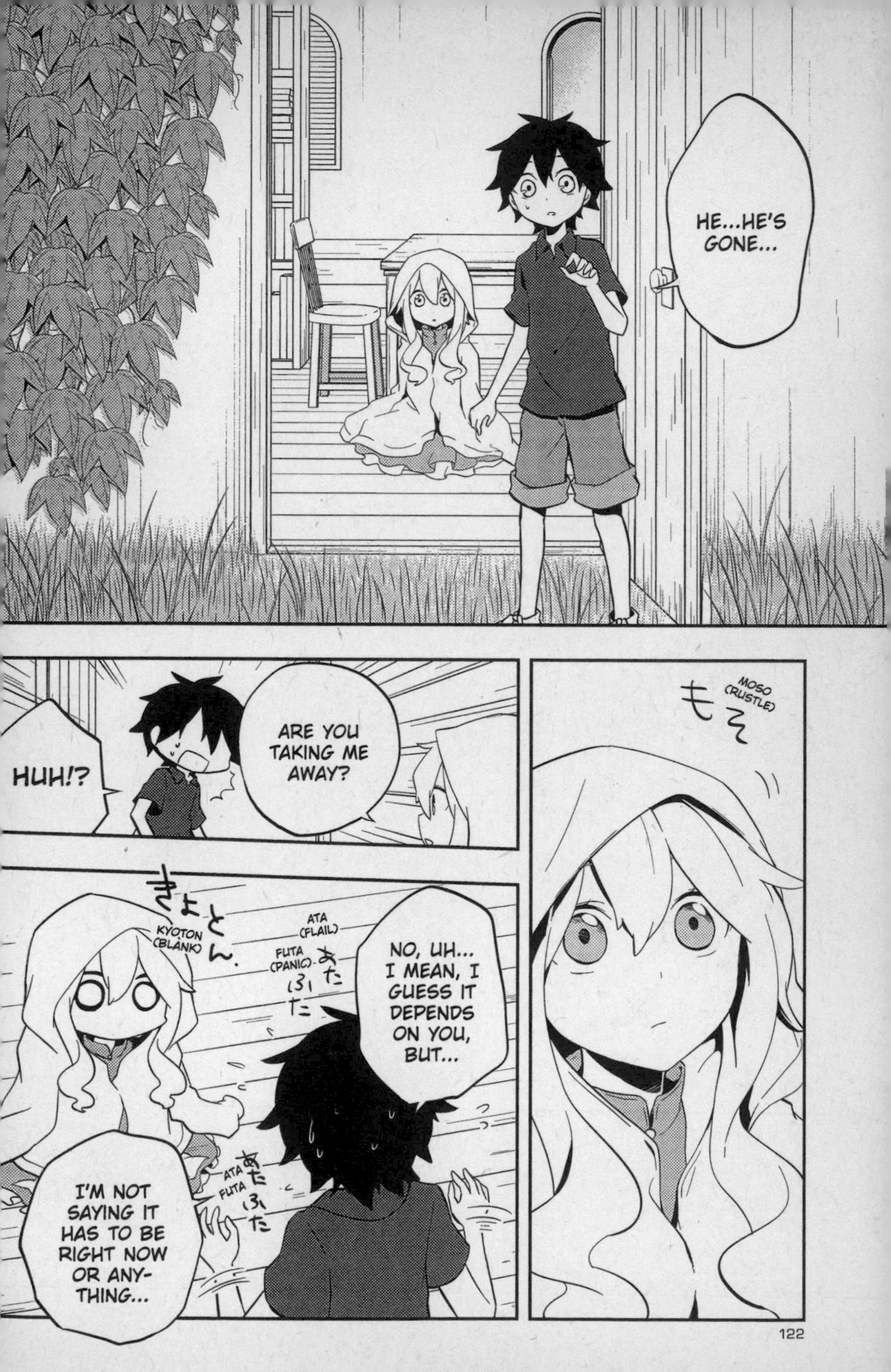
HE...HE'S GONE...
もそ
MOSO (RUSTLE)
ARE YOU TAKING ME AWAY?
HUH!?
NO, UH... I MEAN, I GUESS IT DEPENDS ON YOU, BUT...
あたふた
ATA (FLAIL)
FUTA (PANIC)
きょとん.
KYOTON (BLANK)
I'M NOT SAYING IT HAS TO BE RIGHT NOW OR ANY-THING...
あたふた
ATA FUTA

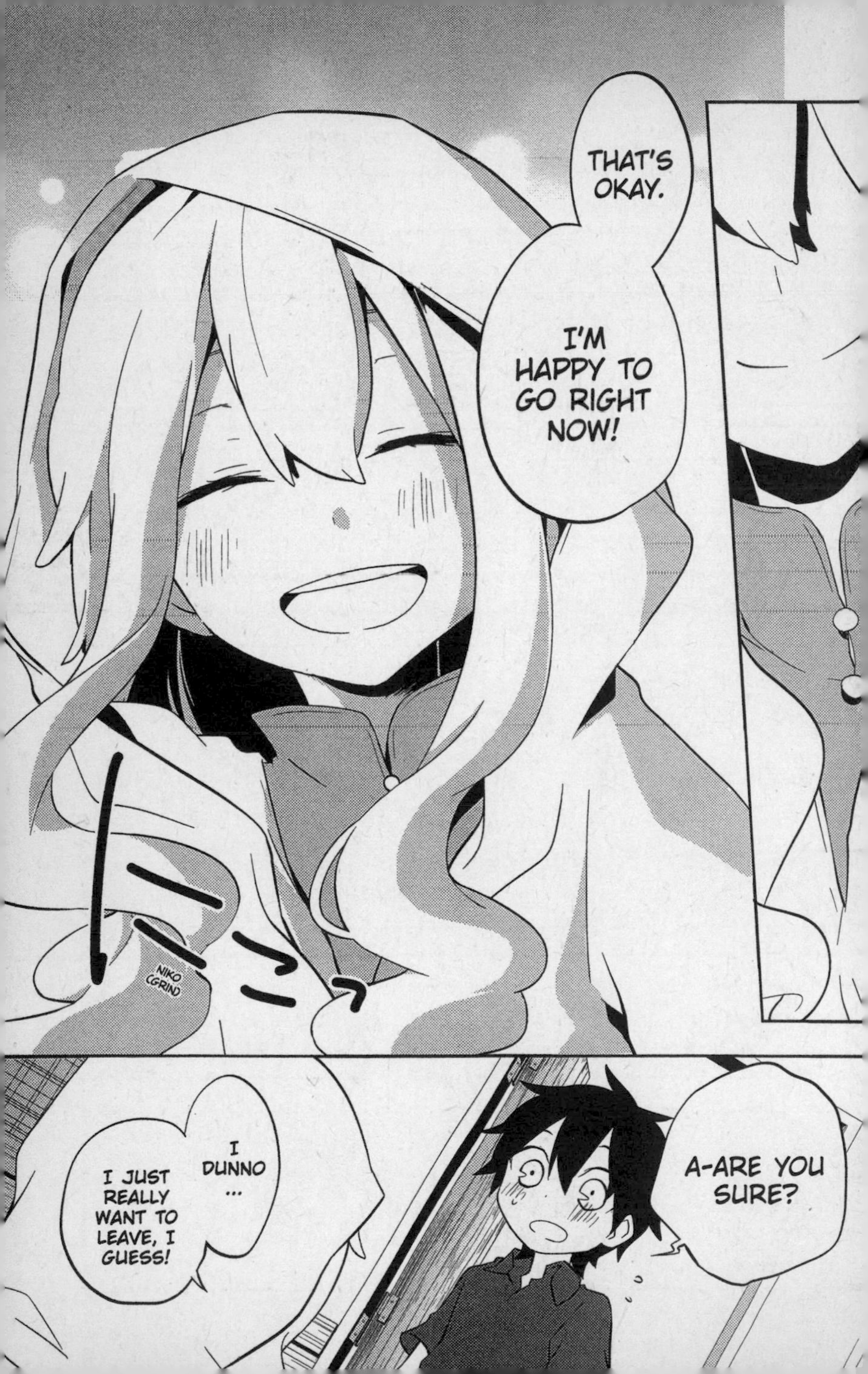
THAT'S OKAY.
I'M HAPPY TO GO RIGHT NOW!
NIKO (GRIN)
A-ARE YOU SURE?
I DUNNO ...
I JUST REALLY WANT TO LEAVE, I GUESS!

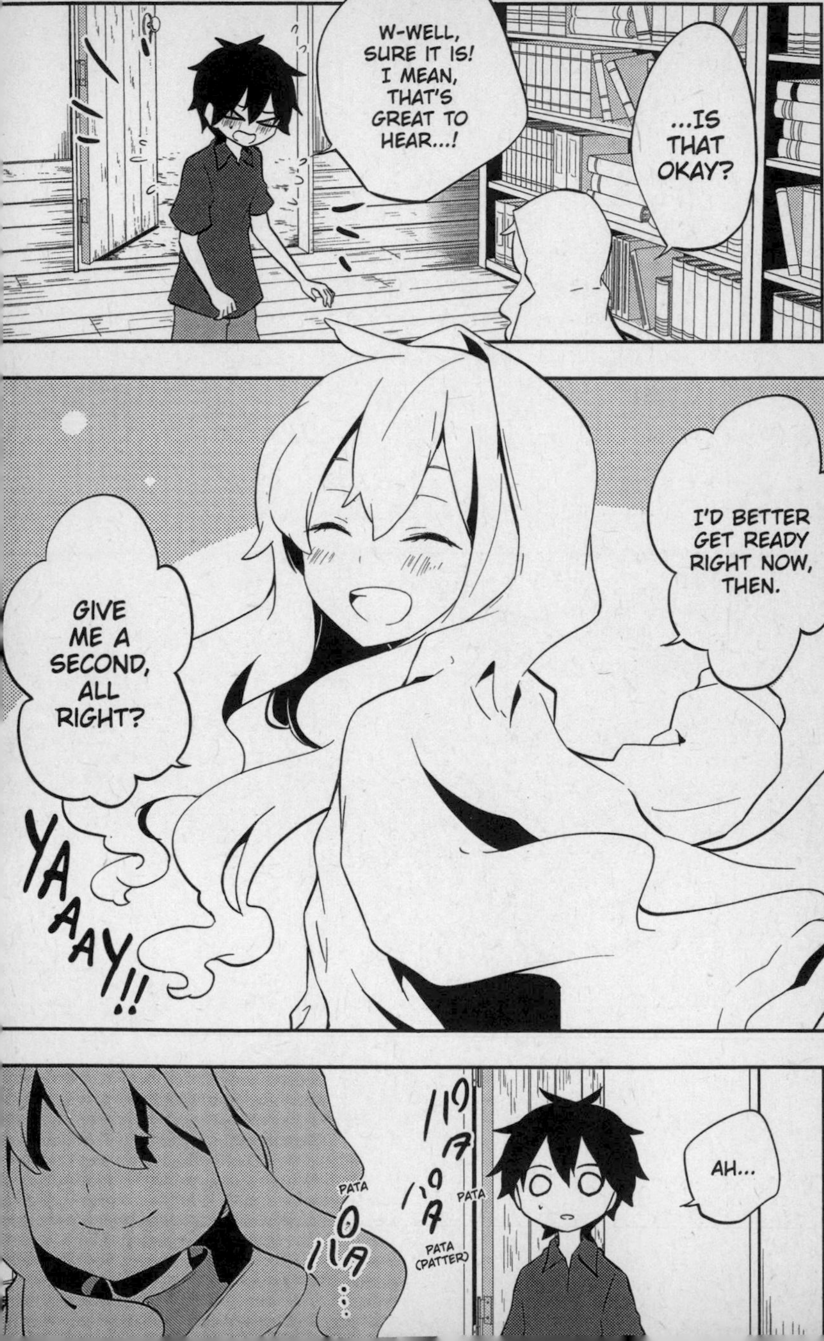
...IS THAT OKAY?
W-WELL, SURE IT IS! I MEAN, THAT'S GREAT TO HEAR...!
I'D BETTER GET READY RIGHT NOW, THEN.
GIVE ME A SECOND, ALL RIGHT?
YAAAY!!
AH...
PATA
PATA
PATA (PATTER)

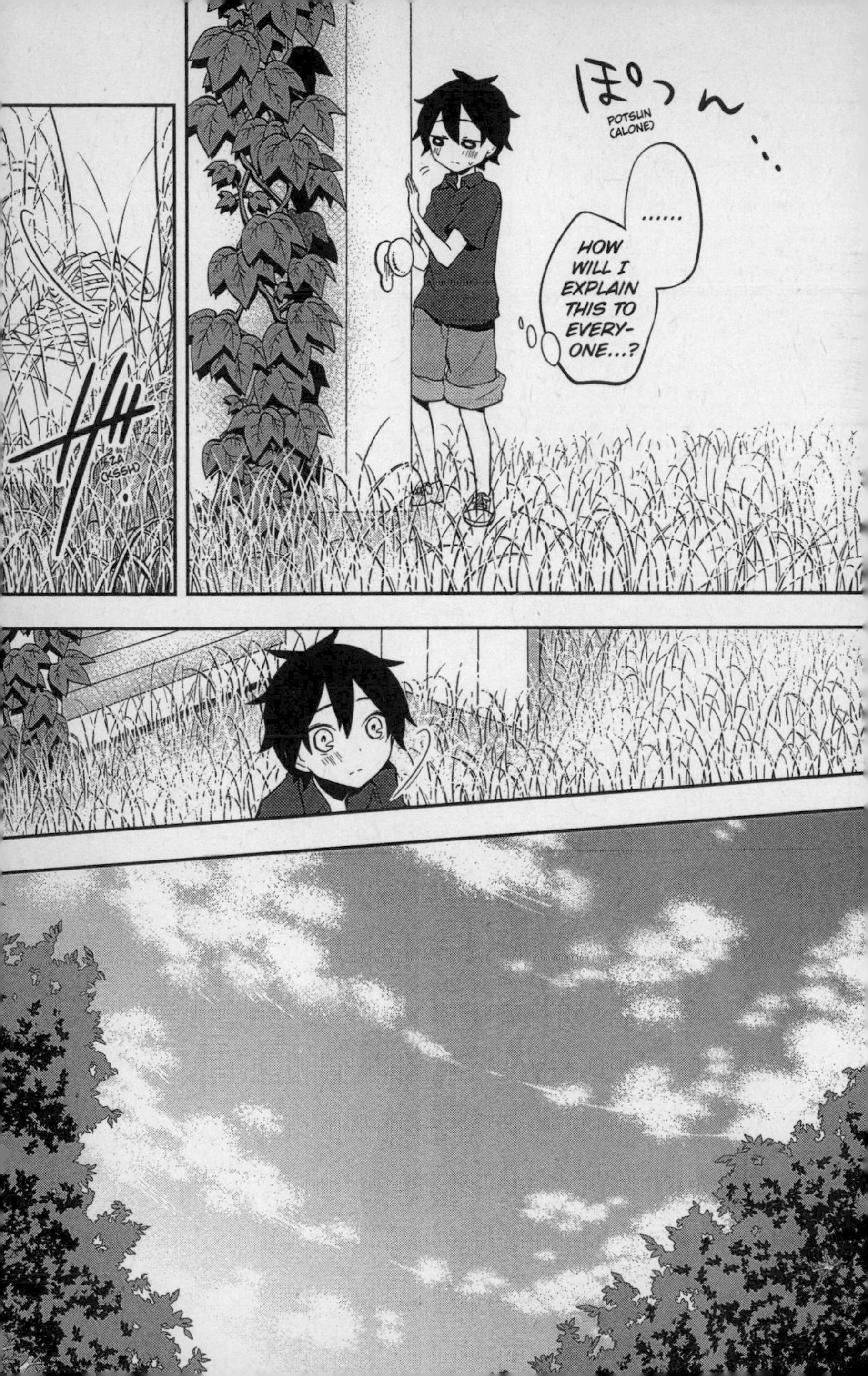
ぽつん…
POTSUN (ALONE)
......
HOW WILL I EXPLAIN THIS TO EVERY-ONE...?
ZA (KSSH)

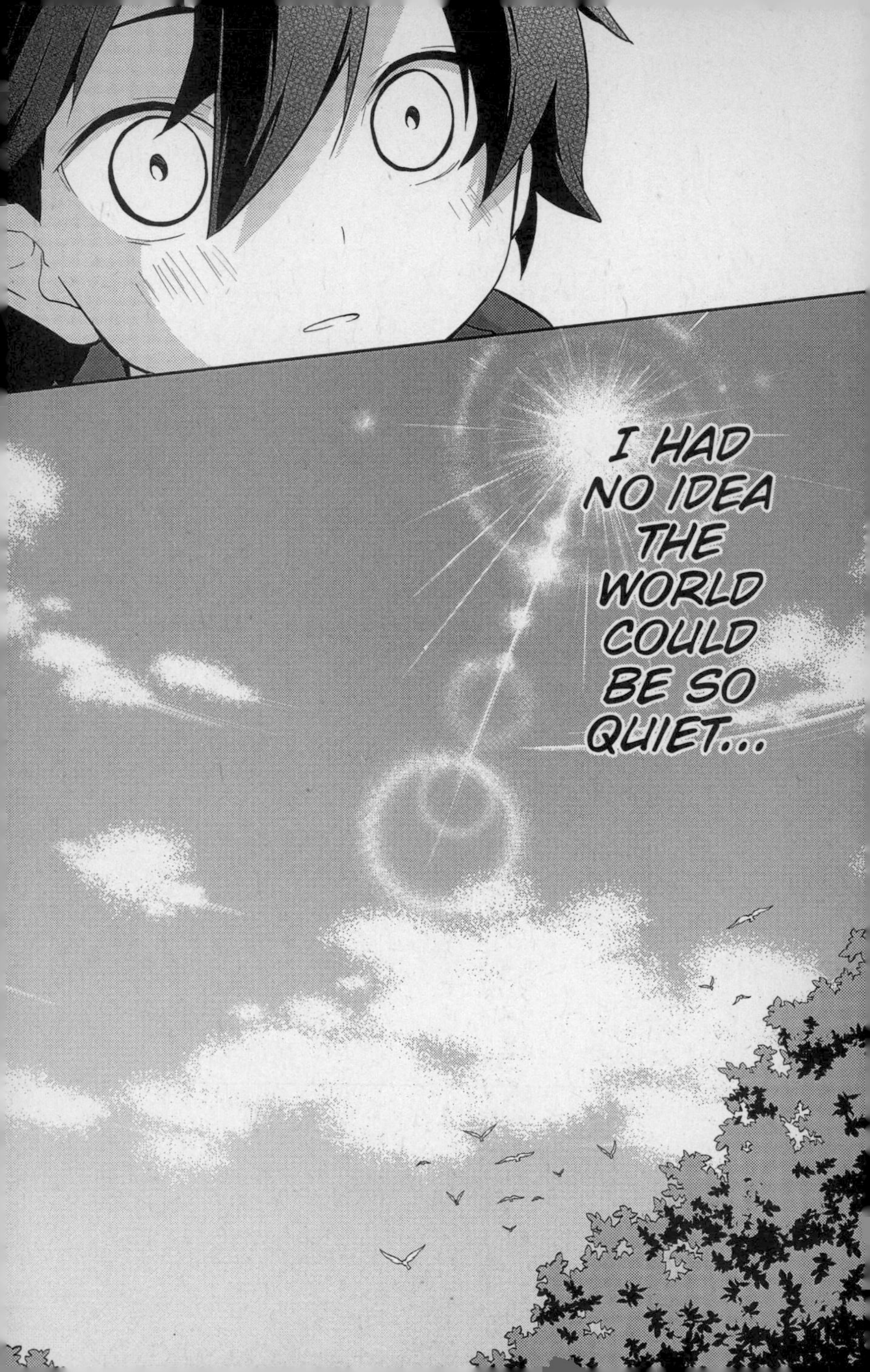
I HAD NO IDEA THE WORLD COULD BE SO QUIET...

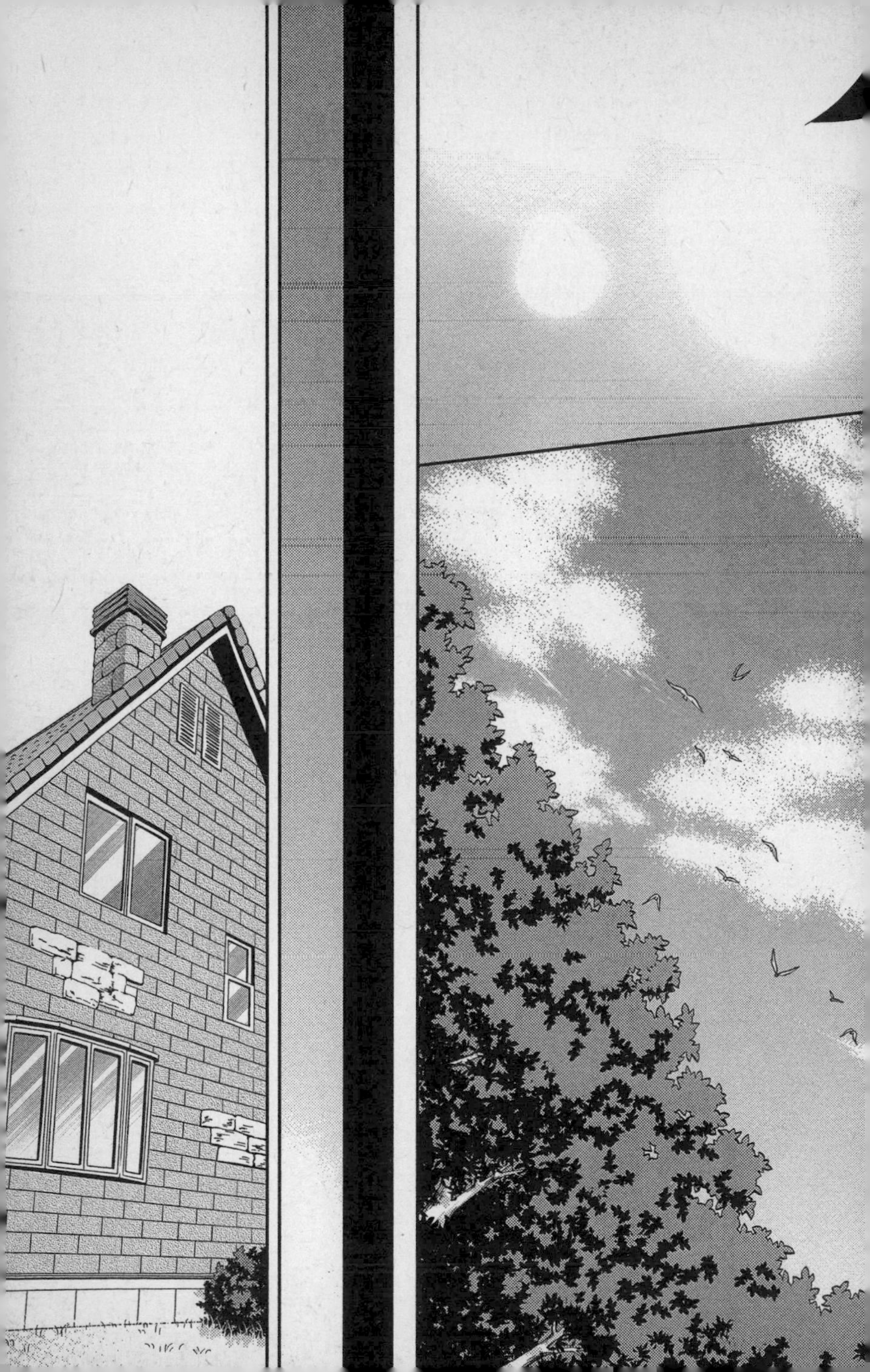

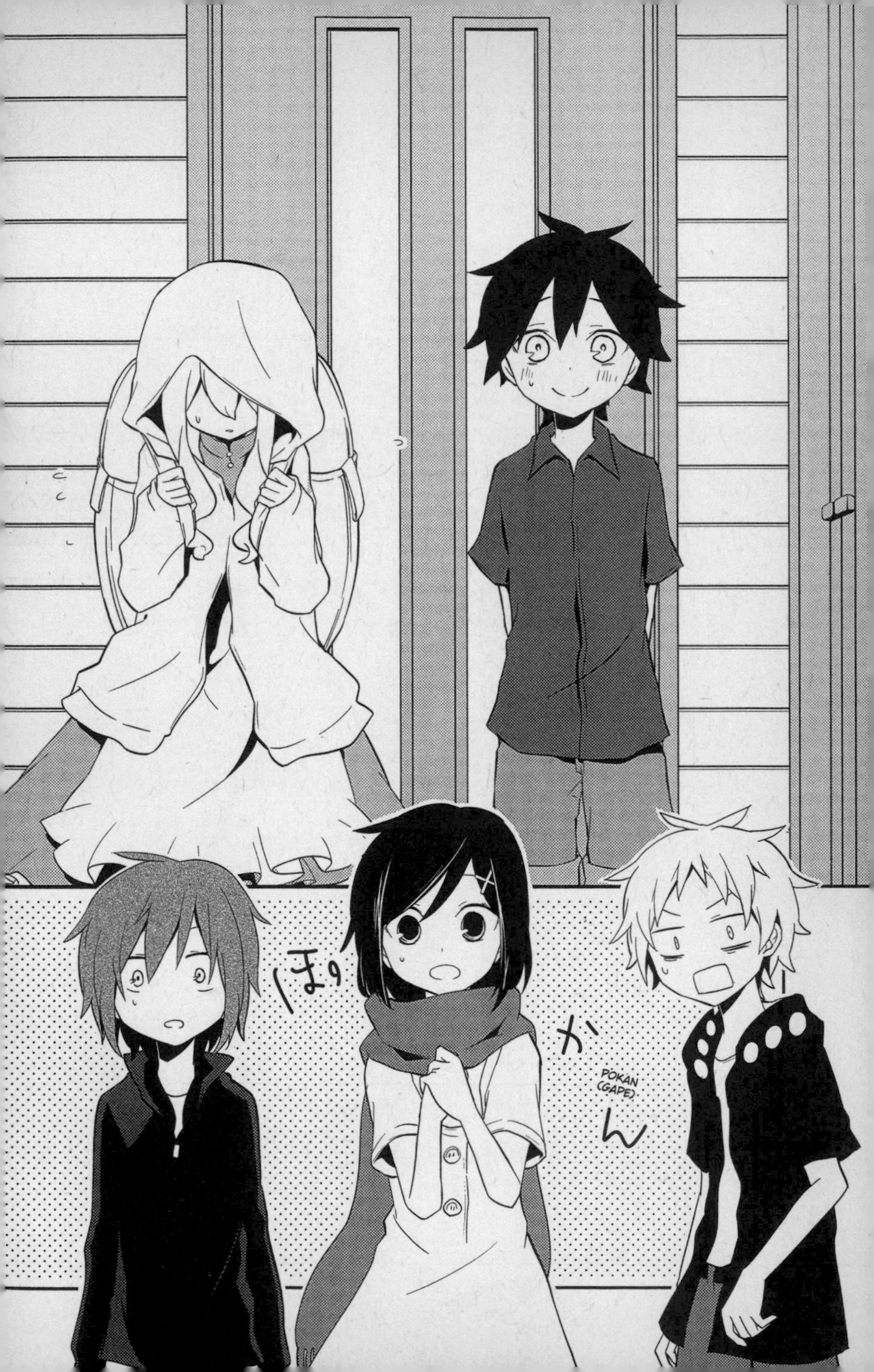
ぽかん
POKAN (GAPE)

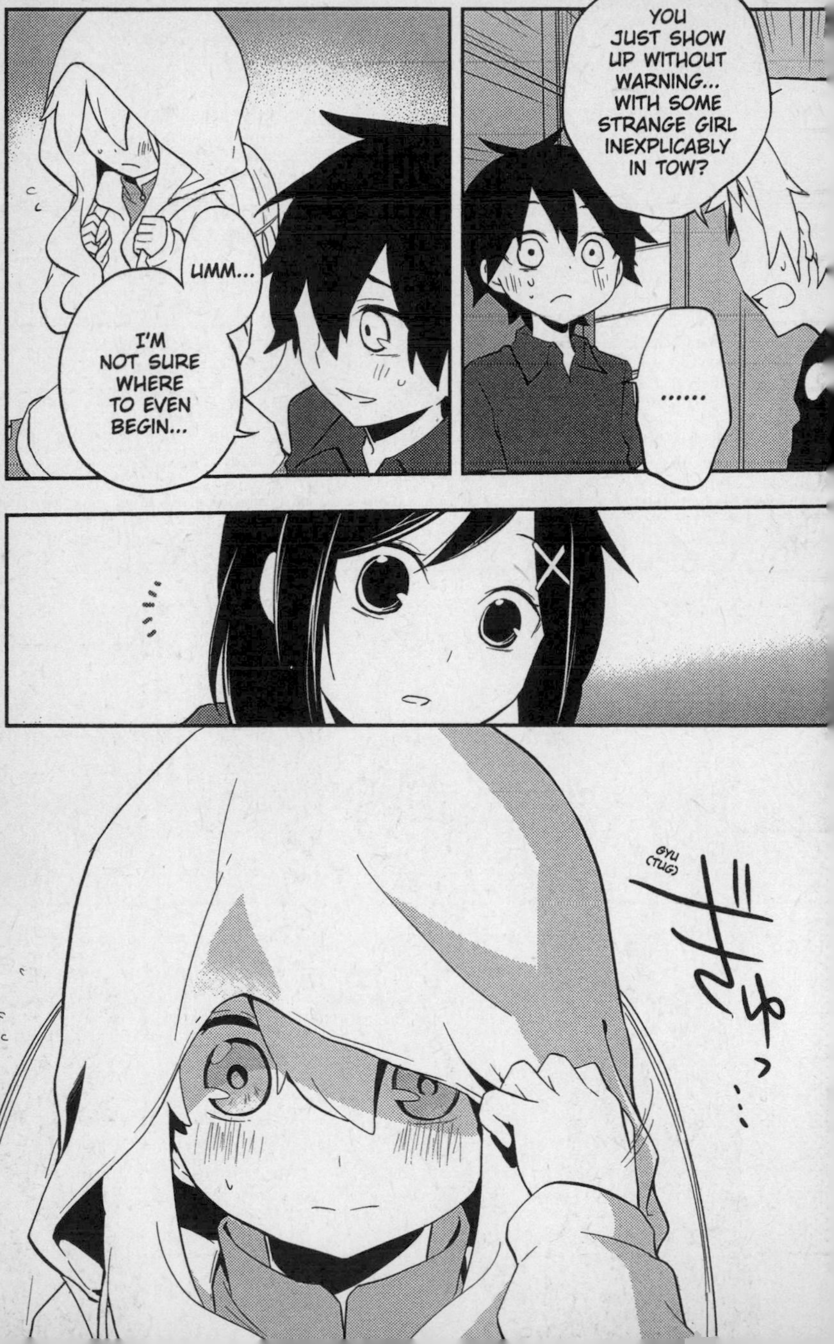
YOU JUST SHOW UP WITHOUT WARNING... WITH SOME STRANGE GIRL INEXPLICABLY IN TOW?
......
UMM...
I'M NOT SURE WHERE TO EVEN BEGIN...
GYU (TUG)

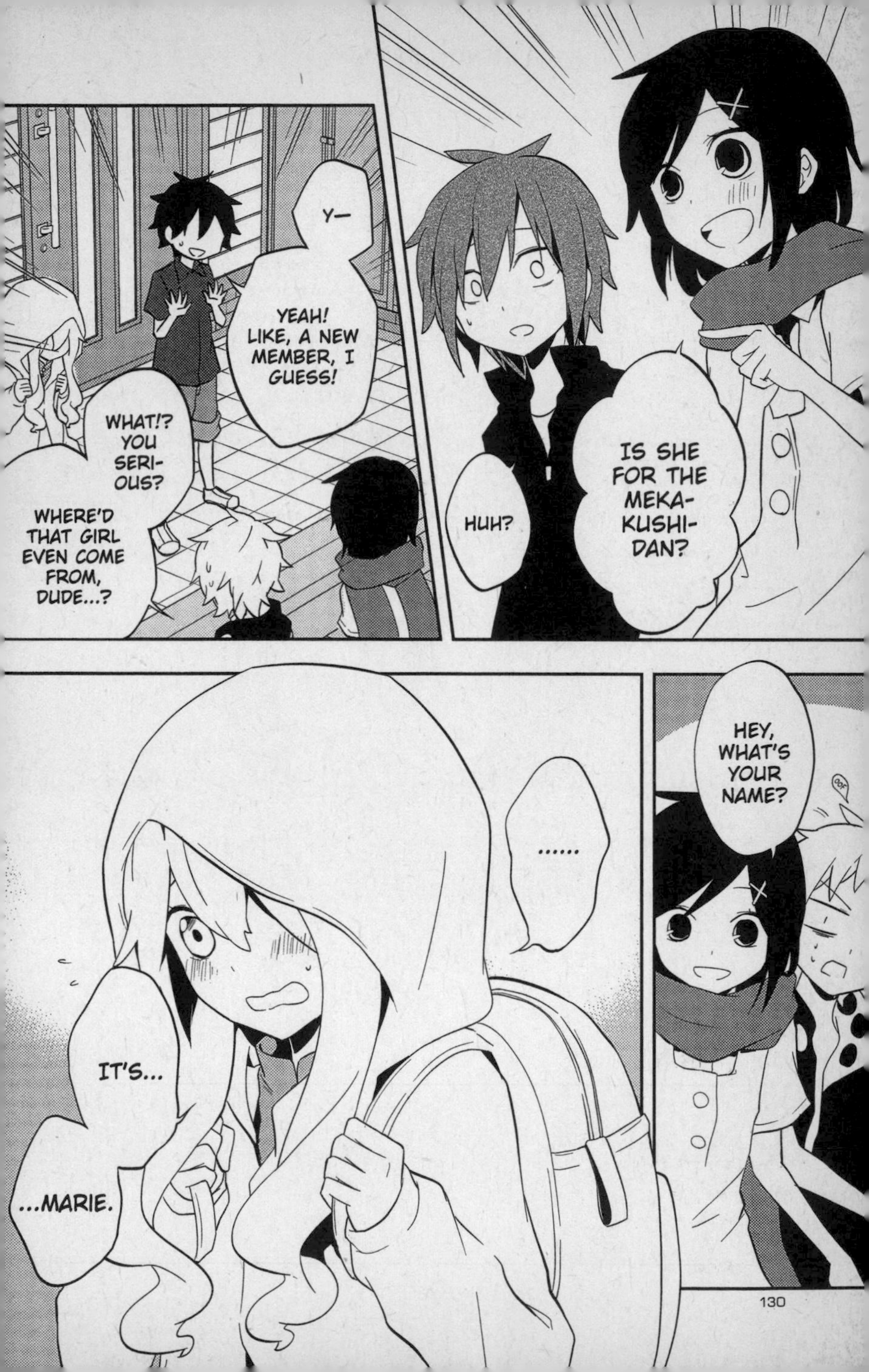
IS SHE FOR THE MEKA-KUSHIDAN?
HUH?
Y—
YEAH! LIKE, A NEW MEMBER, I GUESS!
WHAT!? YOU SERI-OUS?
WHERE'D THAT GIRL EVEN COME FROM, DUDE...?
HEY, WHAT'S YOUR NAME?
......
IT'S...
...MARIE.

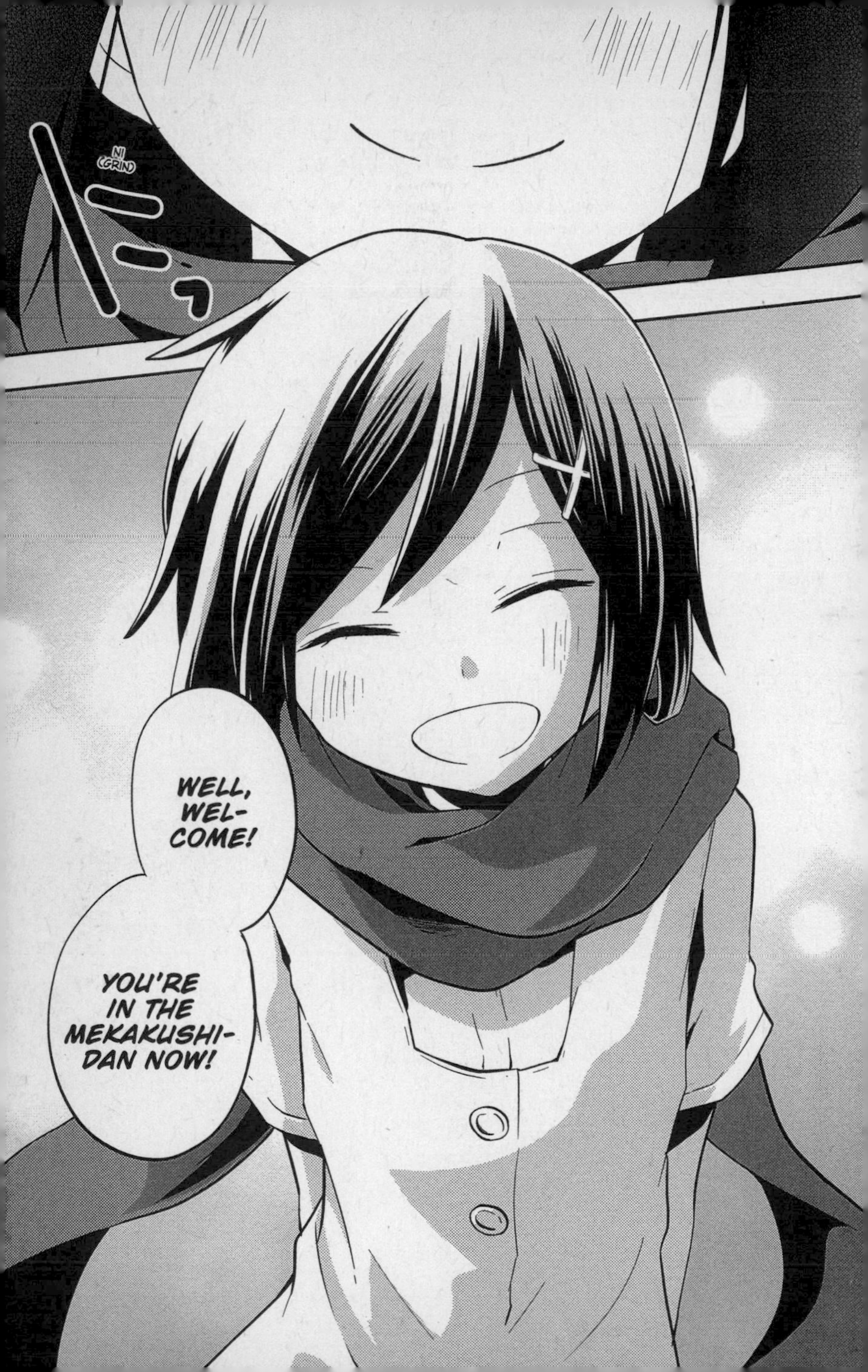
NI (GRIN)
WELL, WEL-COME!
YOU'RE IN THE MEKAKUSHI-DAN NOW!

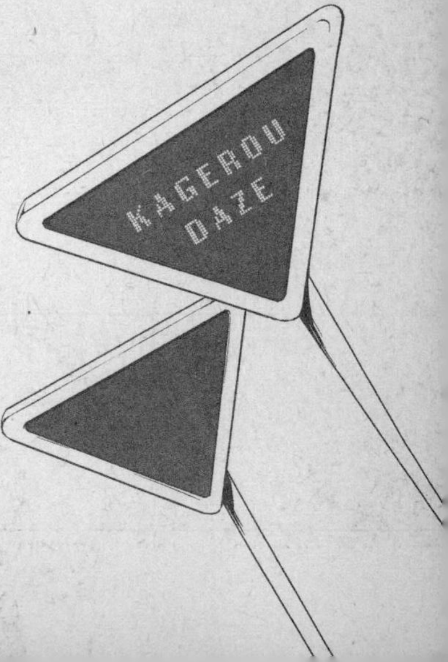
KAGEROU
DAZE

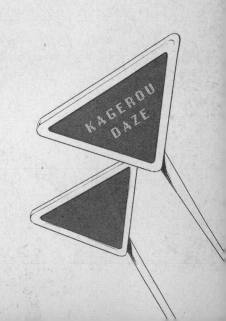

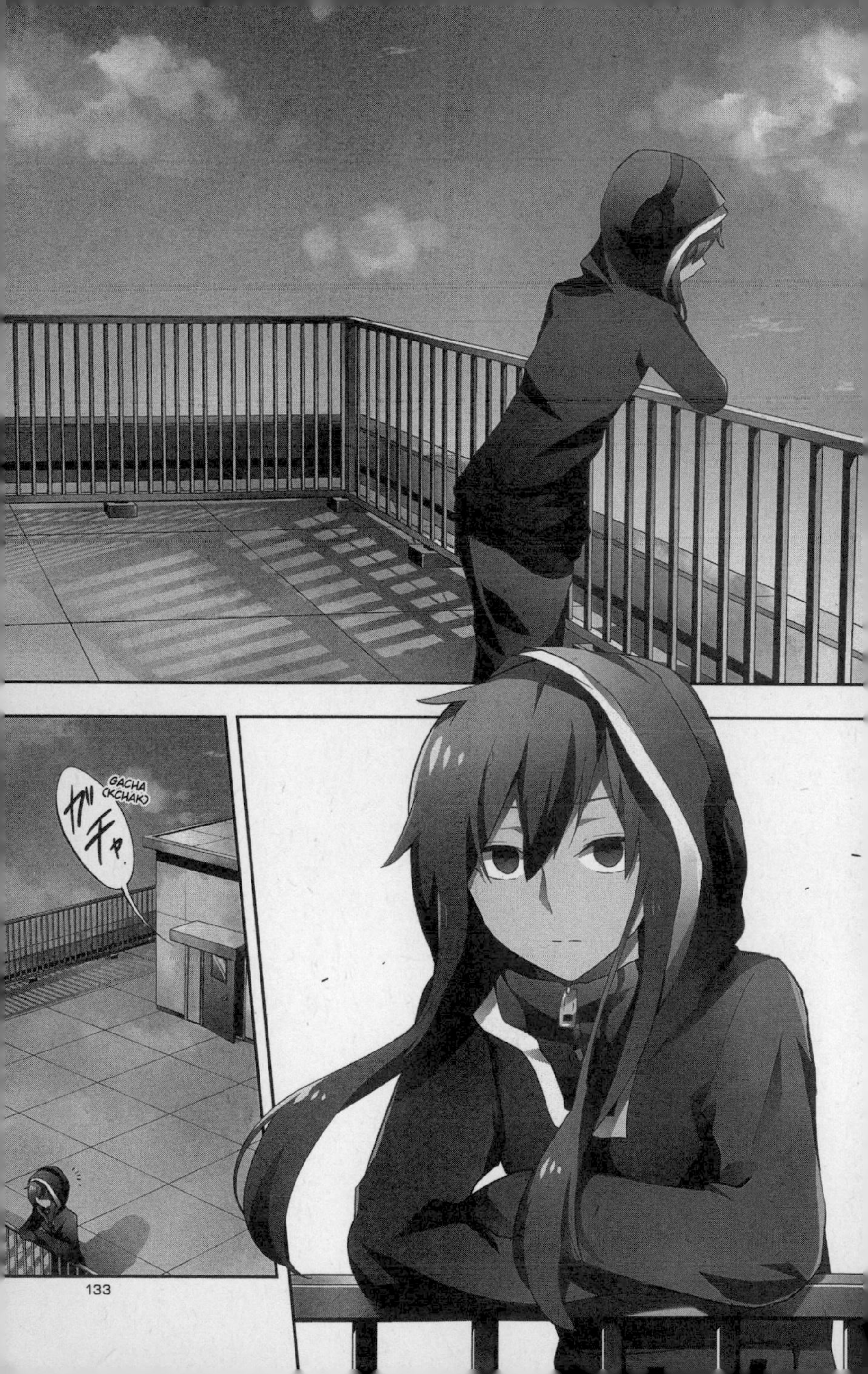
ガチャ
GACHA (KCHAK)

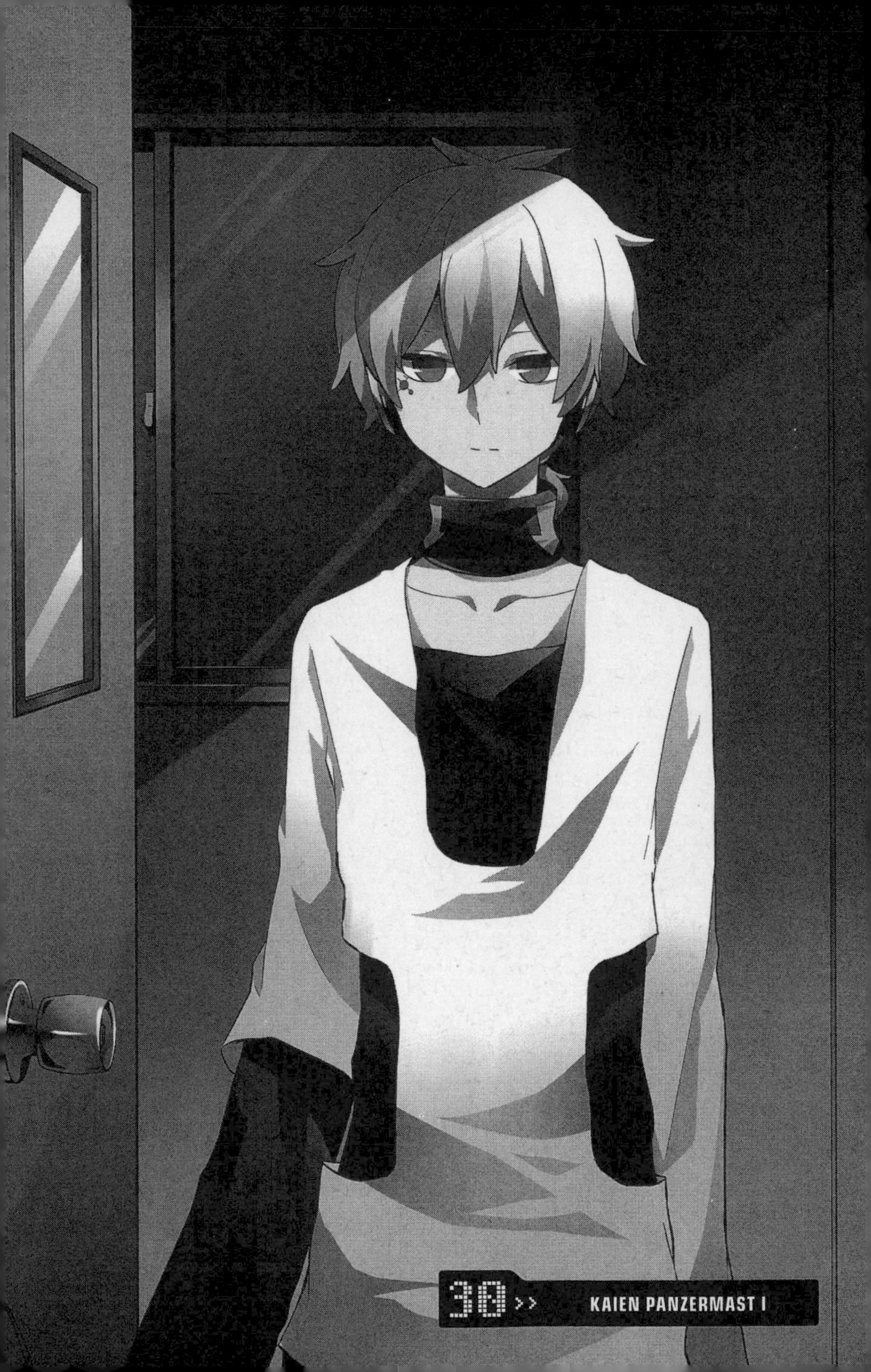

30 >>
KAIEN PANZERMAST I

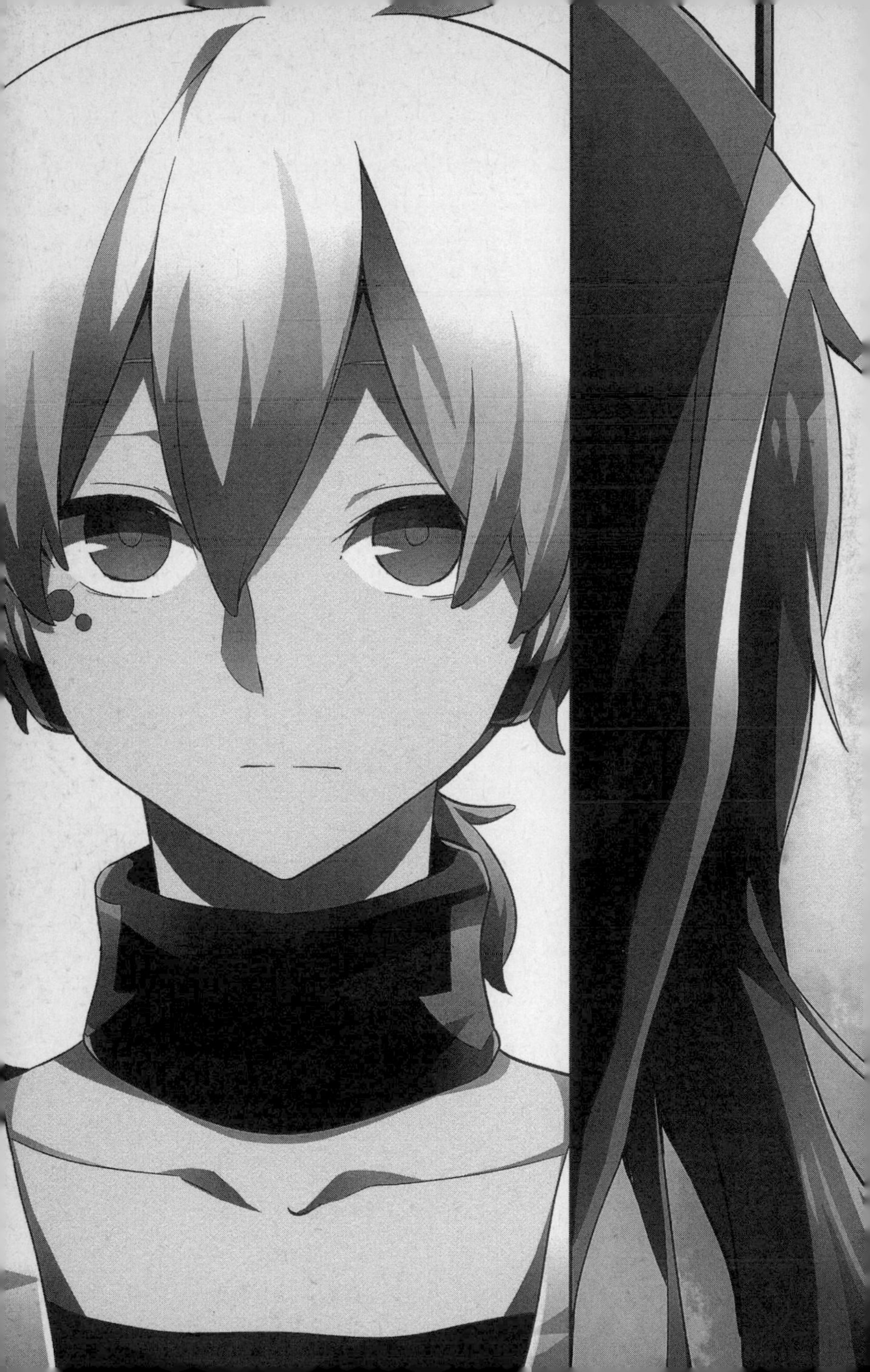

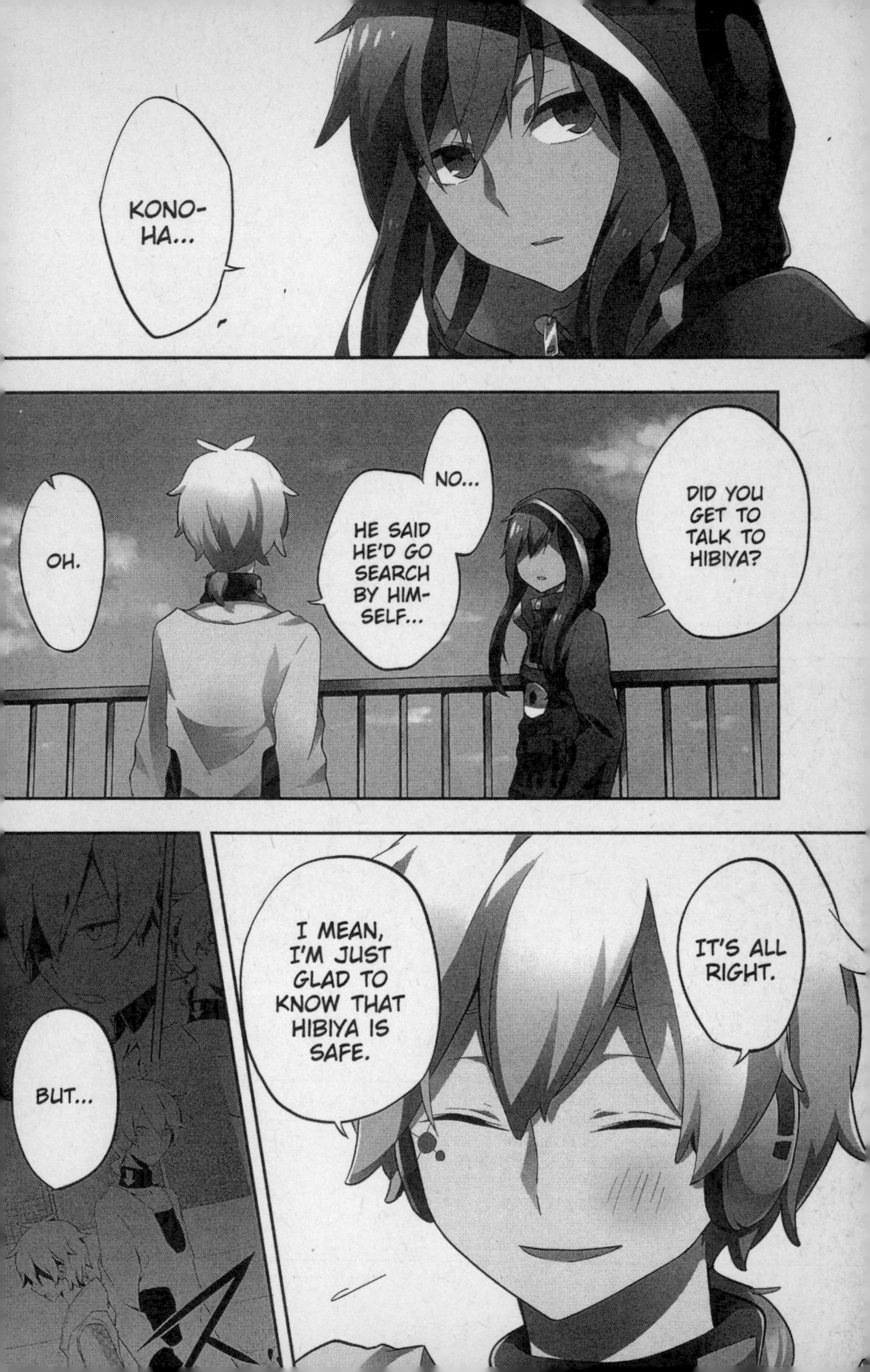
KONO-HA...
DID YOU GET TO TALK TO HIBIYA?
NO...
HE SAID HE'D GO SEARCH BY HIM-SELF...
OH.
IT'S ALL RIGHT.
I MEAN, I'M JUST GLAD TO KNOW THAT HIBIYA IS SAFE.
BUT...

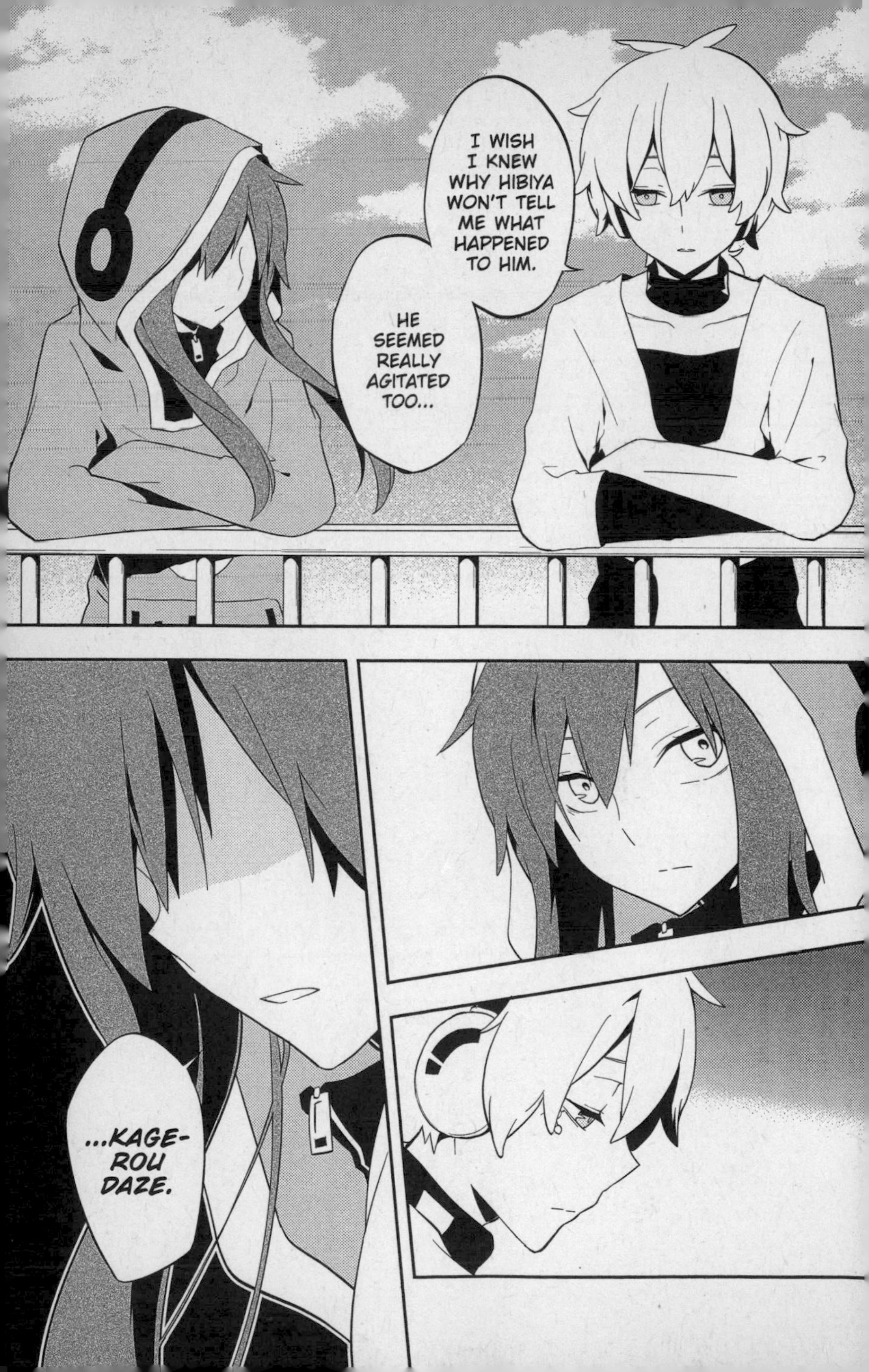
I WISH I KNEW WHY HIBIYA WON'T TELL ME WHAT HAPPENED TO HIM.
HE SEEMED REALLY AGITATED TOO...
...KAGE-ROU DAZE.

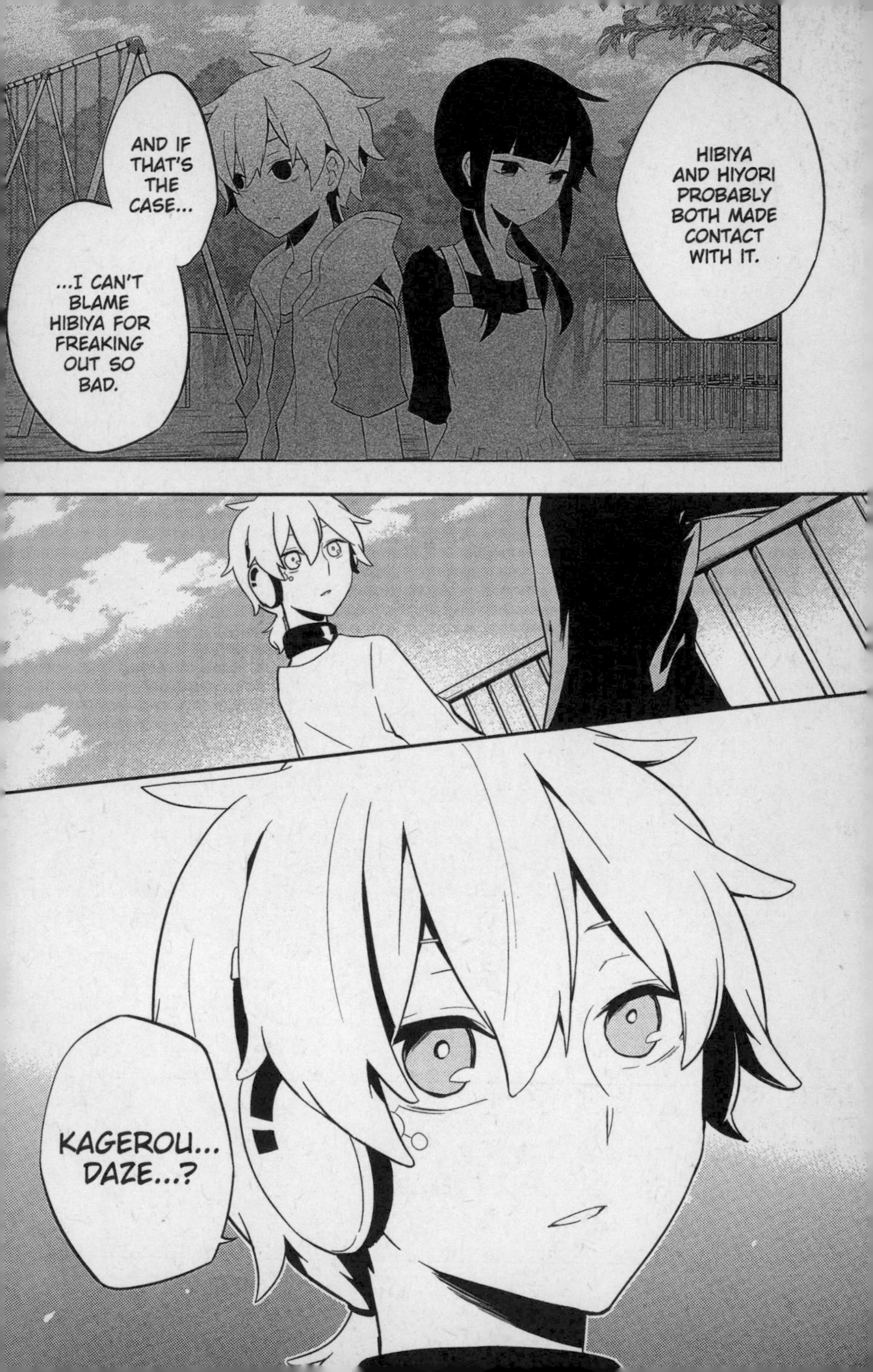
HIBIYA AND HIYORI PROBABLY BOTH MADE CONTACT WITH IT.
AND IF THAT'S THE CASE...
...I CAN'T BLAME HIBIYA FOR FREAKING OUT SO BAD.
KAGEROU... DAZE...?

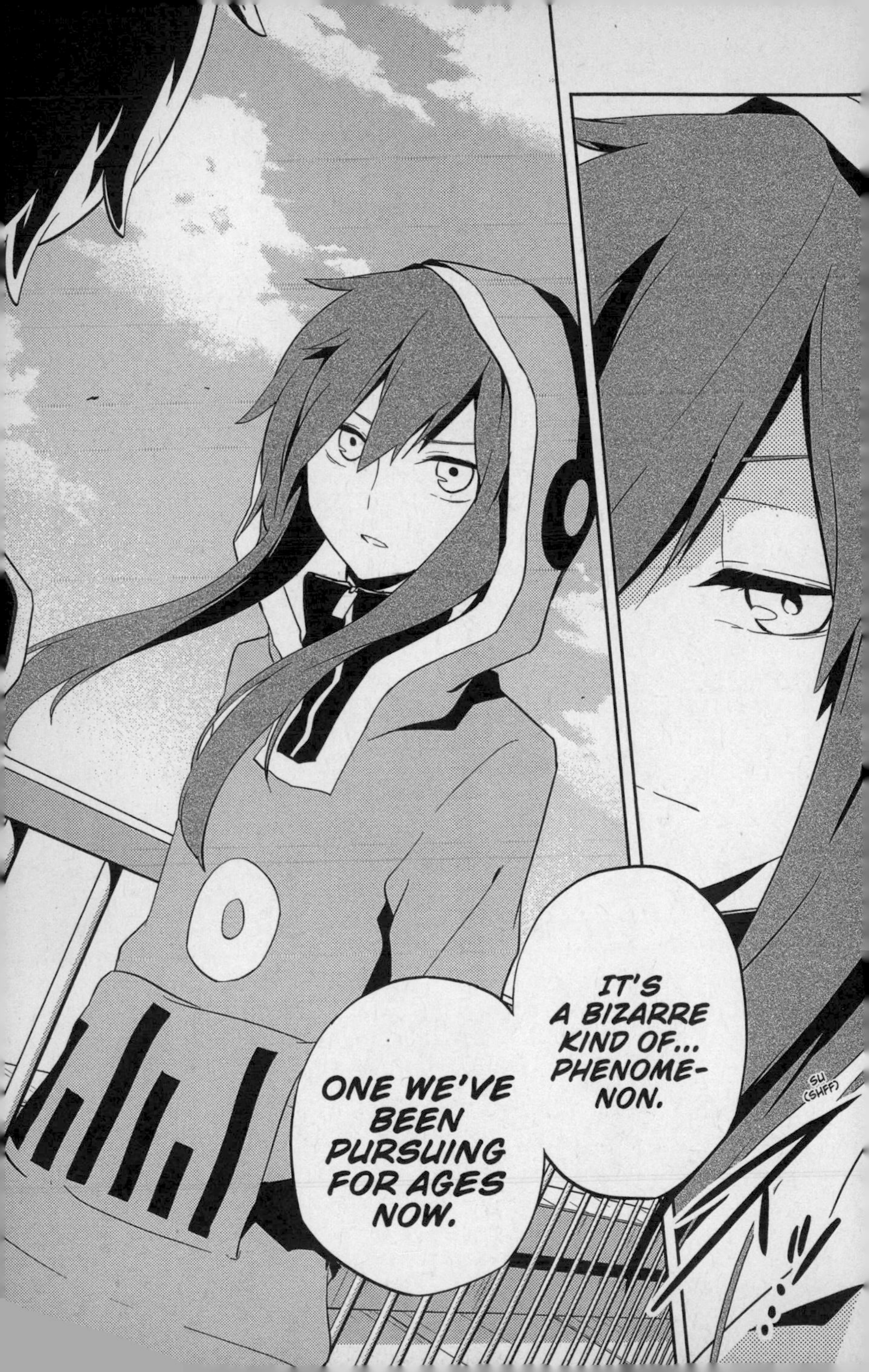
IT'S A BIZARRE KIND OF... PHENOMENON.
SU (SHFF)
ONE WE'VE BEEN PURSUING FOR AGES NOW.

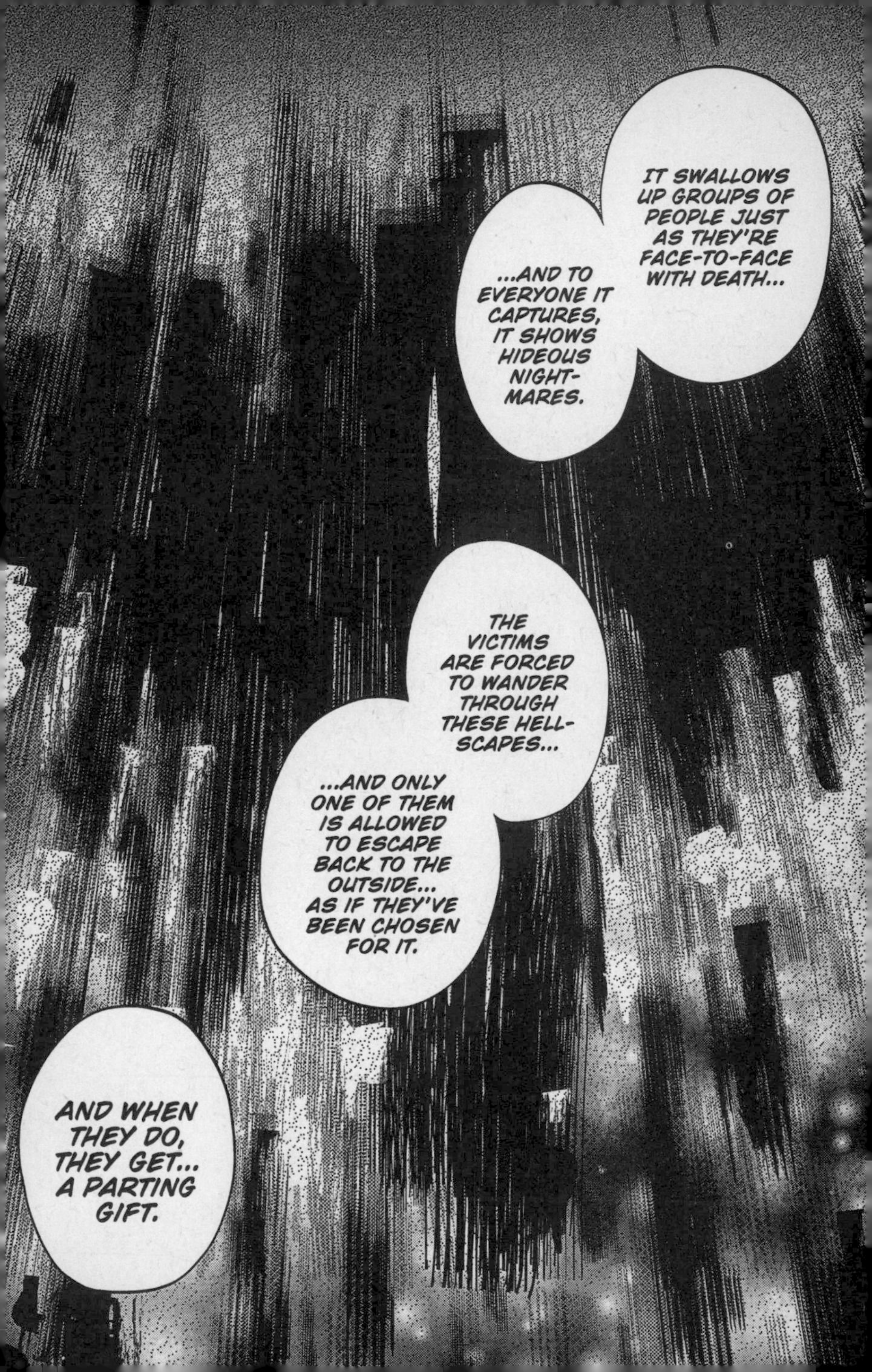
IT SWALLOWS UP GROUPS OF PEOPLE JUST AS THEY'RE FACE-TO-FACE WITH DEATH...
...AND TO EVERYONE IT CAPTURES, IT SHOWS HIDEOUS NIGHT-MARES.
THE VICTIMS ARE FORCED TO WANDER THROUGH THESE HELL-SCAPES...
...AND ONLY ONE OF THEM IS ALLOWED TO ESCAPE BACK TO THE OUTSIDE... AS IF THEY'VE BEEN CHOSEN FOR IT.
AND WHEN THEY DO, THEY GET... A PARTING GIFT.

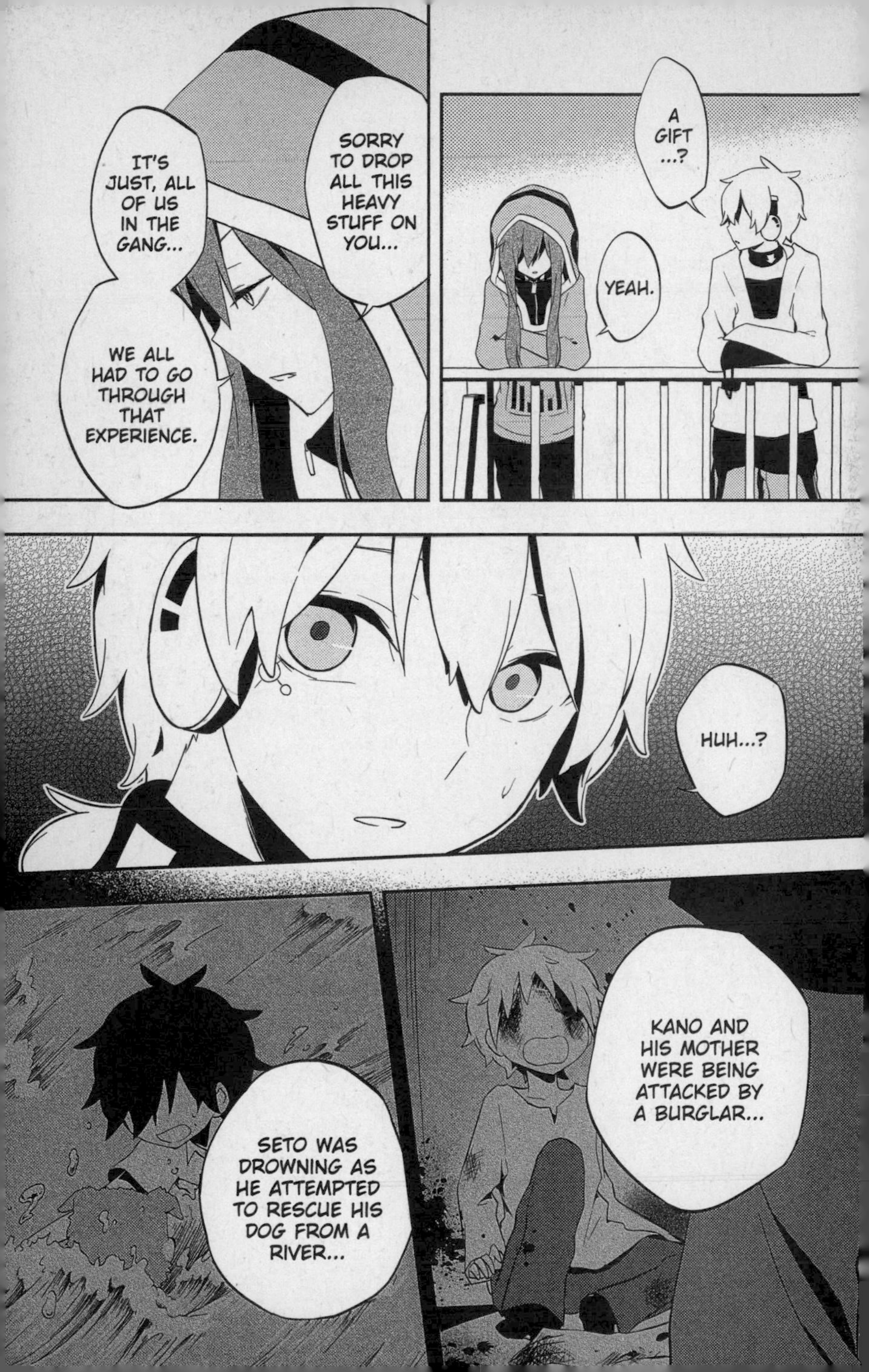
A GIFT ...?
YEAH.
SORRY TO DROP ALL THIS HEAVY STUFF ON YOU...
IT'S JUST, ALL OF US IN THE GANG...
WE ALL HAD TO GO THROUGH THAT EXPERIENCE.
HUH...?
KANO AND HIS MOTHER WERE BEING ATTACKED BY A BURGLAR...
SETO WAS DROWNING AS HE ATTEMPTED TO RESCUE HIS DOG FROM A RIVER...

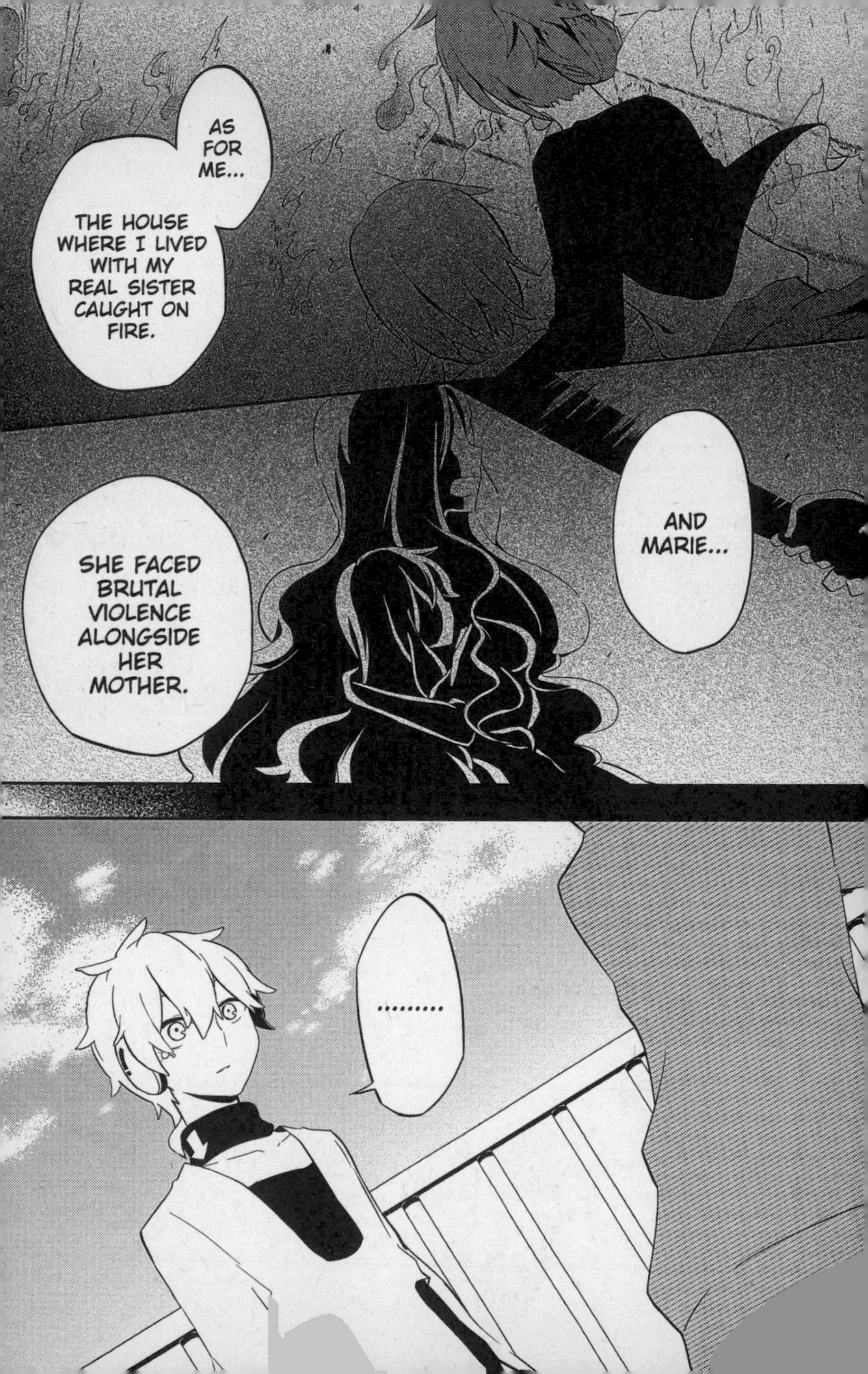
AS FOR ME...
THE HOUSE WHERE I LIVED WITH MY REAL SISTER CAUGHT ON FIRE.
AND MARIE...
SHE FACED BRUTAL VIOLENCE ALONGSIDE HER MOTHER.
....

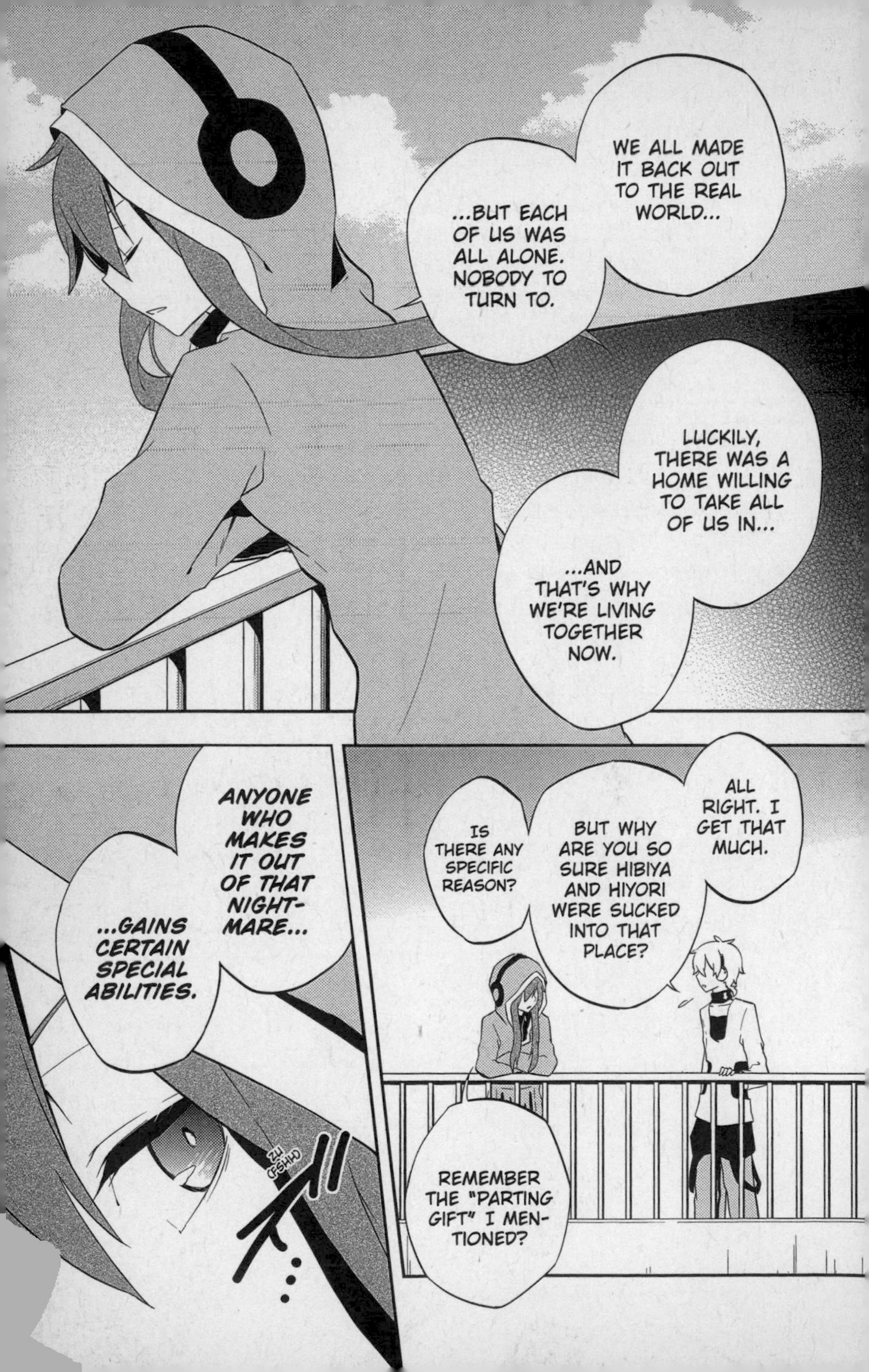
WE ALL MADE IT BACK OUT TO THE REAL WORLD...
...BUT EACH OF US WAS ALL ALONE. NOBODY TO TURN TO.
LUCKILY, THERE WAS A HOME WILLING TO TAKE ALL OF US IN...
...AND THAT'S WHY WE'RE LIVING TOGETHER NOW.
ALL RIGHT. I GET THAT MUCH.
BUT WHY ARE YOU SO SURE HIBIYA AND HIYORI WERE SUCKED INTO THAT PLACE?
IS THERE ANY SPECIFIC REASON?
REMEMBER THE "PARTING GIFT" I MENTIONED?
ANYONE WHO MAKES IT OUT OF THAT NIGHTMARE...
...GAINS CERTAIN SPECIAL ABILITIES.
...

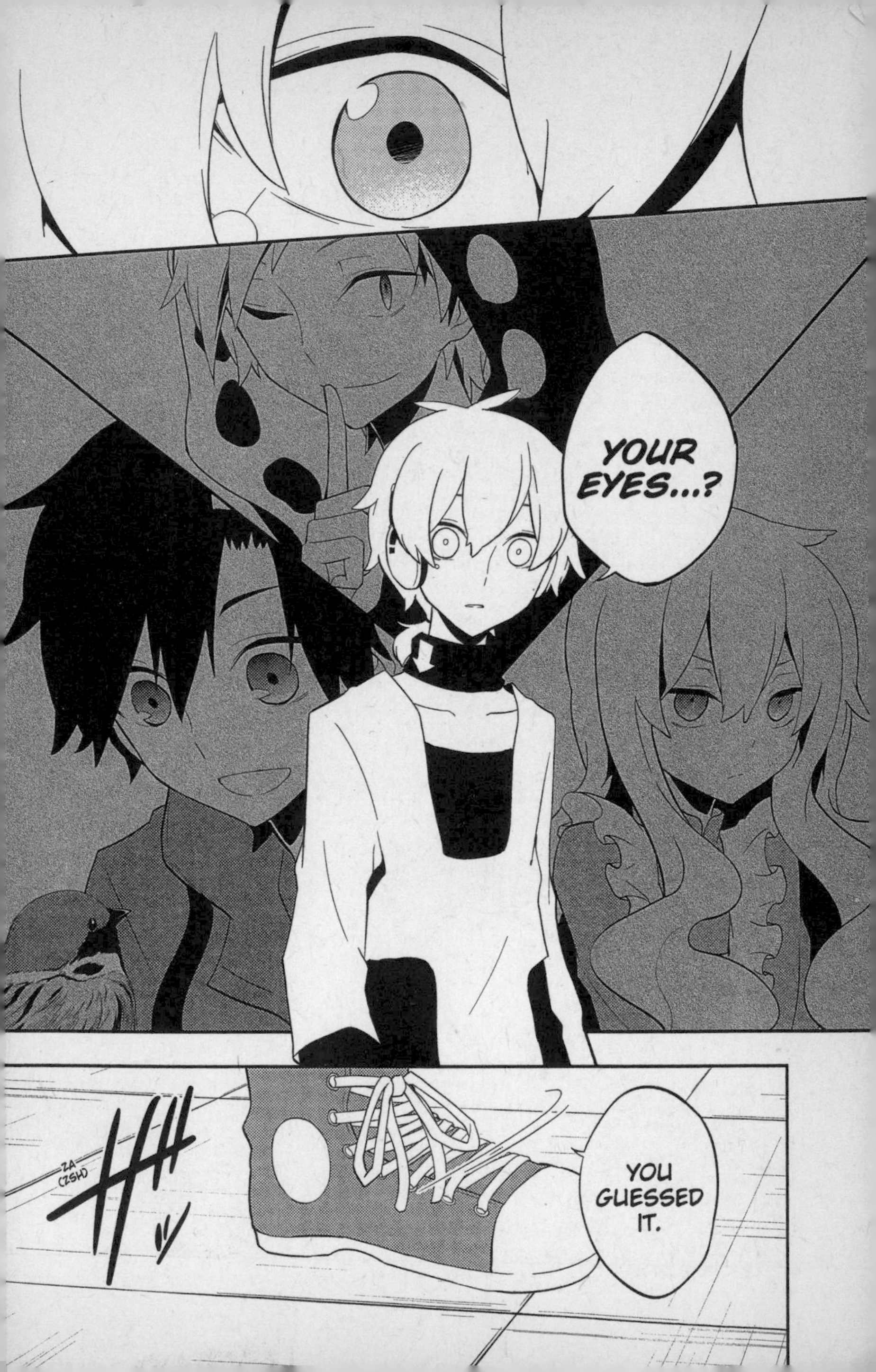
YOUR EYES...?
YOU GUESSED IT.
ZA (ZSH)

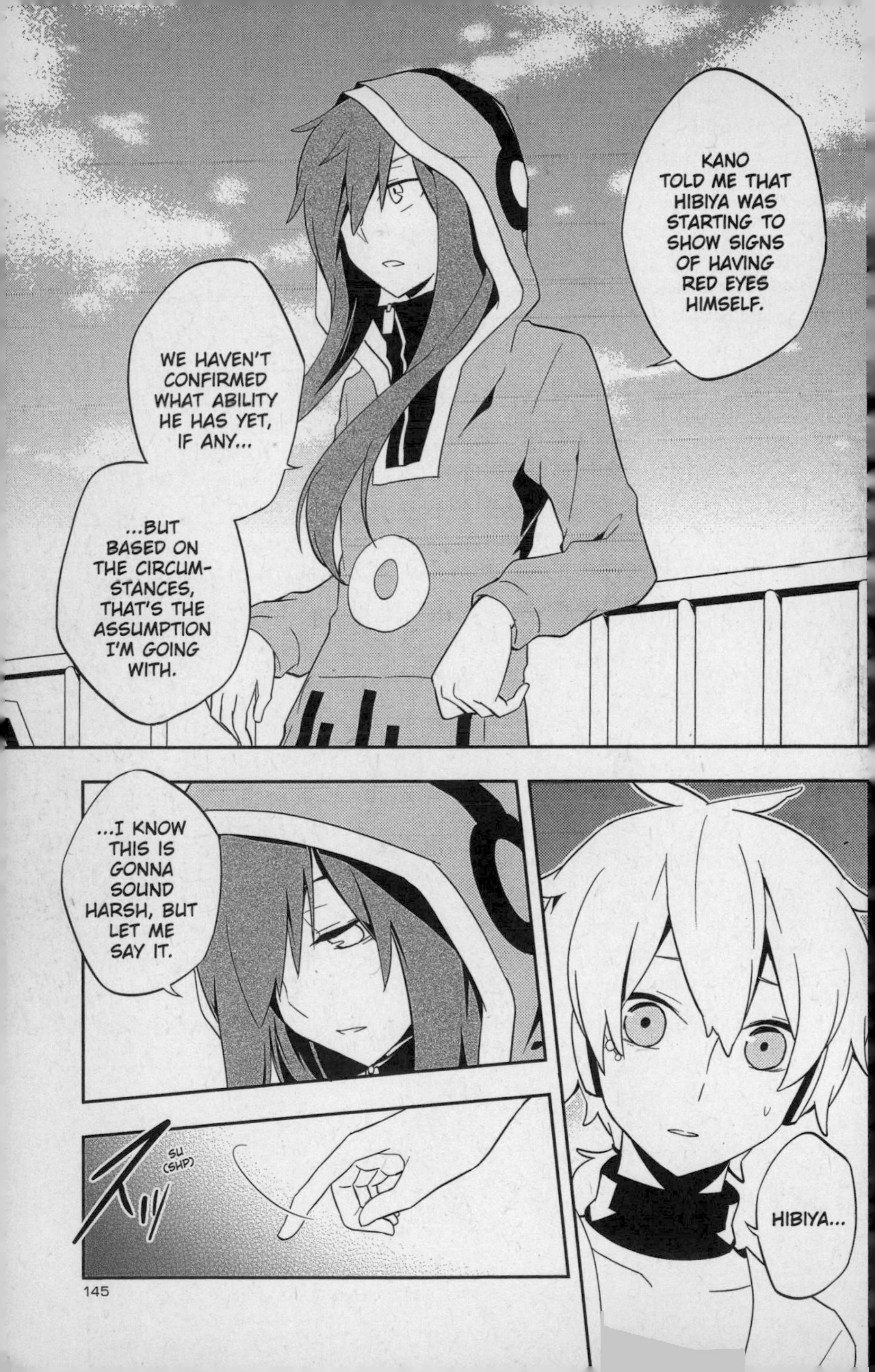
KANO TOLD ME THAT HIBIYA WAS STARTING TO SHOW SIGNS OF HAVING RED EYES HIMSELF.
WE HAVEN'T CONFIRMED WHAT ABILITY HE HAS YET, IF ANY...
...BUT BASED ON THE CIRCUM-STANCES, THAT'S THE ASSUMPTION I'M GOING WITH.
HIBIYA...
...I KNOW THIS IS GONNA SOUND HARSH, BUT LET ME SAY IT.
スッ
SU (SHP)

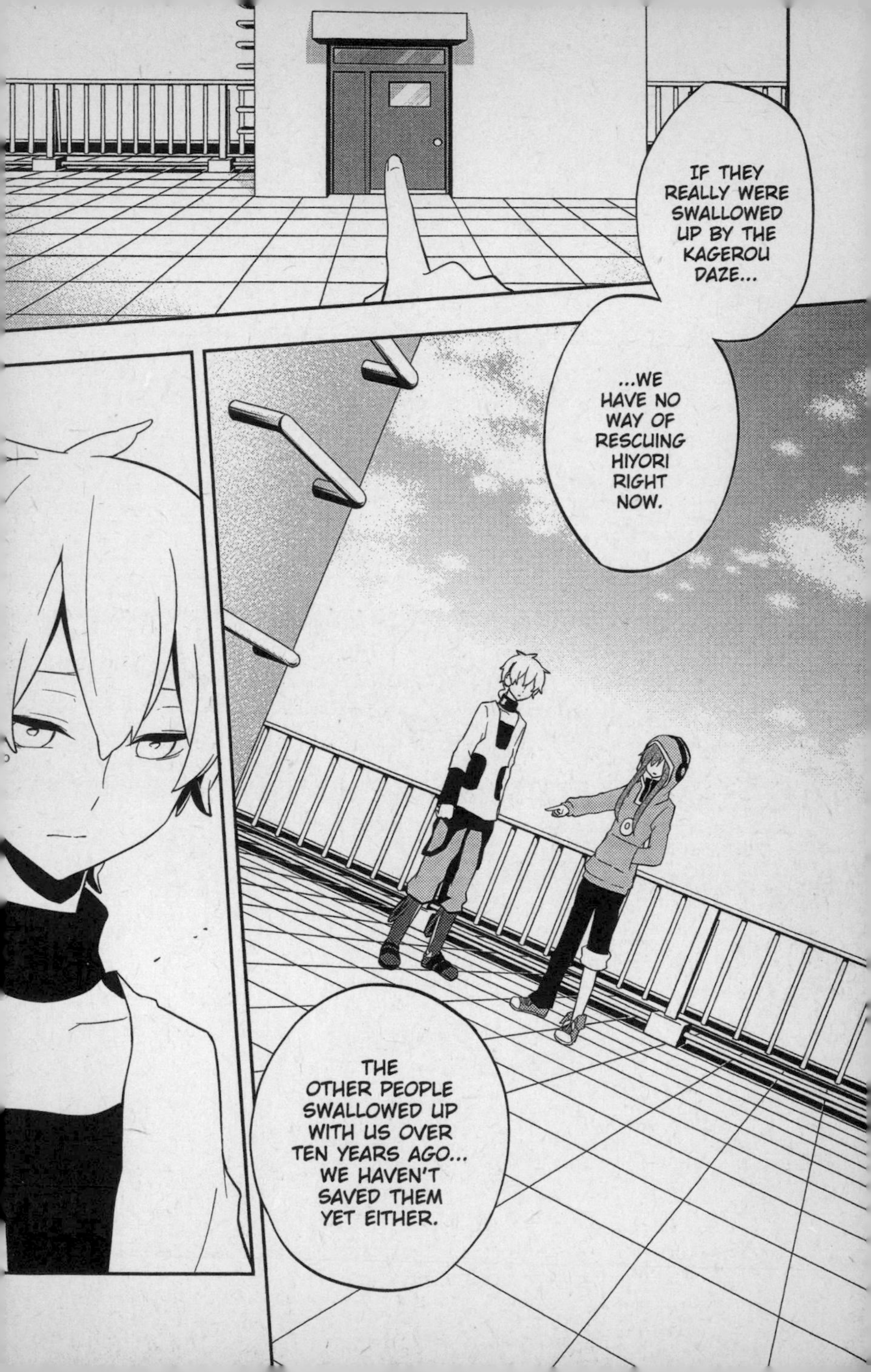
IF THEY REALLY WERE SWALLOWED UP BY THE KAGEROU DAZE...
...WE HAVE NO WAY OF RESCUING HIYORI RIGHT NOW.
THE OTHER PEOPLE SWALLOWED UP WITH US OVER TEN YEARS AGO... WE HAVEN'T SAVED THEM YET EITHER.

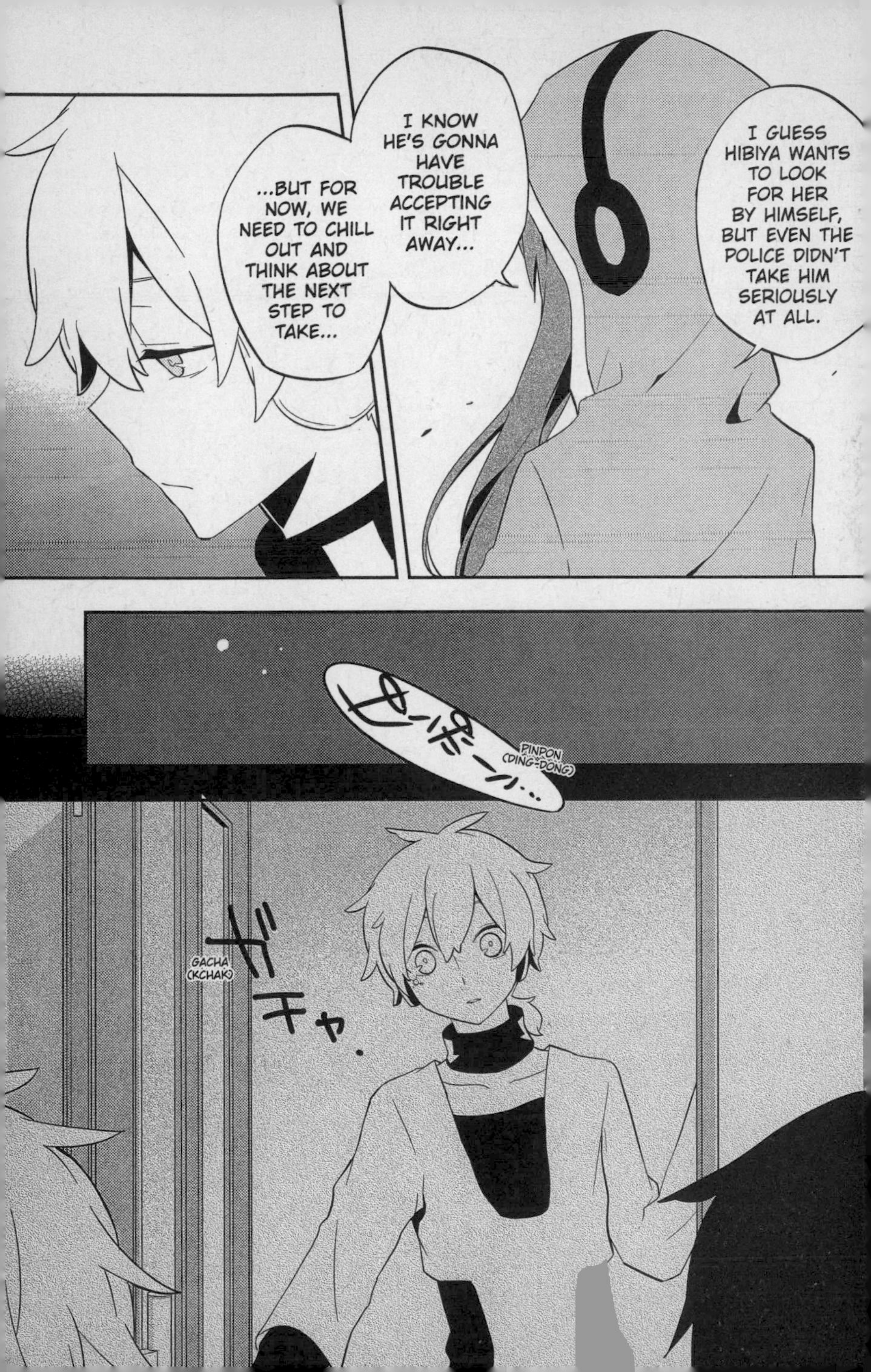
I GUESS HIBIYA WANTS TO LOOK FOR HER BY HIMSELF, BUT EVEN THE POLICE DIDN'T TAKE HIM SERIOUSLY AT ALL.
I KNOW HE'S GONNA HAVE TROUBLE ACCEPTING IT RIGHT AWAY...
...BUT FOR NOW, WE NEED TO CHILL OUT AND THINK ABOUT THE NEXT STEP TO TAKE...
ピンポーン...
PINPON (DING-DONG)
ガチャ.
GACHA (KCHAK)

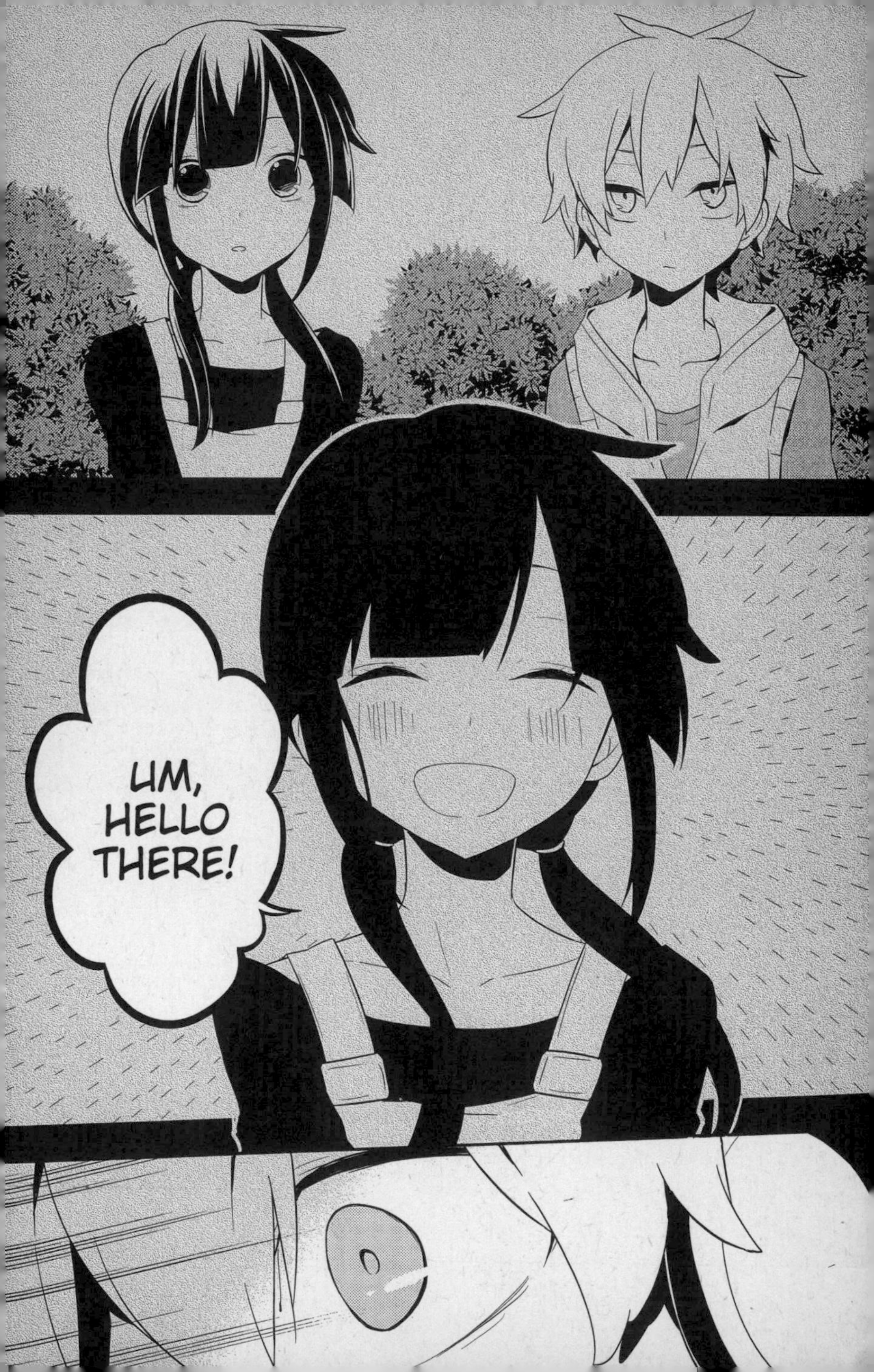
UM, HELLO THERE!

FRIEND

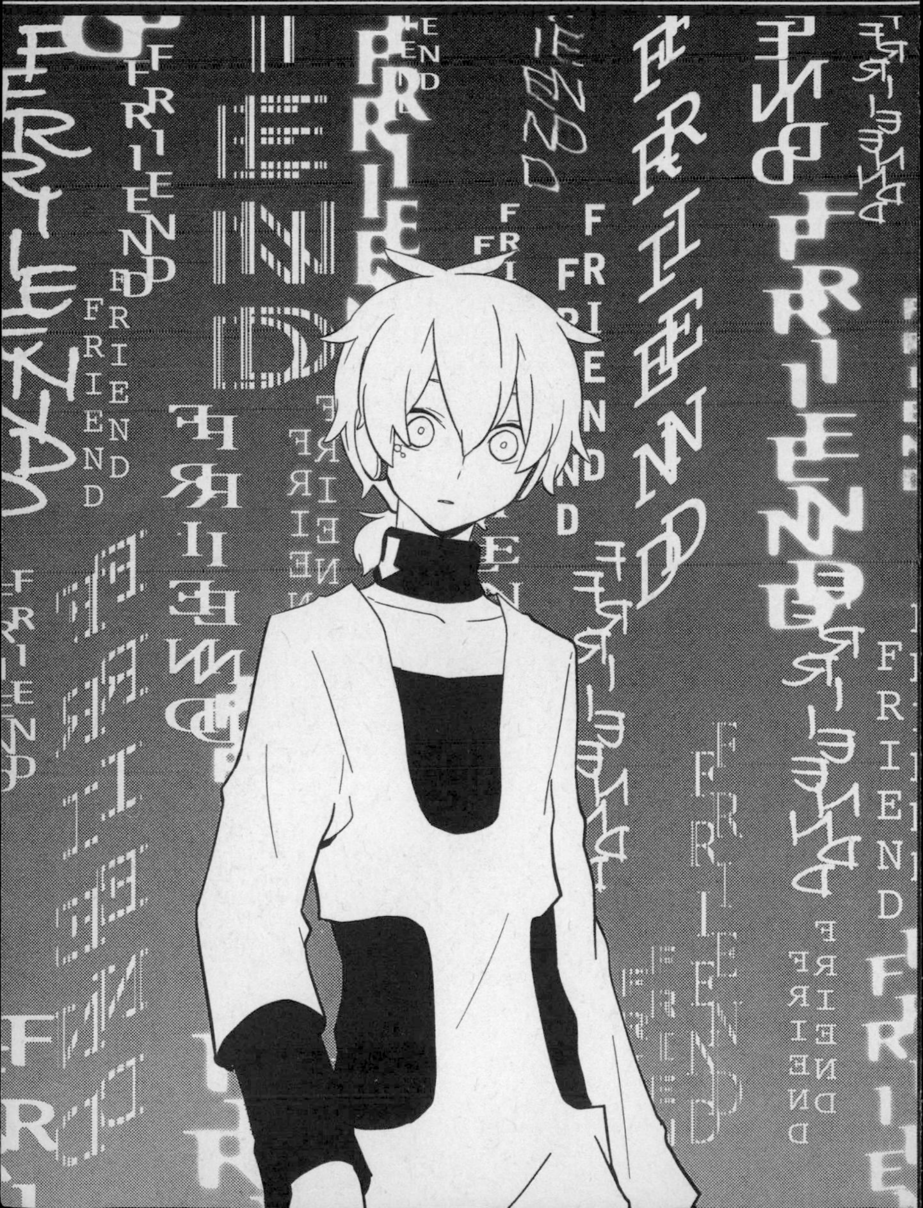

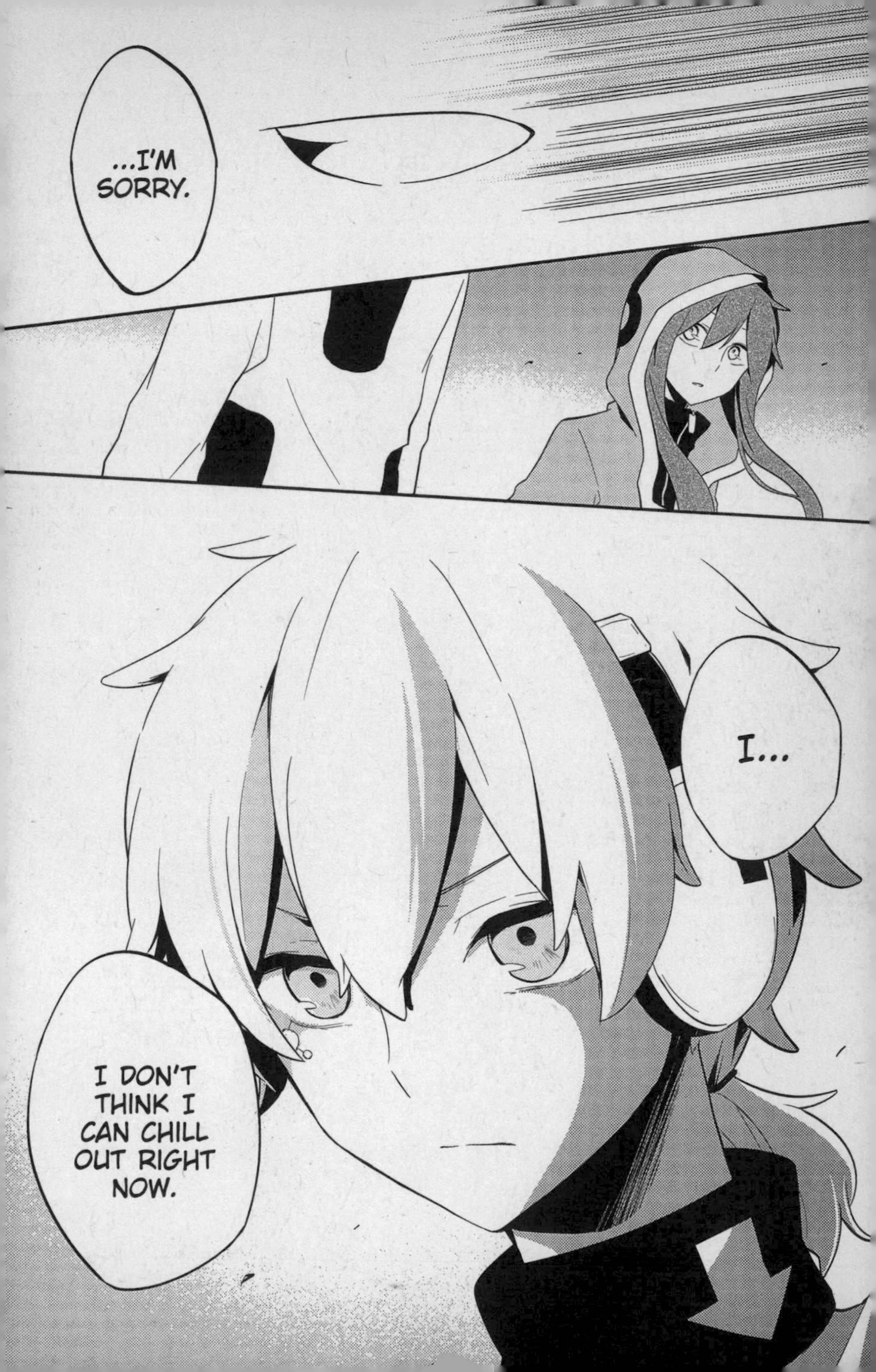
...I'M SORRY.
I...
I DON'T THINK I CAN CHILL OUT RIGHT NOW.

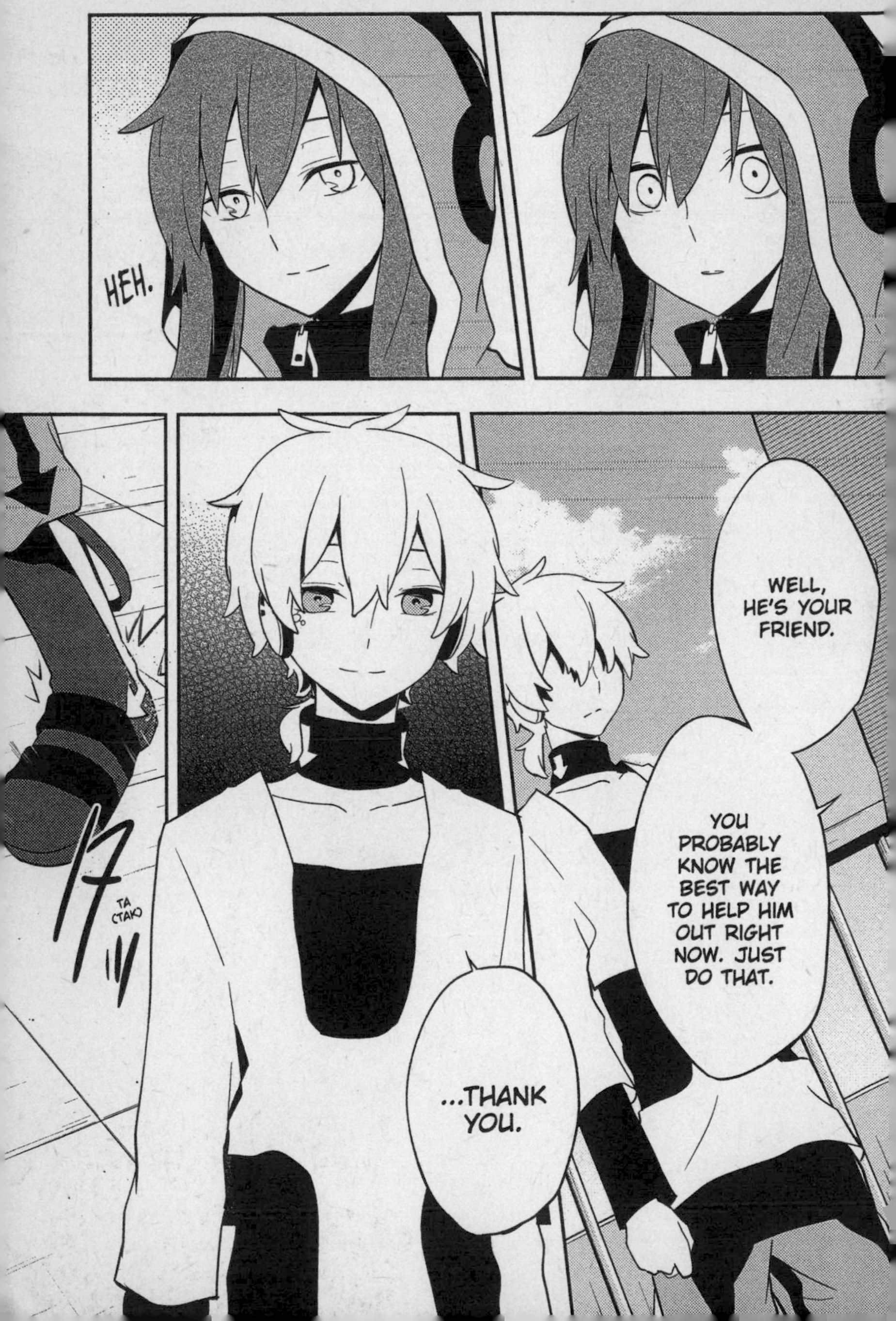
HEH.
WELL, HE'S YOUR FRIEND.
YOU PROBABLY KNOW THE BEST WAY TO HELP HIM OUT RIGHT NOW. JUST DO THAT.
...THANK YOU.
TA (TAK)

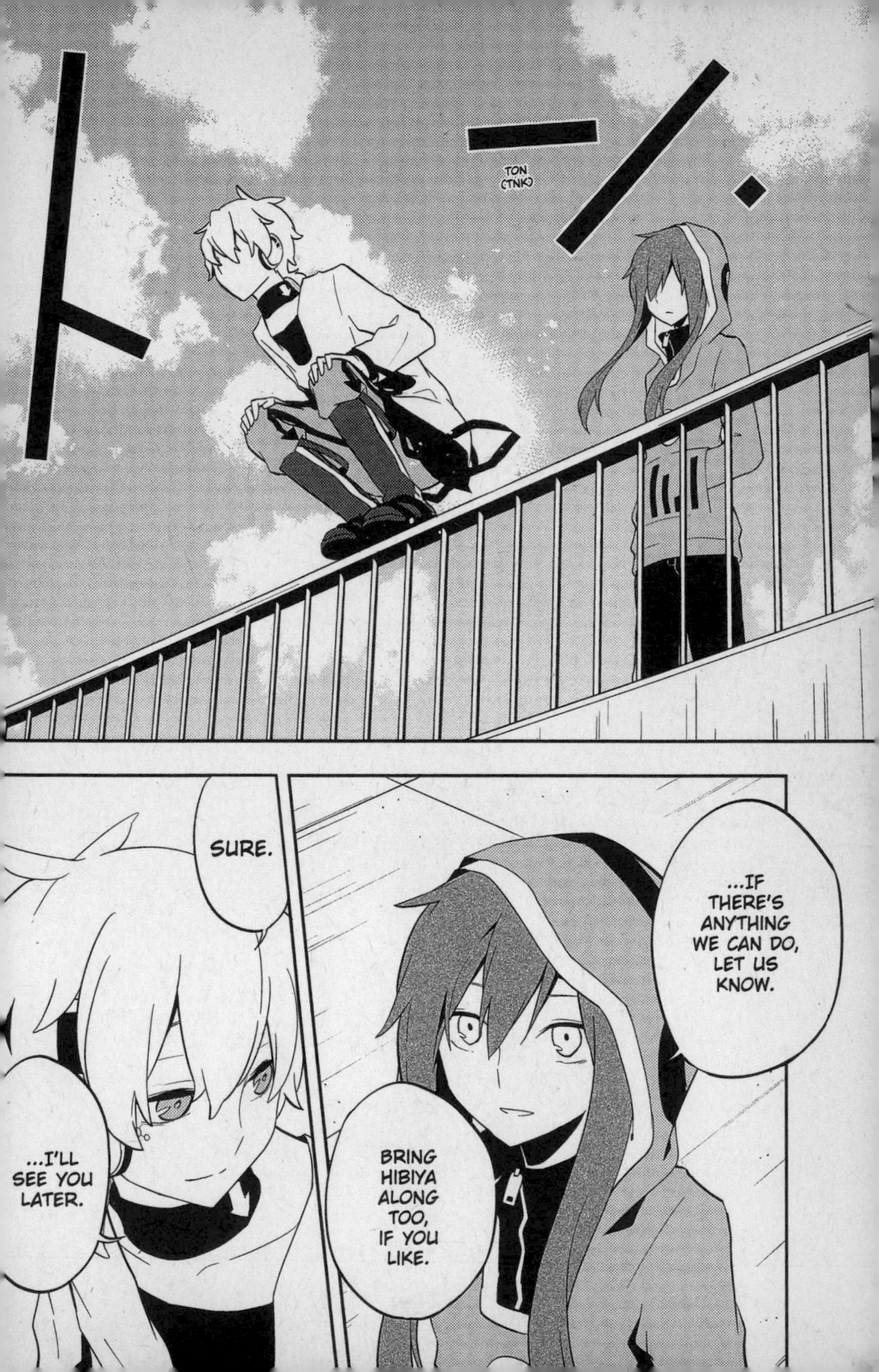
TON
(TNK)
...IF THERE'S ANYTHING WE CAN DO, LET US KNOW.
BRING HIBIYA ALONG TOO, IF YOU LIKE.
SURE.
...I'LL SEE YOU LATER.

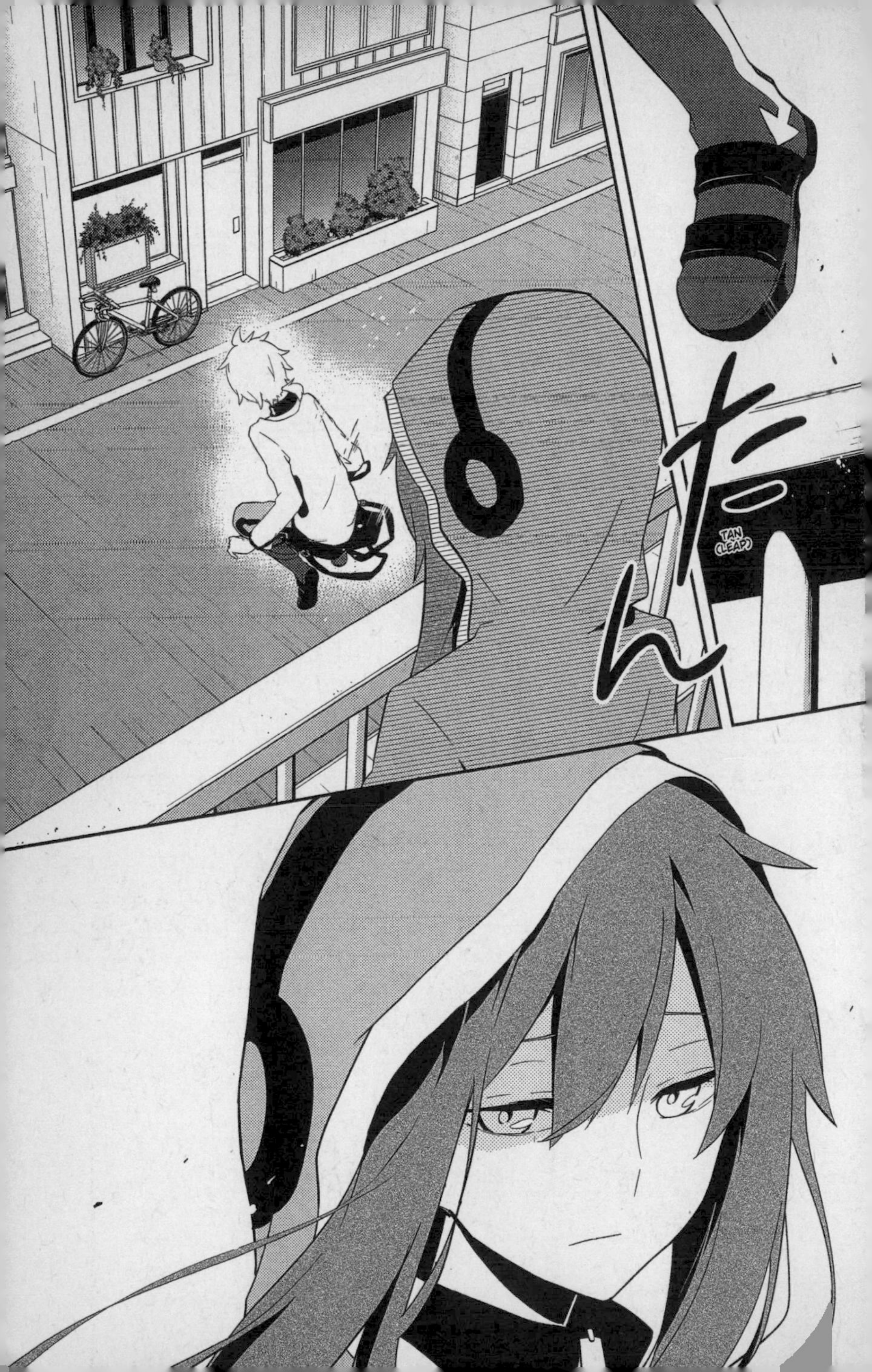
たん
TAN (LEAP)

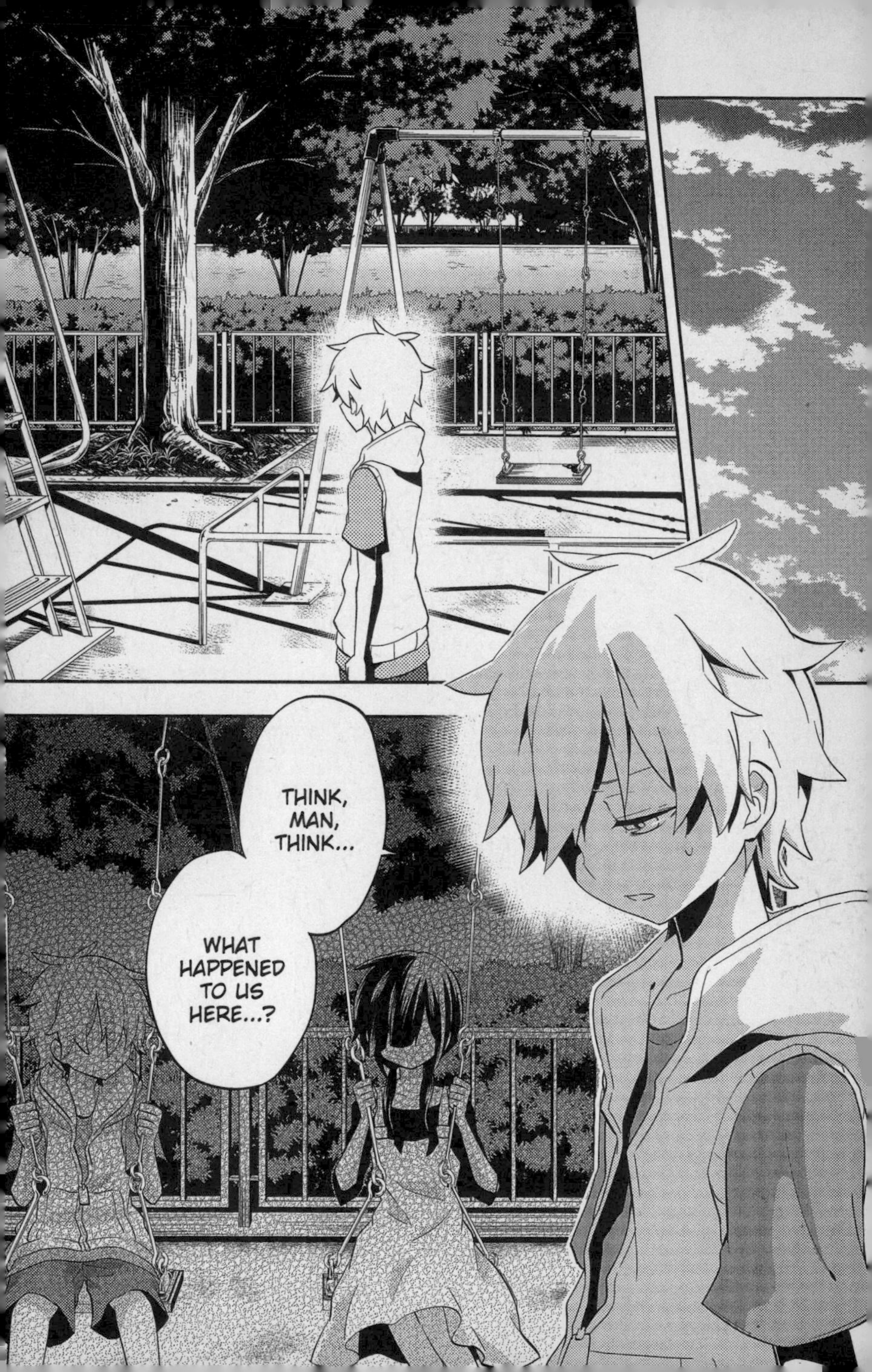
THINK, MAN, THINK...
WHAT HAPPENED TO US HERE...?

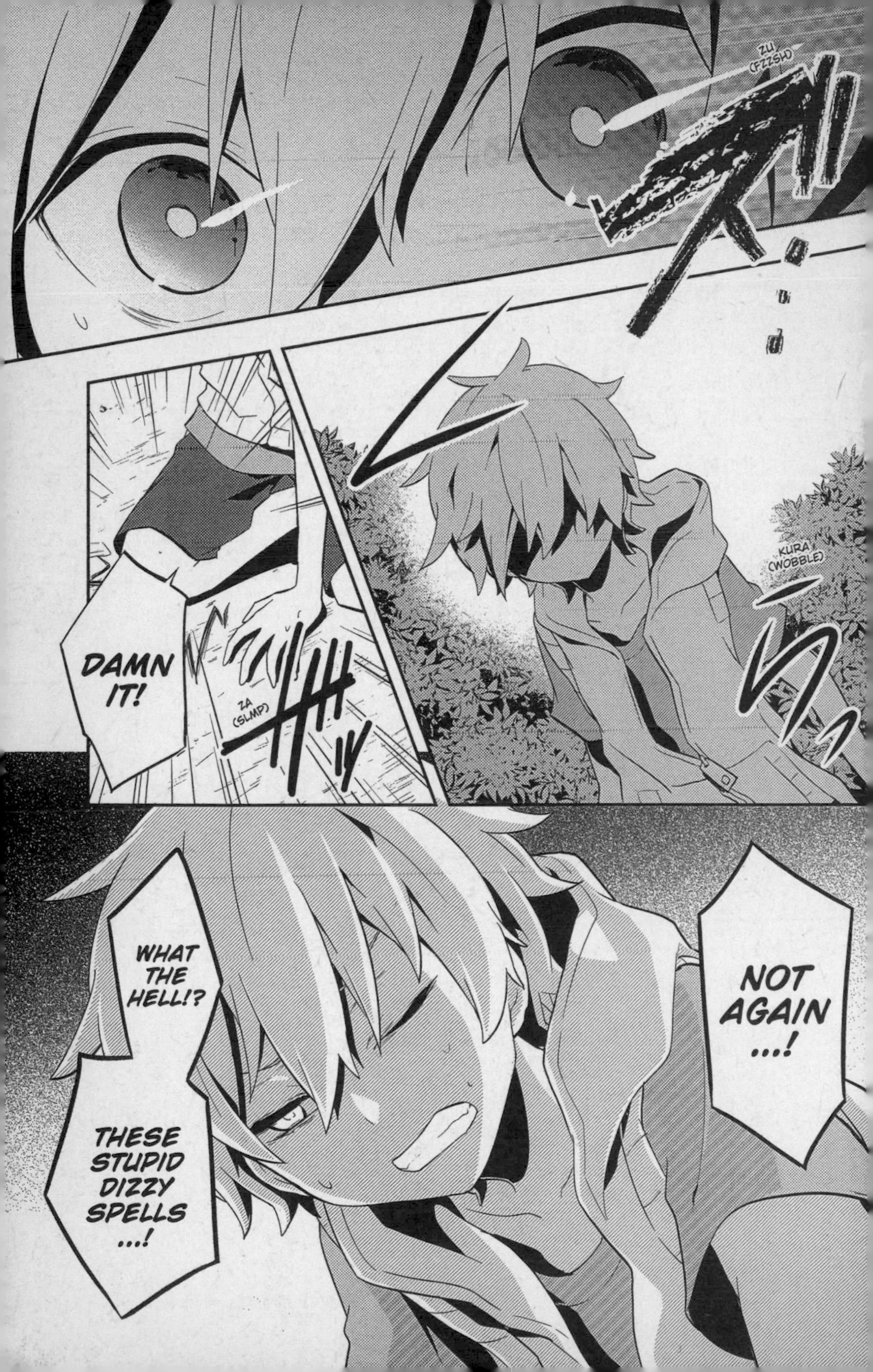
ZU (FZZSH)
KURA (WOBBLE)
DAMN IT!
ZA (SLMP)
NOT AGAIN ...!
WHAT THE HELL!?
THESE STUPID DIZZY SPELLS ...!

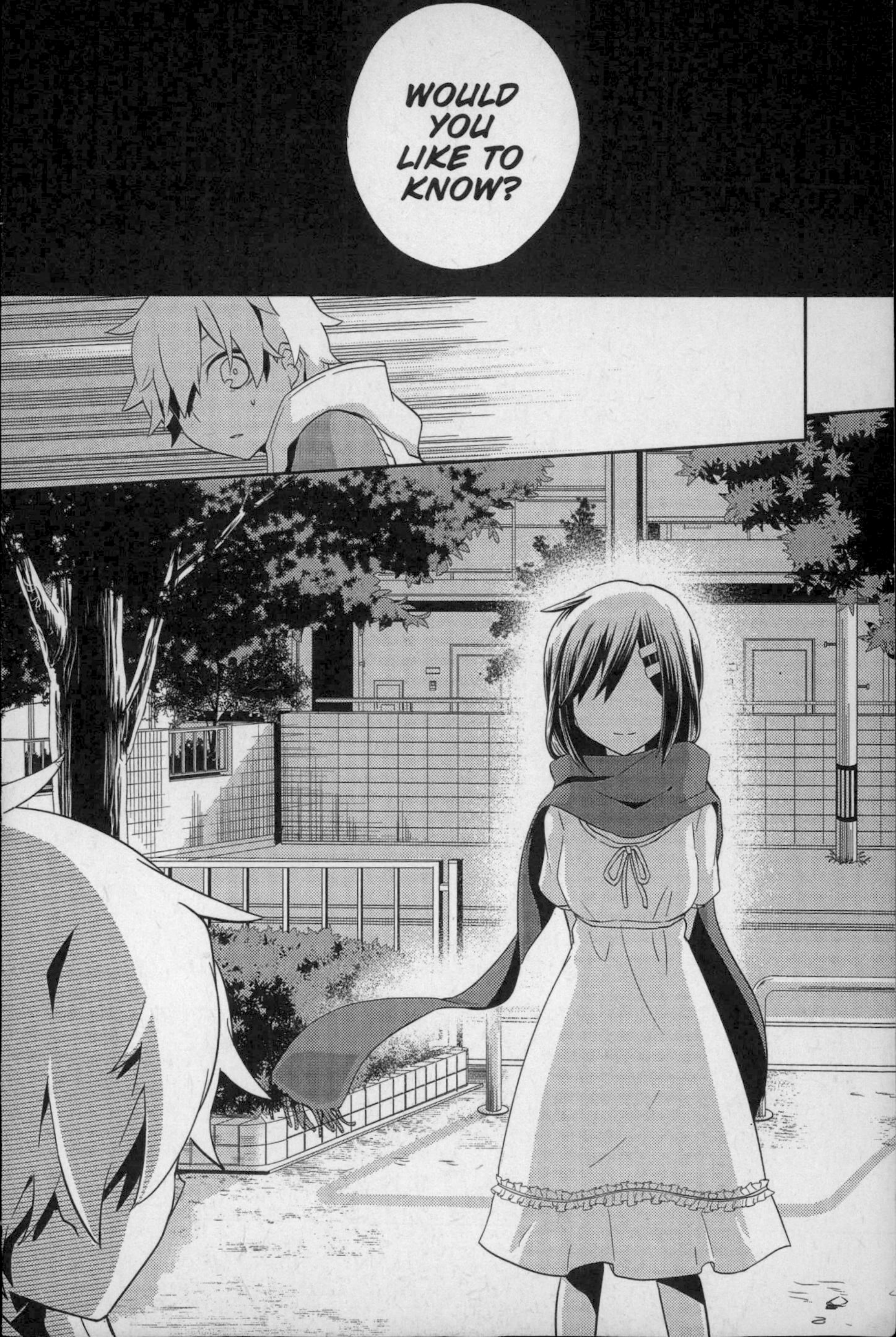
WOULD YOU LIKE TO KNOW?

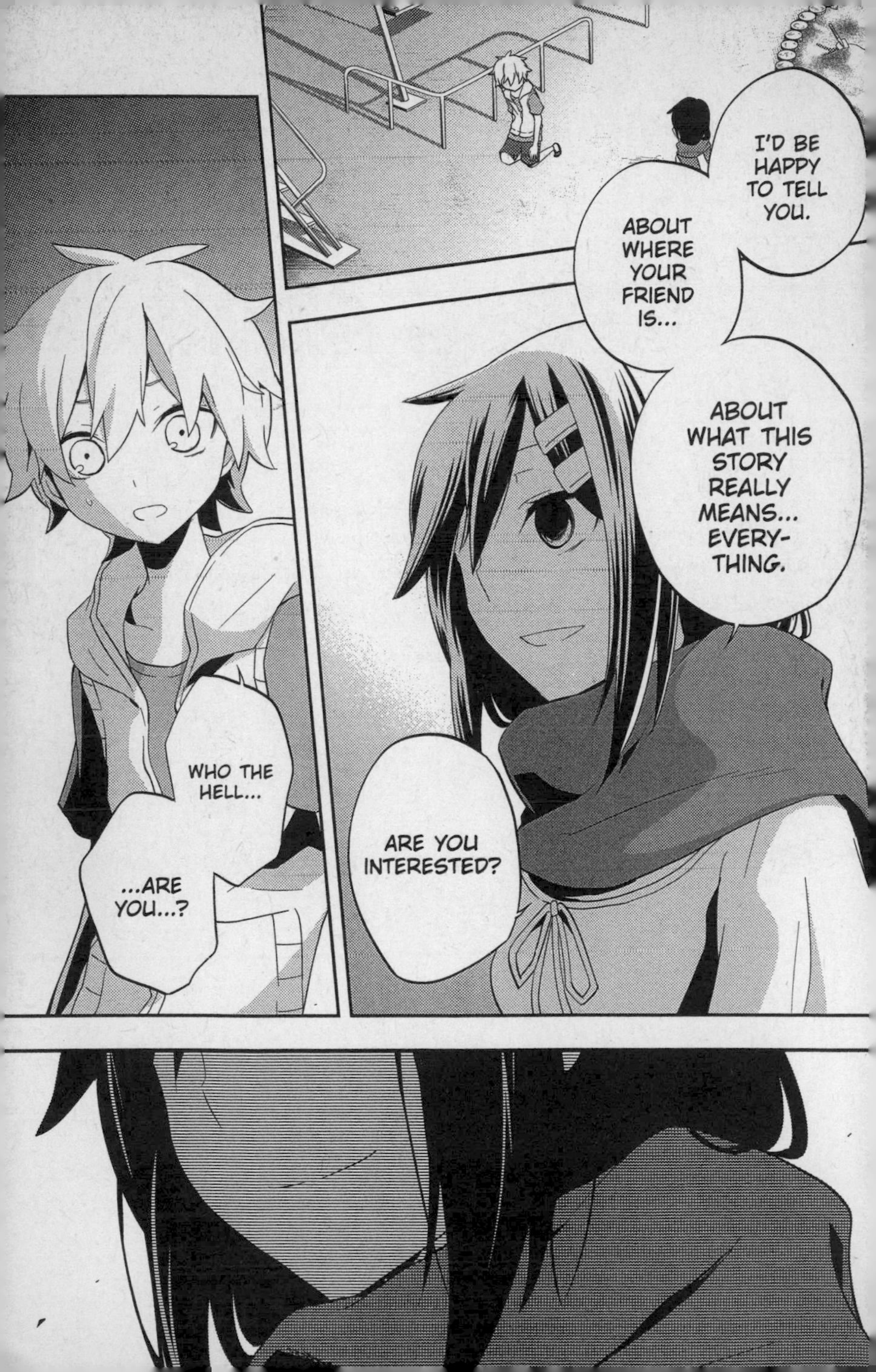
I'D BE HAPPY TO TELL YOU.
ABOUT WHERE YOUR FRIEND IS...
ABOUT WHAT THIS STORY REALLY MEANS... EVERY-THING.
ARE YOU INTERESTED?
WHO THE HELL...
...ARE YOU...?

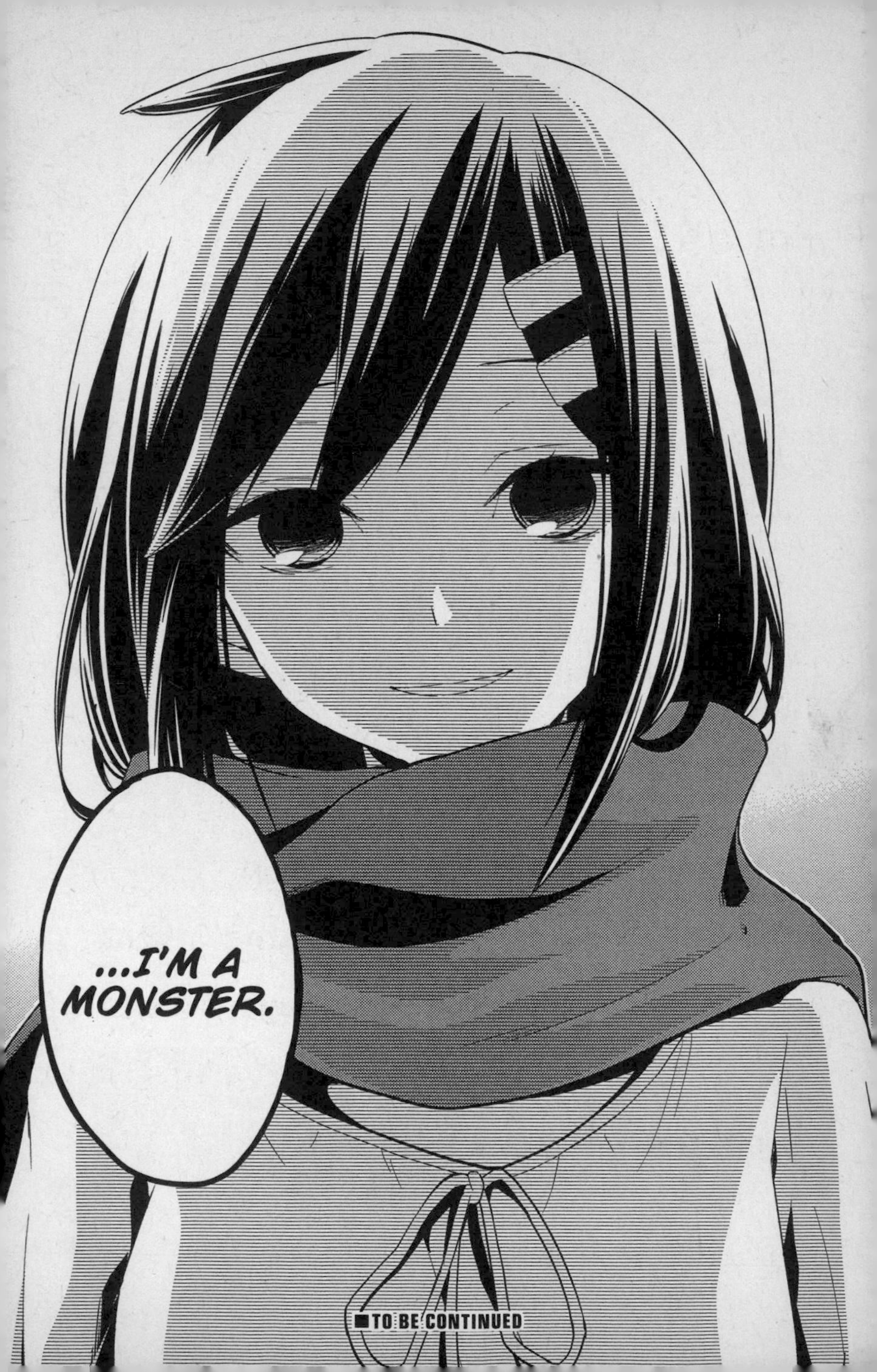
...I'M A MONSTER.
TO BE CONTINUED

Jin's penmanship is utterly tragic!

VOL.6!
CONGRATS!!

Congratulations on releasing Volume 6 of the *Kagerou Daze* manga. I'm having a lot of fun thinking up new developments for the original story depicted in this manga version. Things are going to go south for our heroes starting with the next volume, so I hope you'll all be around to read it.

JIN

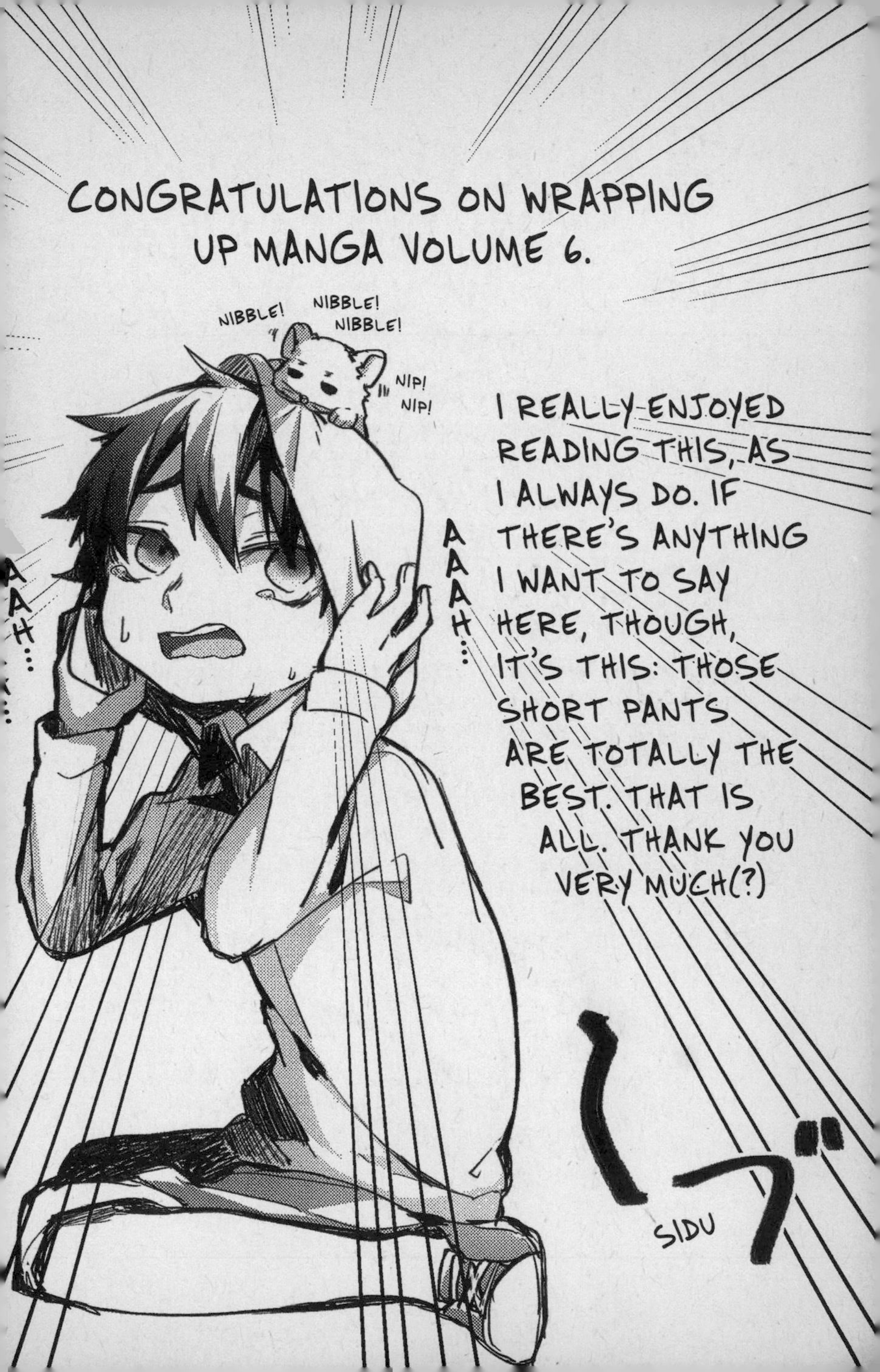
CONGRATULATIONS ON WRAPPING UP MANGA VOLUME 6.
I REALLY ENJOYED READING THIS, AS I ALWAYS DO. IF THERE'S ANYTHING I WANT TO SAY HERE, THOUGH, IT'S THIS: THOSE SHORT PANTS ARE TOTALLY THE BEST. THAT IS ALL. THANK YOU VERY MUCH(?)
NIBBLE! NIBBLE! NIBBLE!
NIP! NIP!
AAAAH...
AAAH...
しづ
SIDU

WE MADE IT TO VOL. 6! THANK YOU SO MUCH!!!

A SERIES OF FREAK EVENTS HAPPENED TO ME AS I WORKED ON THIS VOLUME. FOR EXAMPLE, I TOOK A RIDE IN AN AMBULANCE FOR THE FIRST TIME IN MY LIFE. THE REASON? OH, YOU KNOW. THAT THING. THE THING THAT PRODUCES KIDNEY STONES. THAT THING THEY SAY IS EASILY ONE OF THE THREE MOST PAINFUL EXPERIENCES IN ONE'S LIFE. MY LIFE WASN'T IN DANGER AT ALL, BUT MAN, DID IT HURT A LOT. I HAVE TO APOLOGIZE FOR ALL THE TROUBLE I CAUSED FOR OTHER PEOPLE IN THE PROCESS. I'LL TRY TO MANAGE MY HEALTH A LITTLE MORE CAREFULLY IN THE FUTURE. STILL, I'M JUST HAPPY I MET THE DEADLINE FOR VOLUME 6 SOMEHOW...! HOPEFULLY I'LL STILL BE IN ONE PIECE BY THE TIME WE SEE EACH OTHER IN THE NEXT VOLUME!! ^o^

まひろ
MAHIRO

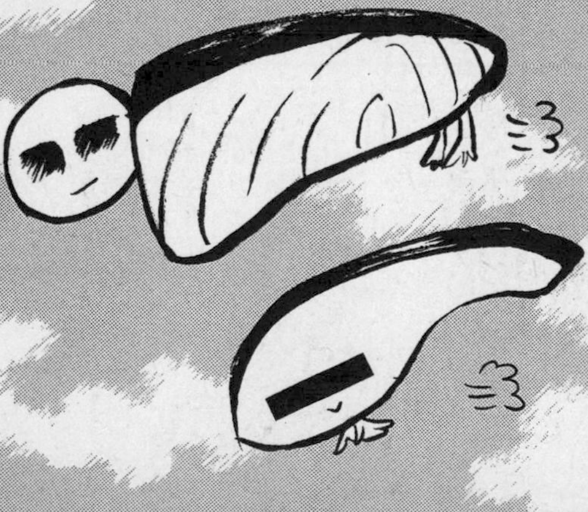

KAGEROU DAZE 06

MAHIRO SATOU
Original Story: JIN
(SHIZEN NO TEKI-P)
Character Design: SIDU, WANNYANPUU-

Translation: Kevin Gifford • Lettering: Abigail Blackman

Kagerou Daze
© Mahiro Satou
© KAGEROU PROJECT / 1st PLACE
Edited by MEDIA FACTORY
First published in Japan in 2014 by KADOKAWA CORPORATION.
English translation rights reserved by YEN PRESS LLC under the license from KADOKAWA CORPORATION, Tokyo through TUTTLE-MORI AGENCY, Inc., Tokyo.

English translation © 2016 by Yen Press, LLC

Yen Press
1290 Avenue of the Americas
New York, NY 10104

Visit us at yenpress.com
facebook.com/yenpress
twitter.com/yenpress
yenpress.tumblr.com

First Yen Press Edition: July 2016

Yen Press is an imprint of Yen Press, LLC.
The Yen Press name and logo are trademarks of Yen Press, LLC.

The publisher is not responsible for websites (or their content) that are not owned by the publisher.

Library of Congress Control Number: 2016297061

ISBNs: 978-0-316-27022-9 (paperback)
        978-0-316-27023-6 (ebook)
        978-0-316-27024-3 (app)

10 9 8 7 6 5 4 3 2 1

BVG

Printed in the United States of America